Dear Reader,

The thinking behind the PEOPLE OF THE PLAINS series is that truth is not only stranger than fiction, but also more exciting. The traditional "Western" gave us gripping tales of gunslingers, cattle barons, clean-cut heroes, fierce Indian horsemen collecting scalps, and the U.S. cavalry racing to the rescue. But, with some notable exceptions, it concerned a frontier as mythic and romantic as Camelot.

Thanks to the work of historians, we now know that what was happening on the western frontier was far more complex than the myths, and far more interesting to today's reader. In the middle years of the 19th century the rules determining who owned that "sea of grass" and the mountains which surround it were being formed. The horse was revolutionizing Indian cultures, tribes were jostling with tribes over hunting grounds, the Spanish frontier was collapsing, and the new Americans were trickling westward looking for their fortune, their freedom, or simply adventure.

Ken Englade is best known for books focused on notable criminal trials. In this PEOPLE OF THE PLAINS series he taps a lifelong fascination with the history of the American frontier to give us a series of novels of this era as it really was. I hope you enjoy this as I have, and look for future titles in the series, coming soon from HarperPaperbacks.

Sincerely,

Tony Hillerman

TONY HILLERMAN'S

~FRONTIER~

PEOPLE OF THE PLAINS

BATTLE CRY

Ken Englade

HarperPaperbacks
A Division of HarperCollinsPublishers

HarperPaperbacks

A Division of HarperCollinsPublishers
10 East 53rd Street, New York, N.Y. 10022-5299

This is a work of fiction. The characters, incidents, and dialogues
are products of the author's imagination and are not to be
construed as real. Any resemblance to actual events or persons,
living or dead, is entirely coincidental.

ISBN: 0-06-100944-X

HarperCollins®, 📖®, and HarperPaperbacks™
are trademarks of HarperCollins*Publishers* Inc.

Cover illustration by Steven Assel

First printing: May 1997

Printed in the United States of America

Visit HarperPaperbacks on the World Wide Web at
http://www.harpercollins.com/paperbacks

❖ 10 9 8 7 6 5 4 3 2 1

For H. J. Englade

*Special thanks to Con Pyle and Larry Podolsky,
experts both.*

PEOPLE OF THE PLAINS

BATTLE CRY

"I don't know what the big secret is," Erich Schmidt grumbled. "The fort ain't that big a place where everybody don't already know everybody else's business."

Jim Ashby raised a stubby index finger to his lips. "You fergit my commandments agin?" he asked in a throaty whisper, his voice made harsh by too many pipes of rough *shongasha* and too much coarse frontier whisky chugalugged straight from the jug.

"N-no, Jim," Erich stammered, his fair cheeks turning a bright red.

"Number One?" Ashby prompted, leaning over his saddle until his lips were only a foot from Erich's ear.

"Always keep my rifle clean and dry."

The scout nodded. "Number Two?"

"Sharpen my knife every night, whether I've used it or not."

"An' number three?"

"Keep my voice down on the trail. Number four . . ."

"Three's enough." Ashby grinned. "I doan wanna strain your brain."

"You're just trying to change the subject. We was talking about the colonel's secret."

"Ain't 'xactly a secret," Ashby replied. "Reckon Kemp jis figgered we didn't need to know is all."

"It's more'n that," the teenager persisted. "I asked Cap'n Harrigan straight out."

"An what'd he tell you?"

"He didn't say nothing. Just gave me that snake-eyed look of his and told me to make sure we got out early. Said don't come back without the backstrap 'cause the colonel needed it for dinner for a 'special guest.' "

"Tha's what he said? 'Special gues?' "

"His words pre-cisely."

"Wail," Ashby drawled, "he's taking a right chance we'll be able to comply. Goin' out and findin' elk ain't 'xactly like meanderin' down to Sevier's. 'Specially now. Normally by this time o' year they'd be up high, grazin' on the new grass. But the long winter kept 'em down on the Plains this year and thar ain't no tellin' whar we might find 'em."

"This winter was a real bitch all right," Erich agreed, digging his heels into the flanks of his chestnut gelding just enough to encourage the animal up the steep bank. "Even the injuns was complaining."

The two had left Fort Laramie well before daybreak, riding westward up into the Medicine Bow Mountains. A few minutes before, they had crossed the normally placid Fish Creek, which was running so high with snowmelt that both men were soaked from midthigh down. But their wet leggins would dry quickly in the midday June sun.

"Where you reckon we should check next?" Erich asked. "We already been to three places."

Ashby pointed to the northwest, where snowcapped Laramie Peak was winking seductively through the aspen and evergreens. Above them, the sky was a bright blue, unmarred except for a few meringuelike clouds with blindingly white tops and soft gray undersides that drifted slowly to the southwest on a gentle wind that was cutting across their right quarter. "'Memer tha' li'l hole we come upon that time we was lookin' fer a shortcut to the Brulé village?"

"Oh, yeah!" Erich nodded enthusiastically. "That would be a perfect place. That valley's just big enough to accommodate a small herd."

An hour later, they topped a small rise and Ashby reigned his pony to a halt. "Looka thar." He smiled, exposing twin rows of chipped, uneven teeth stained berry brown. From their vantage point, Erich could just make out tiny spots of brown in a corner of the clearing.

"I reckon they be all cows," Ashby said. "Takin' their calves up into the hills."

After making a wide half-circle to insure that the wind was directly in their faces, the two men tethered their horses, then set off through the forest, Erich in the lead about ten yards to Ashby's left.

Dropping into a squat, Ashby followed, duckwalking toward the valley, his eyes focused determinedly on the ground in front of him. If he had paused to look up he would have seen the wasp nest anchored solidly to the low-hanging limb directly in his path and would have given it a respectful berth. Instead, he was unaware of the insects until he bumped their home with his shoulder, sending them buzzing angrily in search of the intruder. Silently cursing himself for not being more careful, Ashby tucked his chin to his chest and threw his right arm over his head, fighting back the urge to flail at the insects or turn on his heels and scamper away, putting as much distance between himself and the enraged wasps as possible. Rather than risk spooking the elk, he endured the attack, drawing his head as far as it would go into the neck of the thick buckskin shirt he wore summer and winter.

Sensing the disturbance, Erich glanced over his shoulder. Better him than me, he told himself, watching the wasps swooping down on Ashby.

Scurrying forward as quickly as he could, Ashby slithered under a spruce, where he lay motionless, breathing heavily, trying to ignore the throbbing in his left hand, which already was swelling from a half dozen stings. Once he was sure the attack was finished, he cautiously lifted his head just high enough to get his eyes above ground level. Moving toward him at an angle, close enough where he could hear their stomachs growling, were the advance members of a herd of some three dozen cow elk. Keeping pace step for step with the adults were a group of calves, most of them wearing their spotted coats. The animals were in no hurry, Ashby noted, watching them carefully as they stopped to graze on the ankle-high grass that waved in the breeze. Behind them. coal-black mountains with white tops rose majestically, framed by towering evergreens and budding aspen. The beauty of the scene, however, was lost on the scout. He had only one thing on his mind: fresh meat.

Without moving his head, Ashy let his eyes roam across the open space, letting his gaze settle on a cow some forty yards distant. One of the fattest animals in the herd, she had no calf and was moving slightly faster than the others. As Ashby watched, she turned slightly to her right, exposing her flank to the two hunters. Glancing over his shoulder at Erich, who was crouched at the base of an aspen, his rifle already at his shoulder, Ashby nodded almost imperceptibly. At the signal, Erich fitted his sights on the cow's head. Exhaling slowly, he gently squeezed the trigger.

The cow, attracted by a more inviting clump of grass, had moved just as Erich fired. Instead of striking her just below the ear, the Hawken's .50 caliber round hit low, taking off a fist-sized chunk of the cow's lower jaw. A dense cloud of blood and mud temporarily hid the cow's head, but then she burst startlingly into view, her damaged jaw hanging by a thread. As they watched, she jumped straight up, high enough to clear a pony's back. Bellowing in pain, she bounded away toward the trees on the far side of the small valley.

"*Ach du Scheiße*," Erich cursed, slapping the ground in frustration.

The other animals, panicked by the gunshot and the wounded herd member's screams, began running wildly in a large circle, confused by the echoes that bounced off the surrounding hills. Taking advantage of their indecision, Ashby lifted his Hall and fired, selecting another healthy-looking cow with a calf at her heels. He grunted in satisfaction when his .52 caliber bullet impacted just behind the elk's shoulder blade, sending the cow staggering. Seemingly regaining her feet, she ran for thirty more yards before dropping to the ground as abruptly as if her legs had been cut from under her.

"Thanks, Jim," Erich said, blushing for the second time. "I reckon I mucked that up pretty good."

"Jis goes to show you," Ashby replied, crawling into the opening, "there ain't no sech thang as a sure shot. You gotta be prepared for near 'bout anythang. C'mon. Le's git that backstrap."

"What about the cow I banged up?"

"Wolves'll git her," Ashby said. "Or she'll starve to death. Either way, ain't worth us trying to track 'er down."

"And the calf?" Erich asked, nodding toward a nearby clump of bushes where the offspring of the cow that Ashby had killed was cowering perfectly motionless, believing itself invisible to the hunters.

"Maybe another cow'll let her suckle." Ashby shrugged. "Maybe not. If not, the coyotes'll find her."

Erich nodded indifferently. Ever since Ashby had agreed to let him work at his side so he could learn to be a hunter and tracker, Erich had come to understand only too clearly that life was hard on the Great Plains. Sentimentality quickly gave way to reality, and reality was often cruel. Both people and animals died suddenly, violently and with regularity. It was the way things were.

"Doan stan' there dreamin', boy," Ashby said, not unkindly. "We got work to do." Leading the way in his peculiar, sailorlike, rolling gait Ashby hurried to where the cow had fallen.

Mindful of the instructions Ashby had imparted over the years, Erich gave the elk a quick but keen look. She was about two years old, he reckoned, and by the end of the summer probably would top out at four hundred pounds although she still had a way to go to reach her prime. Showing the consequences of months of little feed, her ribs protruded prominently and she had that scruffy end-of-winter look common among big game in that transition period between seasons. Along her neck, tufts of winter hair stuck up like flatland sagebrush, giving way grudgingly to the slick, smooth summer coat that was just starting to come in.

"She doesn't even look like she's hurt that bad, does she?" Erich said, sticking his finger in the silver dollar–sized entrance wound created by Ashby's bullet.

"Reckon on the other side there's a hole bigger'n my fist," Ashby said disinterestedly. "An' if we was to cut her open, her insides would look like they been stirred with a spoon. Them big slugs are mighty fierce." Laying down his rifle, he crouched at the animal's head. "Le's roll 'er over."

Erich moved obediently to the cow's rump. Grunting,

he pulled the underside rear leg out, spread-eagling the cow's lower end. While Ashby pushed with his shoulder against the cow's neck, Erich extracted the front underside leg. When he was finished, the cow was on its stomach with its legs sticking straight out.

"Not a bad looking elk at all," Erich said admiringly.

"Will you quit chattering an' git to work," Ashby growled. "I wanna git that meat and git outta here."

"What's your hurry?"

"Could be you forgot, but we be right on the edge o' Crow territory. We might'n not be the only ones with a yearnin' fer fresh elk. You do it," he added. "My hand's stove up a bit."

"It sure looks like hell," Erich commented, noticing that Ashby's left hand was swollen almost twice its normal size.

"Goddamn wasps," Ashby spit.

Reaching for his knife, a fearsome looking ten-inch-long weapon he carried at his waist in an oversized beaded sheath, Erich bent to his job. Inserting the tip of the blade into the skin at the back of the cow's neck about a foot left of the backbone, he made a shallow cut straight down the cow's back.

"Jis deep enough to get through the hide," Ashby warned, looking over his protégé's shoulder.

"Jeez, Jim," Erich grumbled. "You don't have to tell me that every time. I reckon I can remember."

"Like you do about whisperin'?" Ashby replied, softening the comment with a wink.

Ignoring him, Erich shifted his position and made an identical cut down the cow's right side, then joined the two with another cut perpendicular to the backbone.

"Yank 'er off," Ashby said.

Erich rolled his eyes. Not bothering to answer, he grabbed a double handful of hair and jerked straight back, stripping the skin from the center of the elk's back like peel from an orange. "Look at that," he said, pointing to the underside of the strip he had just removed. "Hardly any fat at all."

"Too early in the season," Ashby replied. "Wait a couple months."

"Boy, that smells good," Erich said, leaning close to the exposed meat and inhaling deeply. When he lifted his head, his nose was smeared with elk blood.

"Tha's right." Ashby chuckled. "Git your nose down in thar jis' like I learned you. Ain't no smell like it in the world."

Nodding, Erich took his knife and jammed the blade solidly into the meat that ran down the center of the elk's back, the prized backstrap. Pushing until he felt his knife tip strike the ribs, Erich pulled the instrument toward him, moving it parallel to the backbone. Then, inserting the blade so it was parallel to the ribs, he made a second cut with the tip aimed directly at the spine. Finally, he made a third cut straight down the cow's spine. When he was through, he lifted out a rectangular section of loin two inches thick, four inches wide and two-feet long that weighed a little more than twenty pounds.

"Ain't nothing like a good backstrap," Ashby commented, licking his lips. "Injuns rightly love a raw buffler liver sprinkled with gall. Tha' be right tasty, tha's fer fuckin' sure, but give me a good backstrap any day."

As Ashby watched approvingly, Erich repeated the procedure on the cow's other side.

"I'm ready when you are," the youth said, rolling the meat into two cannonball-sized lumps. "If there's Crow in the area they'd better hurry," he added, rising and handing one of the balls to Ashby, who took it with his uninjured hand, " 'cause in a few hours this cow'll be nothing but a pile of bones."

"Le's git the horses," Ashby said. "I doan wanna be here when some Crows come snoopin' aroun'."

"Jim," Erich said earnestly as they left the forested hills behind them, moving comfortably down a little-used trail that would take them to Fort Laramie, "you think we'll ever get those boys back?"

Ashby swiveled in his saddle, staring closely at his friend. Although he was almost eighteen, Erich Schmidt could easily have passed for fourteen with his innocent blue eyes and rosy cheeks that had not yet seen a razor. "You mean them kraut young'uns?" he asked, spitting a stream of tobacco juice into the dust. "No offense," he added.

"Werner and Wilhelm," Erich replied, pronouncing the w's as v's in the proper German manner.

"You mean Puma and Magpie," Ashby corrected. "They ain't white folks no longer. Not after three years with the Cheyenne. What makes you as' 'bout them?"

"They've been on my mind a lot lately," Erich replied. "I guess since Inge married Jean and there's the possibility they'll be having a baby afore too long, it's made me realize how hard it must be to lose your kids."

Ashby rode along for ten minutes before answering, his chin on his chest, deep in thought. Erich was about to ask him if he had heard him when Ashby replied.

"It's always a bitch when you lose someone you love an' that rightly includes chillin. I guess it be doubly hard when you know they be alive but being raised somewhar else. 'Specially when its injuns doin' the raisin' although I ain't personally got nothing again injuns. They do a right better job with their kids than mos' whites I seen."

"That doesn't answer my question," Erich replied crossly.

"I know it doan. Tha's 'cause I doan have no answer. Iff'n I was a bettin' man, I'd say you got a better chance being 'lected king than you got o' gettin' them two young'uns back."

"Kings ain't elected." Erich grinned. "They inherit their titles."

Ashby chuckled. "Tha's wha' I mean. Tha' shows you your chances."

"We came this close," Erich said, holding his thumb and forefinger an inch apart.

"Tha' ain't 'xactly right," Ashby said, shaking his head. "We come tha' close to *maybe* havin' 'em back in the fort for a look-see. But it woulda been up to them whether they stayed or not. Tha' was the 'greement with Short Hair."

"Wasn't Short Hair's fault," Erich said bitterly. "It was that damn fool emigrant. What the hell was his name anyway?"

"Agee? Naw, that weren't it. Akins?"

"Adkins!" Erich said. "Jebediah Adkins! If he hadn't been so trigger happy White Wolf would still be alive and the Cheyenne would have come to the fort."

"Tain't necessarily so," Ashby pointed out. "You might think they was headin' toward Fort Laramie but with injuns you never kin tell. They might 'a been distracted by a herd of buffler or decided to take off after some Pawnee. Lots o' thangs could 'a happened before they got to where you s'pected them to be. Injuns ain't hardly predictable. Anyways, relations with the Cheyenne been gettin' worse and worse ever since then. I heered rumors 'round the stables that even now soljers is on their way from Fort Leavenworth to go out lookin' for the Cheyenne just like that bastard Harney done for the Sioux."

"I heard the same rumors," said Erich. "But I sure hope they're not true. If they are, we'll never see Wilhelm or Werner again."

"You better hope you doan," Ashby replied. "Could be iff'n you do see 'em, they'll be ridin' ponies an' tryin' to take your scalp."

"You think they'd fight against their own kind?" Erich asked in surprise, the possibility never having occurred to him.

"I keep tellin' you and you doan lissen," Ashby said. "They be injun now, not white. Even if they had a choice, I'd wager they'd stay with the Cheyenne. But tha's a useless bit o' spec'lation 'cause I doan figger it's ever goan happen. Mark my words, we attack the Cheyenne, we'll start a war."

"You don't sound too concerned about it," Erich snapped.

" 'Course I be concerned but there ain't nothin' I kin do. Them pissants back East seem determined to keep stirrin' up the injuns until we got us a real shootin' war and there's nothin' me and you kin do about it. I kin tell it ain't much to Colonel Kemp's likin' but he jis takes orders. Now that Cap'n Harrigan is sump'n else. I rightly believe he'd *like* a war with the injuns jis so he could advance his career."

"You don't think much of him, do you?"

"It doan make no nevamind what I think. I jis work for the gov'ment; I doan tell 'em how to do thangs or who to make into officers."

"You don't *have* to work for them. You could always go back to trapping."

"Nope," said Ashby. "The trappers be done fer. Them years have passed. Anyways, I made my bed, now I gotta sleep in it. I ain't goan back East, tha's for fuckin' sure, so I reckon I doan have much of a choice no more."

"You sure sound pessimistic."

"It goes back to what we were talkin' 'bout. Them young'uns. They be part of a different wha' you call it . . ."

"Culture," Erich said, smiling.

"Yep. They be part of a differen' culture now and it jis happens tha' the red culture and the white culture get along like 'Hos and Pawnee, which ain't worth a pile o' steamin' horseshit. The injuns be right 'bout us scarin' off the buffler an' the other game. They be right about us bringin' 'em sicknesses they ain't never had before. They be right 'bout the emigrants choppin' down the trees, an' ruinin' the good pasture. They be right 'bout a lot o' thangs but they ain't never gonna be able to stop the white man. I reckon I be as much injun as I be white and I hafta look at the situation from both sides. When I do, tha' makes me sad. Real fuckin' sad, truth be tol'. I jis doan see no solution."

"That's the closest I've ever heard you come to making a speech," Erich said, impressed. "How come you've waited this long to say those things?"

"Hah!" Ashby said, letting loose another stream of tobacco juice. "Who I gonna say 'em to? Cap'n Harrigan? So I kin have him hoppin' on my ass alla time? Use your head, boy. Man's worstest enemy is his mouth. It even worsen' his dick, which also tends to get him into a hell of a lot of trouble. Man learn how to keep his dick buttoned up and his mouth shut, he do right well by hisself."

"You're quite a philosopher, you know." Erich laughed.

"Tha' ain't no 'losophy. It be the truth."

"In the time I've known you, you're right about most things," Erich said. "Even *Mutter* agrees with that."

"Your ma is a right smart woman," Ashby agreed. "Too bad she's got such a blin' spot about them young'uns."

"I think the possibility of getting them back is what keeps her here."

"Wha' do you mean 'keeps her here'?" Ashby asked, giving Erich a sharp look. "She plannin on leavin' Fort Laramie or sum'in?"

"She got a letter awhile back from Else Hartmann. You remember her?"

Ashby nodded slowly. "Sure I remember her. She were the woman whose husband and kid got kilt in the same raid's your daddy?"

"That's the one," Erich said.

"She went on to Oregon. Why you bring her up?"

"*Mutter* got a letter from her last week. She wants *Mutter* to come out there to join her. Said she met a man and got remarried, that there's lots of opportunity to find a new husband out there."

"Holz? I mean your ma. She be looking' for another husband?"

"It's not that far-fetched," Erich said defensively. "She's not *that* old. Now that Inge's married and I'm growed, I think she may be getting a little restless. In my opinion, the thing that keeps her here is the possibility that we might get Werner and Wilhelm back."

"They ain't hers."

"That don't matter. She's the last one left here of the original group, except for me and Inge of course. But she feels responsible. I can't help feeling she'd go to Oregon if it weren't for the two boys."

"Iff'n she wants to go, she should go," Ashby said with finality. "Them boys ain't never comin' back."

Frau Schmidt stood in the door of the cookhouse that adjoined the bachelor officer's quarters, commonly referred to as Old Bedlam, staring southward across the bare parade ground toward old Fort John, the second structure to occupy the point of land where the clear, fast-rushing

Laramie River flowed into a silty, sluggish stream dubbed the Platte, the French word for "shallow."

A sturdy-looking, large-boned woman with a some-what prominent nose, blond hair flecked with gray, and deep blue eyes that seemed capable of staring into a man's soul, Hildegard Schmidt had become an institution since she dragged into Fort Laramie three years previously, barely conscious as a result of an infection stemming from an arrow wound suffered during an Indian attack. Within hours after her arrival, the post's new surgeon, Jason Dobbs, amputated her left leg just above the knee, thereby immortalizing Frau Schmidt as "Holzbein" or, in the shortened version, "Holz," a nickname derived from the German word for "wooden leg."

Electing to remain at Fort Laramie instead of continuing westward, Frau Schmidt took over as the cook in the officer's mess with her daughter, Inge, then seventeen, as her chief assistant. Except for the "girls" at the Hog Ranch a few miles south of the post, Frau Schmidt and Inge were the only known white women living permanently between Fort Kearny, more than 300 miles to the east, and the Mormon settlement on the shores of the Great Salt Lake 450 miles to the southwest.

Among the post's officers, Frau Schmidt was known as the miracle woman who could turn the toughest piece of bull buffalo into an epicurean's delight and, with the barest ingredients possible, whip up a *Gugelhupf* unrivaled this side of Frankfurt.

The post noncoms, who were not direct beneficiaries of her culinary capabilities, had a slightly different view of Frau Schmidt. As far as the old corporals and sergeants were concerned, it was Frau Schmidt who was the real commander at Fort Laramie, not Colonel Kemp. If they were having a problem with one of the new young officers sent in to deal with the "Indian problem" they dropped a few hints to "Ol' Holz," and the difficulty was quickly resolved.

On the other hand, the young enlisted men, mere boys, really, fresh off the farms in Illinois and Indiana or the urbanized sons of emigrants recently arrived from the Old World, were interested not in Frau Schmidt, but in her teenage daughter, an uncommonly attractive, blunt-spoken, somewhat mysterious figure who reminded them of sisters left behind or helped set their standards for lovers still in their future. Occasionally, a new arrival would take one look at Inge and unthinkingly blurt out a sentence or two relating to an imagined lustful encounter. Invariably, the newcomer was advised by his barracks mates, sometimes forcefully, of the errors in his line of reasoning. It had been years since Inge inquired curiously about the origin of a new man's black eye, shattered nose, or broken tooth.

"What are you looking at, *Mutter*?" Inge asked, glancing over her mother's shoulder.

"Nothing particular," Frau Schmidt replied in German, shaking herself out of her reverie. "I was just marveling at how much Fort Laramie has changed since we've been here. It's almost like a city now. When we first came here three years ago there was hardly anything. Now there are so many buildings and so many people. We even have a trading post and a two-story house for the soldiers."

"That's called progress, mother." Inge sighed. "It's happening all over the West. Jean told me that when the Trail was first opened there were only a trickle of people heading to Oregon and California. Now there are thousands and thousands every year."

"*Ja*," Frau Schmidt said sadly, shaking her head. "I see them come in all full of hope and promise and I wonder if that is what we looked like when your father and the others decided to leave New York for Oregon."

"That seems so long ago." Inge sighed. "So much has happened since then."

When the two were together they habitually spoke in German. Although Frau Schmidt understood English as well as anyone on the post she stubbornly refused to speak it unless pushed. Inge and Erich had long ago given up trying to force her; conversing with her in German was the easiest route.

"It seemed like such an adventure," Frau Schmidt said melancholily. "Your father and I were so excited. From what we had heard Oregon was so wonderful."

"Oh, Mother," Inge interjected. "Don't start getting all sentimental on me."

"Don't tell me about sentimental," Frau Schmidt said crisply. "I'm just trying to tell you how dreams often come crashing down around you. Do you remember that day we left Missouri? How pretty it was? How the road ahead beckoned so invitingly? I remember your father, God rest his soul, was as happy as I'd ever seen him."

"How could I forget?" Inge said, wiping her hands on the stained apron she wore to protect her new calico dress, a store-bought garment Jean had ordered through the sutler, Bertrand Sevier, as a surprise for her twentieth birthday two weeks previously.

Remembering, tears formed in her eyes, which were the exact shade of blue as her mother's. "Unfortunately, I also vividly recall what happened later, after we had fallen behind the rest of the group because Herr Mueller was having trouble with his wagon. We were going to help him fix it, the Hartmanns and us, and then catch up."

"Ja." Frau Schmidt smiled. "And we fixed it, too, something that dunderheaded blacksmith at Fort Kearny had been unable to do. We were so proud of ourselves, Everything seemed so peaceful. For the first time in weeks we were away by ourselves and we could speak all the time in our language without worrying about translating for the others. We weren't in any hurry to rejoin the wagon train, so we decided to have a little picnic to celebrate our freedom. That was when the Indians attacked," Frau Schmidt said, her eyes filling with tears. "It was a nightmare. They came out of nowhere, screaming and shooting arrows at us. "

"I remember," Inge said softly.

"There were eleven of us in the camp," Frau Schmidt continued, her voice rising. "They were so hideous, painted in bright colors and nearly naked. They had no mercy on anyone. They killed Henrich and Johanna and Heinz. Even poor little Emmi. And your father, God bless him. He was a good man."

"It's all in the past now," Inge said soothingly.

"I am so happy you weren't there when the attack came," Frau Schmidt said.

"Yes," said Inge, bobbing her head, making her blond braids bounce on her shoulders. "Jean and I had gone back down the trail to pick some wild berries I had noticed earlier. We were going to have them for dessert. By the time we got back, everything was over. Father was dead and you were sitting beside the wagon with an arrow in your leg. Poor Jean. He thought he was going to get in so much trouble because he had left the train at my insistence."

"You had already set your eyes on him." Frau Schmidt smiled. "Even then."

"Of course, I had, *Mutter*," Inge said, trying to turn the conversation to a more pleasant subject. "He was far and away the most handsome man I had ever seen and the fact that he spoke French as well as English appealed to me. He was just not another dull American."

"You were shameless," Frau Schmidt said, laughing. "I used to think of you as 'my daughter the man-hunter.' "

"Well," Inge replied, smiling beatifically, "I *had* to do

something. That man was *so* dumb. He kept insisting I
was too young to get married but what he really meant
was that he thought *he* was too young to get married. And
he was *twenty-two*."

"A real old man."

"By the time you were twenty-two you had two children," Inge said, ignoring her mother's sarcasm.

"Yes." Frau Schmidt sighed. "But times were different
then."

"*Mutter*," Inge said, her smile disappearing, "do you
think you will ever get married again?"

"*Ach!*" Frau Schmidt said in surprise. "I have not
thought about that in years. What makes you ask such a
question?"

"With Erich and I now out on our own you need someone to look after."

"And who would I marry?" Frau Schmidt said, giving
her daughter a curious look. "One of these young officers
who could be my son? Colonel Kemp who already has a
family Back East? Or maybe an Indian chief? Then I could
go live in a lodge and learn to tan hides."

"Don't be facetious, *Mutter*. I wasn't joking."

"I know you weren't," Frau Schmidt said kindly. "It
was only that I don't want to think about that. Although
this country is full of men, there are very few eligible
ones. At least for me."

"Don't give up hope, *Mutter*," Inge said, hugging her
tightly. "I just want to see you happy. Do you want to do
as Else asked? Go to Oregon?"

"I don't know." Frau Schmidt shrugged. "I feel so lost
sometimes. Your husband is a soldier, he has to go where
the Army sends him. And Erich is going to be a wonderful hunter. But he is gone so much of the time. It causes
me much grief. Every time he leaves the fort I fear he will
not come back."

"Would it make you feel any better if you were in Oregon not knowing what was going on?'

"No." Frau Schmidt smiled. "I think you're right about that."

"Speaking of Erich," Inge said, pointing across the parade ground, "here he comes now."

"*Ach*," Frau Schmidt said, looking across the dusty open space that the troopers used as a parade ground. "Mr. Ashby is with him. Look at them; they look like father and son."

"How can you say that?" Inge laughed. "Jim is small, dark, and skinny, while Erich is husky and blond."

"*Ja*," agreed Frau Schmidt, "but they dress almost the same, both in those dreadful skin clothes and they carry more guns and knives and hatchets than the soldiers."

"That's because they're out on their own a lot," Inge added. "They don't have anyone else to depend upon."

"They move the same way, too," Frau Schmidt continued. "Gracefully, carefully. And their eyes are always looking about, never standing still on a single object."

"Occupational hazard," mumbled Inge, turning back to what she had been doing before she stopped to talk. "Tell me again about this *Bienenstich*. How many eggs?"

Frau Schmidt grunted. "Sometimes," she said, shaking her head, "I fear you will never learn to cook properly. If you don't improve, Jean is going to leave you for *eine Indianerin*."

"A squaw." Inge chuckled. "No chance of that. He knows how good he has it."

"Who knows how good he has it?" Erich boomed, bursting through the door.

"My husband." Inge smiled. "Who else?"

"We brung the backstrap the colonel wanted," Ashby added, proffering the two long strips of loin still rolled into balls.

"There, if you please," Frau Schmidt said in English, pointing at a chopping block that stood in the corner.

"It's my pleasure," Ashby said lightly, strolling across the room. "Iff'n you say it, I take it as an order."

Inge looked up, puzzled. There was something, she thought, in Ashby's tone that was different. What was it? she asked herself. Am I imagining something?

"Who's it for?" Erich asked, dipping a finger, the creases still carrying traces of elk blood, into the batter Inge had been preparing.

"Keep out of that," she said tartly, slapping his hand with the wooden spoon she was holding.

"Ouch," he said, drawing back his hand. "But why did Colonel Kemp send us out at the last minute to get back-strap? We were in such a hurry we left the rest of the elk for the scavengers. What a waste."

"It's because he has a special guest that he wants to impress," Inge said smugly.

"Who is it?" Erich persisted. "Another of those god-damn Washington politicians?"

"Watch your language," Frau Schmidt cautioned in German. "You know I don't like that."

"Sorry, Mother." Erich reddened. "I'm just curious, that's all."

"You mean nosy," said Inge.

"Okay, nosy. But I still want to know who it is."

Frau Schmidt turned away, focusing her attention to the meat.

"We don't know," Inge said. "Some man who arrived while you and Jim were gone. A tiny man," she said, placing her hand on a level with her eyes to demonstrate his height.

"That *is* tiny," Erich said in surprise. "You're only five-feet-two or -three yourself. You sure it wasn't a woman or a boy?"

"No," Inge said emphatically. "It's a man. Mother said so, and she knows because she drew his bath."

"Inge!" Frau Schmidt scolded. "Quit your gossiping and get back to work."

"A real mystery, huh?" Erich grinned. "I like that. Some suspense at the ol' fort."

"Anything else we can do for you, ma'am?" Ashby asked, grinning broadly.

"*Nein, danke*," Frau Schmidt replied in dismissal. Reaching for the meat, she spied Ashby's swollen hand.

"*Mein Gott*," she exclaimed. "What is this?"

"It ain't nothing, ma'am," Ashby replied. "I jist got crosswise with a few wasps."

She looked at Inge uncomprehendingly. "Vasp?"

"*Wespe*." Inge smiled.

"Ah," Frau Schmidt said with concern. "Does it pain?" she asked, taking his hand and examining it closely.

"A mite," Ashby admitted.

"Come," she said tenderly. "I fix."

Inge looked at Erich and raised her eyebrows. "What's this?" she whispered. "I've never seen Mother act like *that*."

"Damned if I know." Erich shrugged. "You're imagining things."

Frau Schmidt looked up. "What is all this whispering?" she asked in rapid German. "You go away," she said, pointing at Erich. "Get out of my kitchen. We have work to do. Colonel Kemp wants to make this dinner a fine affair."

"I'll leave if you tell me who the guest is," Erich teased.

"Go," she said in English, losing her patience. "You act like an old woman. Go eat your horse."

"Feed, Mother." Inge giggled. "He needs to feed his horse, not eat it."

"Just go away," Frau Schmidt replied in German. "He knows what I mean."

2

Lieutenant Jason Dobbs was already seated at the long table when a panting Jean Benoit charged in, buttoning his blouse and cursing under his breath in French.

"By God, it must be nice to be newly married." Dobbs grinned, his blue eyes twinkling. "You're supposed to get dressed *before* you come to dinner."

"Don't give me any crap, Jace," Benoit replied irritably. "Inge had me doing some chores and I lost track of the time."

Sliding into his chair, Benoit wiped a thin sheen of sweat off his forehead and looked anxiously toward the head of the table, fearful a reprimand was coming because of his tardiness. Instead of an angry glare from Kemp there was just Harrigan, wearing his perpetual scowl, involved in a spirited lecture to Grant, who was nodding vigorously. Much to Benoit's relief, Kemp's chair was empty.

"Thank God." He sighed, running his fingers through his thick, dark hair. "Do I look presentable?" he asked apprehensively, checking to make sure he had not missed a button.

Dobbs studied his friend, remarking to himself how

much he had matured since the two of them came west together in 1854. Only twenty-two at the time, Benoit still wore the fresh-scrubbed look that was stamped upon all U.S. Military Academy graduates. He kept his boots shined, his brass polished, and his uniforms immaculately pressed. After three years at Fort Laramie, Dobbs noted with pleasure, Benoit's standards had slipped. His boots, by the West Point gauge at any rate, were scuffed and worn at the heels and his brass belt buckle had a mellowed patina. He had long ago worn his tailored cadet uniforms to tatters and these days clad himself in off-the-rack uniforms, noticeable at once because, thanks to his exceptionally long arms, the shirtsleeves hit him well above the wrist. Benoit's complexion, normally a creamy off-white, had tanned two shades darker and wrinkles had appeared at the corner of his eyes and mouth. With a professional eye, Dobbs also noted a white speck on the iris of Benoit's left eye, a callus that was common to men on frontier service who were exposed daily to the west's bright light and harsh winds. "I guess you look as good as you ever will," Dobbs replied dryly, "although I'll never understand what Inge sees in you. Maybe its your sunny disposition."

"Jesus, what a day this has been." Benoit sighed. "Grant dumped all his paperwork on me."

"Do I detect a wee bit of disillusion in your voice?" Dobbs teased. "You wanted so badly to be promoted and now that you're a full-fledged second lieutenant, sans brevet, all you do is complain."

"I'm not complaining!" Benoit said, offended. "I enjoy being second in command in a company. But, I won't lie to you about this, if Grant tells me one more time about his 'Uncle Ulysses' I think I'll bust a lodge pole over his head. Where's Kemp?"

"Here he comes," Dobbs said, turning toward the door. "He must have heard you."

Seemingly on cue, Kemp sauntered into the room, his arm around the shoulders of a stranger.

Benoit's eyes opened in surprise. Such demonstrations of affection from the post's commanding officer were rare. A burly, barrel-chested man with a head of unruly hair the color of wet straw and a slightly upturned nose, Brevet Lieutenant Colonel Aloysius Kemp was not known for his bonhomie. Even his wife of twenty-odd years elected to remain in Baltimore while her husband completed another tour on the frontier, not his first and possibly not his last. Although he had his genial moods not one of the more than three hundred officers and men at the post thought of him as a kindly man. Even when he was laughing, which was not very often, his eyes remained deadly serious. As black as obsidian, they burned with an intense inner light that signaled he was a driven man, one absorbed with the responsibility of protecting westward-bound emigrants on their journey to Utah, Oregon, or California. He knew that some officers in the other Western posts had a low opinion of travelers bound for Utah, considering the Mormons religious fanatics who were not entitled to be in the same category as other westward-bound emigrants. But Kemp vociferously rejected those opinions. As far as he was concerned, every emigrant, regardless of his religion, was entitled to protection and aid. Equally important, he demanded that his men adopt the same philosophy.

Harrigan broke off his discussion with Grant and popped to his feet. "Atten'hut!"

"At ease," Kemp said easily, motioning them to sit. "Gentlemen," he said with an uncharacteristic smile, "I want you all to meet someone. This is Mr. DeAl . . . oh, excuse me, son," he interrupted himself, looking abashed. "I forgot. This young man is Mr. Biv, the son of my oldest

and best friend and he's going to be with us for awhile.
As long as he's here," he added, unconsciously slipping
into his command voice, "he has the run of the post. I
expect you to give him every assistance. Am I understood?"

Kemp smiled beatifically as the 'yes sirs' echoed
around the room.

While the colonel was no taller than average, he all but
dwarfed his guest, who barely came up to the commander's shoulder. But, despite his abbreviated stature, Biv
had the trim look of a trained gymnast with a powerful
upper torso and an innate grace that made him appear to
be floating as he walked.

"He's sure short, *isn't* he?" Benoit whispered. "I wonder if he's going to sit on a box."

"Don't be nasty," Dobbs whispered back, "you were
probably that height once yourself."

"Excuse me, ladies," Kemp said glancing at Benoit and
Dobbs, his voice turning steely. "Is there something you'd
like to contribute?"

"N . . . n . . . no, sir." Benoit blushed. "I was just chatting with Lieutenant Dobbs."

"Very good, Benoit," Kemp said, pronouncing the
name as he always did, Ben-oight. "Then why don't we
get down to dinner, which smells divine. The peerless
Frau Schmidt has prepared an elk loin in honor of Mr. Biv.
Eat hearty."

Benoit grimaced. "God, I wish he'd stop that. I'll bet
I've asked him a million times to pronounce it in the
proper French way. Why can't he do that one little thing,
for Christ's sake?"

"He loves to ride your ass," Dobbs said, tucking a nap-
kin under his collar, which was much too large for his
skinny, stalk-like neck. "He knows it gets your goat."

"This formidable-looking man on my left," Kemp said,

introducing the officers to his guest, "is Captain Jonathan Harrigan, my executive officer. Harrigan drives the men hard, but he has a heart of gold."

"Gold my ass," whispered Benoit, "lead is more like it. And it's between his ears, not in his chest."

"Next to him," Kemp continued, "is First Lieutenant Harold Grant, commander of Company D. Harry comes from excellent stock, his family has a long military tradition. His uncle, Ulysses, is a colonel in personnel in the War Department."

Pointing, Kemp went around the table: First Lieutenant Zack Adamson, commander of Company C . . . First Lieutenant William Barnes, Company G . . . Brevet First Lieutenant Alexander Hopkins, Company F and his second in command, Second Lieutenant George Strudelmeyer.

"Some men are missing. Companies E and B are on patrol," Kemp explained, "out making the Trail safe for wayfarers. But you'll meet them later. And down there at the end of the table are First Lieutenant Jason Dobbs, the extremely competent post surgeon, and, on his left, Second Lieutenant Jean Benoit of D Company."

"I've had just a smattering of French," Biv said, speaking for the first time, "but is that B-e-n-o-i-t? Isn't that pronounced Ben-wah?"

"It certainly is." Benoit beamed, noting that the guest's voice was deep and rich with just the slightest trace of an East Coast accent. "It's a pleasure to meet someone who appreciates the subtleties of our diverse population."

Kemp glared. "Around here it's Ben-oight."

Benoit opened his mouth to speak, but Dobbs kicked him under the table. "Your name is rather unusual, too," he said quickly to the newcomer. "I don't think I've ever met anyone named Biv before."

"That's because I made it up," the guest said with a

smile, exposing a mouthful of gleaming white teeth that seemed even brighter because of a thick black moustache that drooped down almost to his chin.

"I beg your pardon?" Dobbs asked, raising an eyebrow. "You made it up? Your name is not really Biv?"

"Actually," Biv said, "my given name is Alonzo DeAlonzo. My father, with all respects to Uncle Al here, has a perverse sense of humor."

"Oh, no," Benoit groaned. "Not another fucking uncle."

"Why do you use a made-up name?" Harrigan asked.

"It's a long story," Biv replied.

"Why don't you tell us?" Dobbs urged. "We're not going anywhere and we've all heard each other's biographies so often we can repeat them by heart."

"Okay," Biv said good-naturedly, taking a large bite of elk. "By God, that's delicious," he said, smiling happily. "My compliments to the chef."

"*Danke*," Frau Schmidt said, setting a platter of freshly gathered wild onions in front of Kemp.

"You see," Biv continued, "I'm an artist . . ."

"You mean a painter?" interrupted Barnes.

"Precisely. I specialize in portraits. It's very cumbersome to sign a painting with my given name and I think initials look crass. So I adopted what your countrymen," he said, looking at Benoit, "might call a *nom de pinceau*."

"How's that?" Benoit said, surprised. "A 'paintbrush name?' "

"And why not?" Biv grinned. "If a writer can assign himself a nom de plume, literally a pen name, I see no reason why an artist cannot call himself by a *nom de pinceau*."

"That's a good point," Kemp said. "But why 'Biv?' I imagine your father just about had a heart attack when you told him."

"Well," Biv said, embarrassed, "I didn't exactly tell him. I just made the decision a few weeks ago while I was in Independence waiting for an escort west. But I wrote him. He should know by now."

"That explains the rumble I heard in the east last night." Kemp chuckled.

"I imagine it's going to be more like a meteor shower," Biv added.

"You didn't say why you chose such an unusual pseudonym," Dobbs prompted.

"Actually," Biv said convivially, "my entire new name is Roy G. Biv. Would anyone like to guess why?"

"Roy G. Biv," Dobbs repeated slowly. "You've got me. Should that mean something?"

"As someone familiar with the sciences, I was wondering if you might be able to figure it out."

"Why don't you save us all a lot of time and just tell us?" interjected Hopkins, known to all as the least tactful officer on the post.

"Very well," Biv said easily. Laying down his knife and fork, he reached under his collar and withdrew an ornament suspended on a thin gold chain. "My totem," he said with a hint of pride.

"It looks like a piece of glass," Hopkins said, squinting.

"Crystal," Biv corrected. Holding up the object, which was about two inches long and three-sided, he looked at it lovingly. "This is a prism, a gift from my mother when I was just a toddler. With two other boys under five to look after, she thought it would keep me occupied. I daresay she was right."

"A prism refracts light," Dobbs added for the benefit of the others.

"Indeed it does," agreed Biv. "You see, I was sitting in my hotel room in Independence, bored to distraction, when I found myself toying with my prism, abstractly

making color patterns on the wall. I've always been fascinated by colors; that's one of the reasons I wanted so
much to be an artist."

"What does that have to do with your name?" asked
Hopkins, trying to show he was not disinterested.

"Have you ever looked closely at a spectrum?" Biv
asked him.

"No, I don't think so," Hopkins said skeptically.

"A rainbow then?"

"Oh sure, I've seen lots of rainbows."

"In that case, do you remember the order in which the
colors appear?"

Hopkins scratched his head, looking uncomfortable.
"No, can't say that I do."

"Well, they always follow a pattern . . ."

"Red," interrupted Dobbs, "followed by orange, blue . . .

"You forgot yellow."

"Oops, you're right. Red, orange, yellow, green, blue,
purple . . ."

". . . Indigo and violet," Biv added.

"I still don't understand," Hopkins said.

"That's my new name," Biv said proudly. "Picked from
the first letters of the colors in the spectrum. R for red, O
for orange . . ."

"Ah, I see," said Dobbs. "Red, orange, yellow, green,
blue, indigo, and violet—Roy G. Biv."

"Indeed," Biv said, clapping his hands joyously.
"Pretty ingenious, eh?"

"That *is* pretty clever." Kemp smiled benignly, much as
a father would applaud a young son's accomplishment.

"Absolutely," Harrigan echoed faithfully.

"More like infantile if you ask me," Benoit mumbled
under his breath.

"*Gestatten Sie,*" Frau Schmidt said to Kemp. "You
would like to feed now the sweet?"

"By all means," the colonel replied expansively. "Bring on the dessert. And a fresh pot of coffee, if you please. We have business to discuss."

"Top item on the agenda," Kemp said briskly, "is something we've all heard talk about but up to now have had no details. Harrigan," he added without turning, "hustle over to my office and bring back those documents sitting on my desk. And the mail sack," he added.

As Harrigan hurried out of the room, Kemp reached into his shirt pocket and fished out a thin, black cigar. As addicted to them as Benoit was to Cajun coffee, Kemp always managed a plentiful supply. "Mr. Biv was kind enough to bring along our mailbag, along with some more cigars," Kemp said, searching idly for a match. "In addition to some very important documents from Fort Leavenworth it also includes letters for most of you. You can collect them after we adjourn.

"Ah, there you are," he said as Harrigan returned, breathing heavily. "You have a light?

"Here we go," Kemp said puffing, emitting a dense cloud of pungent smoke. "This is from General Culbertson, commander at Fort Leavenworth. It confirms that the rumors we've heard about an imminent large-scale attack against the Cheyenne are not rumors but, in truth, fact."

"Hot damn," Grant said anxiously, his thin face breaking into a large grin. "Action."

"Not so fast, son," Kemp warned. "Let me finish."

"Sorry, sir," Grant replied, reddening.

"Culbertson is sending twin columns on a search for the Cheyenne," Kemp said, shuffling through the papers. "There's a southern column composed of four companies of the First Cavalry under Major John Sedgwick. Their order of march is southwest from Leavenworth heading toward old Fort Atkinson—a real shabby post that was," he added in an aside, "then west to Fort Pueblo. From there, they go almost due north to Fort Saint Vrain.

"Hmmmm," he said, flipping back a page. "Sedgwick left Leavenworth on May eighteenth. That was almost five weeks ago. I wonder why no one told us before now?"

"You said two columns, sir?" prompted Hopkins.

"Yes," Kemp replied, "the other group is under Colonel Sumner . . ."

"Edwin Sumner?" interrupted Barnes. "Ol' Bull of the Woods? I served under him at Fort Union down in New Mexico. A good man."

"Yes," Kemp said peevishly. "Now if you all will quit interrupting me I'll finish. Colonel Sumner," he continued, "should, by now, be at Fort Kearny . . ."

"Indeed he is, Uncle Al," Biv broke in. "Excuse me for interrupting, but I just left Kearny and Sumner was there trying to whip some recruits into shape."

"Recruits?" Harrigan asked. "Don't tell me they're sending recruits on this expedition?"

"Goddamnit," Kemp said. "Let *me* explain this. All right," he added, after a pause, "Sumner left Leavenworth with two companies of the First Cavalry and he's picking up two companies of the Second Dragoons at Kearny. The recruits are for us. He's just the delivery man. I've been listening to all of you moan about being under strength for a long time so rest a little easier; we're finally getting some more manpower."

"Is that going to be all of Sumner's force?" Hopkins asked worriedly. "Four companies?"

"No, dammit, it's *not* all," said Kemp. "He's also taking three companies from here."

"Thank the Lord," sighed Grant. "Which three?"

"I don't know yet," said Kemp. "I haven't made up my mind."

"When is Sumner going to be here?" asked Benoit.

"Any day now, I gather," Kemp replied. "From here, he moves south to link up with Sedgwick east of Saint Vrain."

"This is a little out of my field," Dobbs said tentatively, "but why is Washington mounting a campaign against the Cheyenne? Don't the politicos feel enough blood was shed against the Miniconjou?"

"This has been building for a long time," Kemp replied. "Remember that incident at Renshaw's Bridge about fourteen months ago."

"As I recall it, that was hardly the Cheyenne's fault," said Dobbs. "We had some trigger-happy soldiers. That poor son of a bitch they took captive . . ."

"Wolf Fire," added Benoit.

"That's the one. He died right here just two months ago. Just plain wasted away. Couldn't stand captivity."

"Fortunes of war," said Harrigan.

"We're not at war," Dobbs said hotly. "Our job here isn't to fight the Indians. It's to protect the emigrants . . ."

"Which means fighting Indians," argued Harrigan.

"Gentlemen, gentlemen," Kemp said, raising a hand. "What happened at the bridge was not the only incident. Remember that attack by the Cheyenne against a wagon train on the Little Blue a year ago? *Plus*," he said sternly when he saw Dobbs was about to interrupt, "there was that incident at Grand Island *and* that other attack on the Utah-bound wagon train soon afterwards. Then they killed Babbit—remember the secretary to the Utah Territory?—and the slaughter of that woman captive. There have been a *lot* of incidents in the last couple of years."

"That hardly constitutes enough reason for us to send, what was it, nine companies . . ."

"Eleven," said Grant, "counting the three from here, . . ."

"Right!" said Dobbs. "Eleven companies against a handful of Indians who have been mainly peaceful, even after that fuck-up with Adkins . . ."

"*Lieutenant*," Kemp said, his patience running out, "you don't make policy! And neither do I, for that matter. These orders came straight from Jefferson Davis himself."

"The *honorable* Secretary of War isn't always right," grumbled Dobbs.

"And neither are you, lieutenant," Kemp said sharply. "We do what we're told and right now we're being told to take part in an expedition against the Cheyenne. And . . . we . . . will . . . do . . . it," he said, spacing the words carefully.

"Actually," he added, his tone lightening, "*you* will do it because I'm going to be gone for awhile."

"What do you mean, 'gone'?" Harrigan asked, frowning.

"That's something else I just learned today. It seems that Senator Fontenot was so impressed with what he learned on his visit here that he is having his committee study long-range plans for dealing with the Indian problem."

"It's not an Indian problem; it's a political problem," Dobbs whispered to Benoit.

"I've been called back to Washington to testify before the group. I'm leaving as soon as Sumner gets here. While I'm gone, of course, Captain Harrigan will be in charge."

"Oh, that's just great," Benoit said under his breath.

"Now that business has been taken care of . . ."

"I have a question," Grant said meekly.

"Yes, Harry, what is it?"

"Do the orders say what we're to do with the Cheyenne when we catch up to them?"

"Yes," Kemp said heavily. "Kill them."

"Just like that?" Dobbs asked. "An unprovoked attack? Like Harney at Blue Water?"

"Just like that." Kemp nodded.

"*Mein Gott!*" Frau Schmidt whispered to her daughter. "That means kill Werner and Wilhelm as well."

"Don't worry, *Mutter*," Inge replied soothingly. "I'm sure the soldiers aren't going to murder two young white boys."

"How will they know they're white?" Frau Schmidt asked. "From what Mr. Ashby says they are probably more Indian than white by now?"

"Don't worry, *Mutter*," Inge frowned. "I'll talk to Jean and we'll think of something."

"Frau Schmidt!" Kemp said loudly. "Break out that keg of brandy we've been keeping. Let's all have a drink and then I'll distribute the mail."

"Can you believe Jace?" Benoit asked Inge when they were alone in their tiny quarters. "God, I'm supposed to be the troublemaker around here and he starts picking a fight with Kemp. I thought the Old Man was going to bust a blood vessel."

"That was certainly unusual on Jace's part." Inge laughed. "Help me with this, will you?" she asked, turning her back.

"'Unusual' isn't the word for it," Benoit said, crossing the room with his head at a tilt to keep it from brushing the ceiling. When the tiny adobe they were assigned was constructed by imported labor from New Mexico, the tiny-statured builders did not foresee that it's first occupant would be six feet tall "Rare is more like it. Why," he frowned, fumbling with the tiny buttons, "do women make it so difficult for themselves to get out of their clothes?"

"So they can ask a man to help them," Inge said slipping

the dress over her shoulders. "Who did you get post from?" she asked pointing at the two letters sticking from his pocket.

"This is from my sister," he said, looking at the return address of the one on top.

"What does she have to say?"

"Huh?" Benoit asked, watching as Inge stepped out of her underclothes.

"The *letter!*" Inge smiled. "What does it say?"

"It'll wait," Benoit said, yanking his blouse from his trousers.

"It will *not*," Inge said sternly.

Benoit looked up in surprise. She sounded exactly like her mother.

"Tell me what Marion has to say."

Benoit sighed, watching as she dropped her clothing in a pile and bent over to pull back the light quilt they kept on the bed even in the summer because western nights were typically cool. Benoit studied her perfectly rounded derriere and felt himself getting hard.

"Aw, Inge, it'll keep."

"So will I. I'm not going anywhere. I'm here every day but it isn't every day we get mail. Now," she said, blowing him a kiss, "What's your sister say?"

Benoit ripped open the envelope and glanced hurriedly at the contents.

"The usual stuff," he mumbled impatiently. "Mamman seems finally to have recovered completely from my father's death ... Theophile is coming home on his summer break from the Naval Academy ... Marie ..."

"Arrrgh," Inge said, making a face, "that slut."

"Don't be catty." Benoit smiled.

"What about her?"

"Ummm," Benoit said, "Marion says she's very excited because her father has started hinting at retirement."

"Why should she be excited about that?"

"Because, according to Marion, the plan is for Senator Fontenot to time his retirement so Cle can be appointed to his seat."

"Cle!" Inge said forcefully, pronouncing it 'Clay' as her husband had done. "In the Senate!" She rolled her shoulders, letting the quilt slip down to reveal two erect pink nipples. "That gives me goose bumps. What are you groaning about?" she asked, looking curiously at Benoit.

"Nothing," he said softly, beginning to unbutton his blouse.

Inge pulled a hand from under the bed covering and slowly shook her finger. "No, no, no," she said. "Not until you finish with the post. Is that all Marion had to say?"

Benoit grunted. Picking up the letter, he frowned as he tried to decipher a section where the ink had been smeared. "No. She says she and Armand have set their wedding date for next spring."

"Spring?"

"Well, April, actually. The twenty-seventh. And," he added, turning the page. "That's about it. Now," he said, ripping off his blouse, "ready or not, here I come."

"Not yet!" she said, holding up her hand, palm outward. "What about the other one?"

"Jesus, Inge!" Benoit wailed. "What are you trying to do to me?"

"I'm trying to teach you patience and control," she said sweetly. "You can come to bed soon enough."

"God*damn*," he grumbled, picking up the other envelope. "I'll be dipped," he said, thrusting the envelope under her nose. "Look at this! Speak of the devil."

Inge read the lettering on the outside of the envelope: *The Honorable Clement Couvillion, Member, House of Representatives*. "What does Cle want?" she asked curiously.

"Let's save it until tomorrow," he said hoarsely.

"Jean Francis Xavier Benoit!" she said in the schoolteacher voice she sometimes adopted when she wanted him to do something . . . or not do something. "Will you just open the damn letter before I get angry."

"Just joking," he said lamely. Ripping the end off the envelope he extracted the single sheet that was inside.

"Well?" she said when his expression turned serious. "Please don't tell me he's sending Marie back here."

"No," Benoit replied. "We should be so lucky."

Inge's eyebrows rose. "And just what do you mean by *that*?"

"Oh, God." Benoit blushed. "I just meant that would be an easy problem to solve. But this is difficult."

"What is it? Is something wrong."

"Yes and no," Benoit replied. "You've heard all the talk over dinner and between me and Jace about the situation between the North and the South?"

"Of course. That's why there's so much trouble in Kansas, too."

"Exactly. A lot of people, I guess you could say most people, are expecting a war. They think the North and South are going to fight."

"Do you think so, too?"

Benoit took a long time to reply. "Yes," he said slowly, "I guess I do. But not for awhile yet. Maybe something will be worked out."

"Well, what does that have to do with Cle's letter?"

Benoit read the brief letter again. "He says some people he knows very well—he doesn't name them but I have a good idea who he's talking about—are forming a military group in New Orleans because they think a war is inevitable and they want to be prepared. They can't call it an army so they call it a militia."

"What's the difference?"

Benoit shrugged. "Not much. I guess you could say that a militia is an army in training."

"And what does that have to do with you? With us, I should say."

"He's offering me a job," Benoit said somberly.

"A *job*?" she said, her eyebrows skyrocketing upward. "You already have a job. You're a second lieutenant."

"Well, Cle wants to promote me. He says if I resign my commission in the Army and return to New Orleans he will guarantee that I'll be named a captain in this new group."

"Leave the Army? You? Don't make me laugh."

"It's not that I haven't thought about it. There's a lot of talk among the other officers, many of whom are from the South. In fact, it's a very hot issue."

"Well, if you did that," Inge said, "there is a possibility that one day you would be fighting against Jace and all your other friends."

"On the other hand, I may be fighting against all the boys I grew up with. Even Theophile."

"Oh, God," Inge gasped. "I didn't think of that."

"It could happen." Benoit nodded. "He's only a second-year plebe but he may be thinking about joining the militia, too. They must be desperate for men. They'd probably make him an ensign. After all, New Orleans is still much more his home than it is mine."

"Oh, Jean," Inge said sadly. "this *is* serious, isn't it?"

"Very," he agreed solemnly. "But," he added, brightening. "It isn't something we have to decide right now. There's no sense wasting a good night talking about politics."

"Why ever not?" she asked coyly. "Did you have something else in mind?"

"You might say that." Benoit grinned. "If I can just get these damn boots off, I'll show you what I have in mind."

"Since when," she said, giggling, "did you ever worry about taking your boots off?"

Biv stood somewhat shakily on the rotting wood planking, gazing solemnly at the littered ground in front of him and the crumbling wooden walls of the old fort.

"It's amazing," he said soberly. "I must have viewed Miller's sketch a thousand times, yet I never thought I'd actually be standing here, exactly where he was."

"Are you an admirer of Miller's?" Dobbs asked.

"An admirer?" Biv said ardently. "No, not an admirer. I'm a worshiper. As far as I'm concerned he's the best of the Western artists. Up to now, of course," he added with a grin. "Now that I'm here the situation may change."

"Why do you like him so much?" Dobbs asked, studying Biv to see if he were joking.

"I actually met him once," Biv replied. "He's a native of Baltimore, you know. Just like me. After he got back from his European sojourn he more or less went to work for William Walters, making copies of his original works for twelve dollars each. Walters, naturally, hung them in his gallery, which was not more than a couple of miles from my home. I was there so much people used to think I was an employee. One afternoon—I'll never forget, it was October 30, 1855—I was daydreaming in front of Wimar's *Indians Approaching Fort Benton* when Walters himself called me into his office. 'Alonzo,' he said, 'here's someone I want you to meet.' And there, just like that, I was shaking hands with Alfred Jacob Miller."

"It must have been quite a thrill," Dobbs said.

" 'Thrill' is hardly the word to describe it," Biv gushed. "I was in ecstasy. Although I'm also very impressed with Wimar and Stanley and, of course, the fathers of the Western theme, Catlin and Bodmer. Bodmer's illustrations

in von Wied-Neuwied's *Reise in das innere Nord-Amerika
in den Jahren 1832 bis 1834* were pure genius. But for
some reason, I've always been particularly drawn to
Miller. Maybe it was because I actually shook the hand
that made him famous. Tell me, Lieutenant Dobbs . . ."

"Most people call me Jace. Why don't you?"

"Excellent! Jace it is. Tell me, Jace, are you a lover of
Western art?"

"Oh, I like it all right," Dobbs conceded, "but I haven't
allocated it the attention it deserves. I'm more a student of
anthropology, archeology, and history."

"History, eh. That's very interesting. Tell me about this
place," Biv said, sweeping his arm in an exaggerated gesture. "I have to confess, I'm quite disappointed. When I
finally put together enough money to make this trip I was
so looking forward to getting to Fort Laramie. I expected
it to look exactly like Miller's sketch."

"That's hilarious," Dobbs said, laughing heartily. "I
guess most people Back East just figure that's what Fort
Laramie is today. What you're seeing—where we're
standing right now—was originally called Fort William,
after the renowned trapper William Sublette. The first
timbers were laid in 1834, not too long ago, actually, as far
as history goes."

"Yes," said Biv, "that's what Miller entitled his sketch.
Fort William."

"It didn't last very long," Dobbs continued. "The cottonwood they used for lumber rots too quickly. Another
group, the American Fur Company, took over in 1841 and
built Fort John, just over there," he said, pointing to the
south. "I'll give you a tour of it when we leave here but
it's in even worse shape. It was named after John Sarpy,
one of the stockholders who played a major role in the
company's development."

"When did this finally become Fort Laramie?"

"Not until 1849," Dobbs said professorially. "After the government bought Fort John for four thousand dollars they decided to abandon both structures and start fresh with a brand new fort. The difference," he added, warming to the subject, "is that the first two—Fort William and Fort John—were built by traders out to make their fortune in the fur trade. But about that same time the number of emigrants started rising rapidly and Washington decided some soldiers were needed out here to protect the hordes headed west."

"Where did the name come from? Who was Laramie?"

Dobbs smiled. "A French trapper. Killed by the Arapahoes not far from here. I've seen his name spelled three or four ways but the most common is capital *l*, small *a*, capital *r* small *a*, *m*, double *e*. LaRamee. Jacques LaRamee."

"But there were never any walls around the new fort?"

"Contrary to popular belief, no. What good would they do? The soldiers are outnumbered by the Indians a hundred, two hundred or more to one. No one knows for sure because no one has ever taken an Indian census. But there's a hell of a lot of them out there. Besides, walls are too expensive. The War Department doesn't want to spend a lot. They can replace men but the dollar supply is limited."

"That's pretty callous," Biv said. "Have you ever been attacked?"

"No." Dobbs laughed. "So the theory remains untested. However, we came close once, after a hotheaded young lieutenant named Johnny Grattan thought he could take on the whole Lakota Nation and got himself and all his men killed. If the Brulé and the Miniconjou had attacked then, they could have overrun us easily."

"But they didn't?"

"No, thank God, they didn't."

"Don't you worry that they might?"

Dobbs paused, trying to decide how to answer the question.

"Not really," he replied at length. "Right now the Indians are more interested in attacking easier targets, like small groups of emigrants. They don't, praise be, have many rifles, and they're still not confident of their ability to take us on. But things are changing by the day. There are a few groups of renegade Indians roaming around trying to stir up trouble. Probably the most prominent is headed by a real mean Brulé bastard named Blizzard. But the older, wiser members of the tribe are still trying to work out a peaceful solution."

"You don't sound very optimistic."

"I'm not," Dobbs said softly. "The Indian and the white cultures are too different; they won't be able to exist side by side. Eventually, the whites will win but it's going to be a nasty, bloody fight."

"There's a lot of demand in Baltimore, and I guess everywhere in the States, to subdue the savages."

"Yes." Dobbs nodded. "Sadly, that's true. They think of the red man as uncivilized and cruel when that is really far from the truth. When you've been out here awhile you'll begin to wonder who really are the savages."

"I personally don't think of them as savages," Biv said. "That's why I came out here. Miller's portraits of the Indians are absolutely exquisite. They make me want to know them. To paint them. I want to see if I can even come close to rivaling his work."

"That's a very ambitious undertaking," Dobbs said. "But I'll warn you that it isn't going to be easy. There are a lot of Indian-haters around. You and I are in the minority."

"Does that include many of the men at the fort?"

Dobbs nodded. "Jean—that's Lieutenant Benoit—me,

Ashby, our chief guide, Lieutenant Adamson, and probably Lieutenant Battaglia, feel that way. The others are
either neutral or virulently anti-Indian."

"And Uncle Al?"

Dobbs looked blank. "Oh, Colonel Kemp," he quickly
added. "He doesn't like what's happening but there's not
much he can do about it. He has to follow orders. The
low-ranking officers, like me and Jean, can criticize
Washington but the colonel has to keep his mouth pretty
much shut."

"The you disagree with the so-called expedition against
the Cheyenne?"

"Absolutely!" Dobbs said emphatically. "The
Cheyenne are wonderful people and I can't understand
why they have earned the enmity of those pissants in
Washington. They're proud. They're excellent warriors.
And they don't take any crap from anybody. Come to
think of it, that's probably why they're on the War
Department extermination list."

"I surely would like to paint some Cheyenne portraits,"
Biv said wistfully. "Do you think there's any chance?"

"Phew," Dobbs exhaled. "That's going to be
tough. Especially now with the expedition forming up.
The Cheyenne aren't stupid. They've probably
known something was in the wind long before we
did."

"Isn't there some way it could be done?" Biv pleaded.
"God, that would be wonderful."

"I don't know," Dobbs said. "Let me talk to 'tienne."

"Who?"

"Etienne Legendre. He's one of our interpreters and a
former trapper. He was married to a Cheyenne. He has a
son, a boy named David who's about ten now, who's just
about been raised by the tribe. Maybe he can arrange it but
don't get your hopes up too high. These are tense times."

"I've sensed that," Biv replied. "This place is bustling like the Baltimore docks."

"That's true enough." Dobbs chuckled. "When I first came out there wasn't much. Old Bedlam was about it. Now the number of troops has just about tripled. We've got a bakery, a blacksmith shop, a sutler's store . . . you name it."

"Seems like you have everything but a place for entertainment," Biv said. "What do you do for fun?"

Dobbs grinned. "Funny you should mention that," he said. "You can come with me; I need to perform a little medical work."

"Go with you where? What kind of medical work?"

"You'll see." Dobbs beamed. "Let's go find you a fresh horse and I'll give you an exclusive introduction to the Hog Ranch."

"Ranch?" Biv asked, puzzled. "I didn't know there were any ranches around here."

"Your Western education is about to begin," Dobbs said, chortling.

3

"You aren't listening to what I'm saying, Captain . . ."

"Please. Call me Jon."

Ellen O'Reilly stared keenly at Harrigan. As madam of the only whorehouse between Independence and San Francisco, she was accustomed to dealing with strange requests from men. But Harrigan's proposal had come as a shock, as unexpected as a balmy day in February.

"Maybe I misunderstood, captain," she said slowly, pointedly ignoring his request to move their relationship to a more intimate level. "Please tell me again what you're suggesting."

Harrigan stiffened in his chair, throwing back the thick shoulders that helped contribute to his image as a man ful-filling his destiny as a ranking military officer. Deliberately he crossed his legs. Over the edge of the desk in the tiny room she called an office, Ellen could see the toe of Harrigan's right boot. A beam from the lantern on the wall behind her flashed off the shiny surface, looking to her like an obscene wink. Although of only average height, Harrigan had a booming, parade ground voice and a way of sitting a horse that made him look as if he had been born in the saddle. An intelligent and educated man—he had,

Ellen had heard, finished second in his class of twenty-six at West Point—he also had been blessed with an innate astuteness and a facility for organization that made him ideal to be Colonel Kemp's second in command. Leaning forward, he let his hazel eyes bore deep into hers. "It's very simple," he said, using the same tone he would in telling a dull private how to clean his rifle, "I've been watching you for quite a while and I'm impressed. You're a very handsome woman and you have a good head on your shoulders to boot."

"Skip the flattery," Ellen said somewhat impatiently. "Get to the point."

"I find you physically attractive. I would like to get to know you better, man to woman."

"You know, of course," Ellen replied, "that I just run the Hog Ranch as a business, that I personally don't entertain men. That's what my girls are for."

"Has my money offer offended you?" Harrigan asked without apology. "Wasn't it enough?"

"Thirty dollars a month is nothing to sneeze at," Ellen replied, knowing that many of her girls earned less than a third of that. "If I were hungrier and ten years younger, I might be sorely tempted. But I'm not. My business is doing very well. Besides, it's the fine print I'm having trouble with."

"You mean my insistence on exclusivity?"

"Those are fancy words, captain. You want *me* to be *your* woman and nobody else's. You need to know that I'm *nobody's* woman."

"What about Jason Dobbs?" he asked, smiling craftily.

Ellen's eyes widened. He has a point, she admitted to herself. She and Jace had been having a relationship for more than two years, ever since she nursed him back to health from a bout with pneumonia that almost killed him. Certainly, her alliance with Dobbs could be called exclusive.

"Lieutenant Dobbs and I enjoy each other's company," she said frostily. "Money has nothing to do with it."

"Maybe not for you," Harrigan continued. "But how about for Dobbs? He has a good thing going. He can fuck you . . ."

Not one to ordinarily be offended by explicit language — how could she be, she asked herself, and still operate a the kind of business she did—she nevertheless felt her Irish temper rising. "I don't appreciate that kind of language," she said hotly, interrupting him. "I know I'm not in much of a position to sound prudish, but this is my establishment and as long as you're a guest . . ."

"Customer."

"All right, customer. As long as you're a customer here you'll abide by the rules."

"I like that, too." Harrigan grinned. "Spunk. You've got gumption."

It was Ellen's turn to sigh. While she had known Harrigan ever since she came to Fort Laramie from Minneapolis as a twenty-seven-year-old widow three years previously she had never had any close dealings with him. What she knew was basically gossip. There was not much that went on at Fort Laramie that did not reach Ellen's ear and what she had heard about Harrigan was sufficient to make her both wary and uncomfortable.

The word among the enlisted men who flocked to her establishment was that the captain was not the dashing military figure he appeared. While Colonel Kemp was universally respected among the men as a tough but fair commander, that view did not extend to his executive officer, who, thanks to a quickness to anger and a not-so-deeply buried touch of sadism, was more feared than admired. Openly and aggressively ambitious, the captain had a reputation as an unforgiving authoritarian more interested in his career than in his responsibility to

the troopers. It didn't help that he also was perceived as
a sycophant, shamelessly kowtowing to Kemp by opening his doors, lighting his cigars and agreeing with
the commander's every utterance. A standing joke
among the enlisted men who flocked to Ellen's sporting
house was that Harrigan would welcome the opportunity to wipe Kemp's ass if the commander would only
ask.

"Captain," she said, adapting the most businesslike
tone she could muster, "I'm flattered by your offer but I
simply cannot accept. I think it's better for both of us if we
keep things on an impersonal basis. You're welcome to
come down at any time and pay for my girls' time—as
long as you abide by the rules," she added, giving him a
sharp look, "but I think you and me are out of the question. I run this establishment, I don't work here."

"Is it the fact that I'm only a captain?" Harrigan persisted. "That won't be forever. When Kemp is reassigned
in another year or two, I'm almost certain to be named
post commander. In fact, that's a position I hold temporarily from time to time already. Like when Kemp
leaves for Washington . . ."

"The colonel is going to Washington?" Ellen asked in
surprise.

Harrigan smiled, feeling he had drawn blood. "Yes,"
he said lightly, elated that he had won an unexpected
point. "He's been called to testify before Senator
Fontenot's committee which is investigating the Indian
problem. He'll be gone for a couple of months at least.
And while he's absent I'll be in command."

The first thought that popped into Ellen's head was,
Why haven't I heard this? The second was more prag-
matic. "Just what are you trying to say, captain?"

Harrigan shook his head. "I'm just pointing out that it
will be entirely up to me, for the next couple of months, to

decide what privileges the men will have. If I think it's for
their welfare to put the Hog Ranch off limits . . ."

"Is that a threat, Captain Harrigan?"

"God forbid. Why would I want to threaten *you*? I'm
just saying that it's a lot of responsibility being in charge
of the welfare of more than three hundred horny troopers.
If, for example, there is an outbreak of pox . . ."

"My girls are clean. You know that. That's why
Lieutenant Dobbs examines them once a week."

"But with new girls coming in all the time, one can
never be too careful."

"I don't like the tone this conversation is taking," Ellen
said angrily. "I think you'd better leave."

Harrigan's eyes narrowed. "Are you kicking me out?"

"If that's what you want to call it."

The captain slammed his fist angrily on Ellen's desk. "I
don't appreciate being treated this way," he fumed. "I
came here with a legitimate offer . . ."

"Which I rejected . . ."

". . . and you have no right to insult me."

"I'm not insulting you, captain," Ellen said softly. "I'm
just turning down your proposition and trying to tell you
that the discussion is finished. Don't take it personally."

"How the hell am I supposed to take it?" he said, rising
and stomping wrathfully around the small space.

"If I've learned anything in this profession it's how to
deal with men whose delicate feelings are supposedly
shattered," she said as calmly as she could. "Let me make
it clear that I don't intend to let you intimidate me. You
could be the Secretary of War himself, which you're not.
Now," she said, pointing to the tumbler of bourbon that
sat on the edge of the desk, "I'll thank you to finish your
drink and get the hell of out here."

Harrigan glared at the nearly full glass. Ellen watched
him closely, recognizing such anger in his eyes that she

feared he was going to hurl the whisky in her face. If he does that, she thought, I'll get my pistol out of the drawer and shoot the son of a bitch.

As quickly as Harrigan's temper had risen, it seemed to subside. Laughing, he lifted the glass and offered it to her in a toast. "I like a lively woman," he said half mockingly. "But women are like horses. They don't come so full of spirit that they can't be broke. Your day is coming, madam, and I use that word literally, when you'll be *glad* to see me walk through that door."

"And why do you think that will be?" she asked testily.

"Because I'm the closest thing to a real man you've got available. Dobbs may be a good surgeon but I suspect he's not much under the quilts. If he were really interested in you physically, he'd do the right thing by marrying you."

"I can't see where that's any of your business, captain."

"Maybe not," he said, tipping the glass and draining it in one long swallow. "But I want to give you fair warning that if anything ever happens to Dobbs I intend to be back knocking at your door. And next time I don't intend to take no for an answer."

"That'll be the day," Ellen replied, striving for the last word. "I would rather mate with that cutthroat Brulé who's been terrifying the emigrants."

"You mean Blizzard?" Harrigan asked in astonishment. "What in hell do you know about him?"

"Only that his heart is blacker than a chunk of Pennsylvania coal and colder than a January night on the summit of Laramie Peak. Which means that he's one step above you."

"Goddamnit!" Harrigan swore. "That's too much. if you weren't a woman . . ." He stopped in mid-sentence, distracted by a sharp knock on the door.

"Come in!" Ellen said briskly, not taking her eyes off Harrigan.

"Hi, Ellen," Dobbs called out cheerily, swinging the door open. "I've brought along . . ."

Seeing Harrigan, Dobbs paused. "I'm not interrupting anything am I?" he stammered, taking a half step backward.

"Heavens, no!" Ellen said in relief. "Do come in. Captain Harrigan was just leaving. You *were* leaving, weren't you, captain?" she asked, staring at him coldly.

Without responding, Harrigan tromped out of the room, shouldering Dobbs aside.

"What the hell was *that* all about?" Dobbs asked, turning to Ellen, his question punctuated by the sound of the outer door slamming loudly.

"Nothing," she said tiredly, walking behind her desk and slumping into her chair. "Just part of the exciting life of a struggling proprietress. What was it you were so anxious to tell me?"

"I didn't want to tell you anything. I wanted to introduce you to someone. Come on in, Roy," he said over his shoulder.

Biv sauntered into the room, his white teeth gleaming like shards of ivory. "Is this place what I think it is?" he asked exuberantly.

"Indeed it is." Dobbs laughed. "The only place of its kind you're likely to see for a long, long time. And this is the lady who makes it all possible. Roy Biv, meet Ellen O'Reilly."

"My pleasure," Biv said, walking forward and extending a tiny hand. "What beautiful green eyes you have," he said, staring into Ellen's face, "complemented perfectly, if I may say so, by your dark hair. Is it naturally that color?"

Ellen gave him a bemused look. "That's getting rather personal and I don't even know you. But if you're going to talk about physical attributes, you certainly aren't what anyone would refer to as a giant, are you?"

Biv roared. "Only in my heart, Miss O'Reilly. My body may be small but my heart is as big as the Great Plains."

Ellen looked at Dobbs. "Good God, Jace, where did you find this man? You don't know how refreshing it is to meet a gentleman, especially after that experience with your soon-to-be commanding officer."

"Oh, he told you, huh?"

"Well, I certainly couldn't have waited to hear it from you."

"Aw, Good God, Ellen, have some sympathy. I didn't know myself until last night."

"In that case," she said, smiling, "you're forgiven." Swiveling in her chair, she looked into Biv's eyes, which were only a few inches above hers even though she was seated and he was standing. "Tell me, Mr. Biv . . ."

"Roy. Nobody calls me Mr. Biv, especially since hardly anyone knows me by that name."

"Now that sounds like an interesting story," Ellen said graciously. "But whatever is an obviously cultured man like yourself doing on the frontier?"

"Indians," Biv said simply.

Ellen frowned. "Let's go back. How did Indians get into this conversation?"

"You asked me what I was doing here?"

"So I did. But what kind of an answer is 'Indians'?"

"It's why I'm here. I came from Baltimore to see Indians."

"I see," she said, looking at him as if he were retarded. "You traveled fifteen hundred miles to see a bunch of savages."

"I don't think they're savages, Miss O'Reilly . . ."

"Ellen."

"Okay, Ellen. To me they aren't savages at all. They're a handsome, nomadic people who deserve respect, not censure."

"Oh Jesus," she said, rolling her eyes. "Jace, you goddamn didn't bring me another Thunder Tongue, did you?"

Dobbs laughed heartily. "Would I do that to you,
Ellen?" he asked, gasping for breath.

"Who's Thunder Tongue?" Biv asked.

"Also known as the Reverend W. Cleveland Longstreet," Ellen replied.

"All right, who's Reverend Longstreet?"

"He was a crazy, lecherous old man who thought Good
God was a Cheyenne warrior," Dobbs interjected.

"*Was?*"

"Yes, *was*. He died a couple of years ago of lockjaw."

"Thank Good God for that," Ellen said. "Or I might
have had to kill the bastard myself. Preferably slowly and
painfully."

"I take it you didn't like him," Biv said, grinning.

"Like him . . ."

"He tried to rape her," Dobbs interrupted. "Then he
ran off to live with the Cheyenne."

"As I want to do."

Dobbs rubbed his chin. "I hadn't thought of that. In a
way there are similarities. Both of you seem obsessed with
the Cheyenne, for one thing."

"Do you want to convert them, too?" Ellen asked.

"Good God, no," Biv said quickly. "I'm a painter, not a
preacher."

"A painter."

"Of portraits. I'm a great admirer of some of the artists
who've painted the Western Indians and I'd like to do the
same."

"And you want to go live with the Cheyenne?" Ellen
asked.

"It's what I had hoped for."

"Don't you know how tense the situation is right
now?"

"I've tried to explain it to him," said Dobbs. "But it seems as if his mind is made up."

"I've been called stubborn once or twice." Biv grinned.

"I think I'm going to like your friend," Ellen said to Dobbs. "He knows what he wants and he's not afraid to go after it."

"I didn't say I wasn't afraid . . ."

"But not too afraid to try?"

"No."

"That just shows you're not stupid," Ellen said. "Tell me, Roy, when do you plan to leave on this, uh, excursion?"

Biv shrugged. "I don't know exactly. Jace," he said, nodding at Dobbs, "is trying to help me set it up. I hope in a week or so."

"In the meantime, you need some help in combating your loneliness. Is that right?"

Biv blushed. "Well, gee. I haven't really had time to think about that."

"You *do* like girls, don't you?"

"Ellen!" Dobbs said in surprise. "That's a hell of a thing to ask."

"Well, you know how it is, Jace. A lot of the artistic types, writers and painters, seem to prefer boys."

"I'm not one of those!" Biv said emphatically.

"Wonderful!" Ellen clapped her hands. "Then I think we can do some business. Tell me, do you like blondes, brunettes, or redheads?"

"I like 'em all," Biv said. "But liking has nothing to do with it."

"What do you mean?" Ellen asked.

"I mean, the trip out here ate a big hole in my budget. I spent more than I thought I would."

"Ummmm," Ellen replied, drumming her hands lightly on the desktop. "I'll tell you what," she said, after a pause.

"You do have your painting stuff with you, don't you? Brushes and paints, paper . . ."

"Canvas."

"Canvas. Whatever. You have all your equipment?"

"Of course."

"Then we may be able to work a trade."

"What kind of trade?" Dobbs asked, fascinated by the glimpse of a side of Ellen O'Reilly that he had not yet seen.

"Yeah," echoed Biv. "What kind of trade?"

"Let's say service for service." Ellen smiled. "I'll provide you with an, uh, companion, to help you while away the long days before you leave, and you provide me with a nice portrait that I can hang on the wall over the bar. Give the place some class."

"That sounds fair to me," said Biv.

"Wait a minute," said Dobbs. "A portrait of whom? I've seen barroom paintings before."

"Well," Ellen said briskly. "I think that choice should be Roy's. He's the one who's going to be doing the work."

"More than fair." Biv nodded. "Let's shake on it."

"Agreed." Ellen laughed, extending her hand for the second time. "Excuse me just a moment."

Walking to the door, she stuck her head out. "Narcissa," she called. "Will you come in here for a moment, please?"

Biv turned to Dobbs and raised his eyebrows. "Narcissa?"

Dobbs shrugged. "Must be new. I don't know her."

"Roy," Ellen said, leading a woman in her early twenties into the room. "I want you to meet Narcissa Chandler, newly arrived from Richmond."

Biv looked up. And up. And up. "My good God!" He gasped. "You must be six-feet four."

"Six three and a half, actually," Narcissa said, throwing back her broad shoulders. Two perfectly formed breasts quivered in the air more than a foot above Biv's head. "I'm the runt of the family."

"In that case, I'd sure hate to meet your brother in a dark alley," Biv said.

"Don't have no brothers," Narcissa said, shaking her head, setting two long braids swishing like twin horses' tails. "Just three sisters. Two older. One younger."

"Are they all as beautiful as you?"

Narcissa's dark eyes twinkled and she smiled, revealing deep dimples in each of her rosy cheeks. "Pret' near."

"Don't you just love it, Jace?" Ellen gushed.

"What do you mean?" Dobbs frowned.

"Them." Ellen pointed at Biv and Narcissa. "The perfect couple. When they're toe to toe, his nose is in it. When they're nose to nose, his toes are in it."

"You're impossible, Ellen," Dobbs erupted. "Sometimes I wonder why I don't make an honest woman out of you."

Ellen looked at him, her glance turning somber. "Sometimes I wonder, too."

Dobbs was well into the familiar nightmare, the one where his wife Colleen was plaintively calling him to her side, begging him to do something to stop the pain. But Dobbs was standing across a raging river so swollen by the spring rains that it was impossible to cross. Staring at the water, Dobbs could tell it was dark and cold, filled with uprooted trees whose twisted roots stuck up like the grotesquely rigored limbs of soldiers killed in battle. Although he had saved many lives as a battlefield surgeon, he had lost a lot of men as well. And he knew, although he was stripping off his shirt and boots and preparing to plunge into the swollen stream, that he was going to lose Colleen as well. But he had to try, not only for her sake but for the sake of his children.

Most people's dreams are a strange mixture of fact and fantasy, and Dobbs's was no exception. In reality, his wife, Colleen, did indeed die, but Dobbs was nowhere near when she passed away. He had been in Mexico as a surgeon with an infantry company. And he did, indeed, have two children, Mary Margaret and Patrick. Although he had not seen them since he came west in 1854, three and a half years before, they wrote him regularly, at least as regularly as he could hope to hear from children aged fourteen and eleven. But he knew they were well. Colleen's sister, Agnes, and her husband were taking good care of them, raising them on their New England farm as proper little Yankees.

In his dream, Dobbs had both his boots off and was undoing the heavy Army buckle at his waist when he realized that it was not Colleen screaming at all, but a man who was yelling not so much in pain as in anger. Springing upright, he was halfway out the door when he heard Ellen's caution.

"Don't take any dumb chances, Jace," she said with the wisdom of someone who has witnessed such incidents many times. "This happens all the time. The best thing to do is stand back and let them fight it out. If you try to get in the middle they might turn on you."

Dobbs nodded. Although he was six-feet-two he hardly had the build of a brawler. Starving-man thin with a long chin, pointed nose, and oversize head that rested precariously on a reedlike neck, Dobbs was smart enough to know his limitations. His exceptionally long fingers were skilled at sewing up wounds and amputating limbs and he wisely restricted them to those uses. He was paid to mend, not to fight, and he willingly abided by that dictum. "Don't worry," he said, winking at Ellen with an ice-blue eye, "I'll climb under a table until it's all over."

Running down the hall, he screeched to a stop just inside the room that served as the Hog Ranch's bar. Nose to nose, screaming at each other at the top of their voices, were two privates. One of them, Dobbs knew, was Carmine LaRossa, son of an Italian immigrant and a member of Benoit's company. The other was a new arrival that Dobbs did not know well, only that his last name was Venezia and obviously of Italian descent as well.

"Welcome to the show," Biv said excitedly.

Dobbs turned. The artist was sitting on top of Narcissa's shoulders, like a child being lifted up to watch a parade. He was so high, Dobbs noted, that he had to duck his head to keep it from bumping against the ceiling. "Air's great up here," Biv said, giving Dobbs a thumbs-up sign. "Now I'm beginning to see what I've been missing."

"*Succhiatore!*" the new man screamed, red faced.

Dobbs frowned. "What the hell is that?" he said half to himself.

Biv grinned. "Don't forget my real name is DeAlonzo. I speaka da language like a true Roman. The one on the right just called the other one a cocksucker."

"*Vaffanculo!*" LaRossa screamed back, shoving the other man's shoulder.

Dobbs raised an eyebrow.

" 'Fuck you,' " Biv translated.

"They certainly are imaginative, aren't they," Dobbs mumbled dryly.

"*Uno che va in culo a sua madre!*" hollered Venezia, shoving back.

"Ooh," Biv hissed. "It's getting nasty. That means motherfucker."

"*Tua madre is da per ninete.*"

"Literally, 'Your mother gives it away,'" said Biv, enjoying himself immensely.

"Lei e'un cafone stronzo!" LaRossa yelled, a vein in his forehead pulsing like a snake under a blanket.

"Loosely," said Biv, "he just called him a piece of shit."

"Testa di merda!" Venezia screamed, swooping up a chair and aiming it at LaRossa's head.

"Uh-oh," Dobbs ejaculated. "Now comes the rough stuff."

LaRossa, who had backpedaled in anticipation, lifted his arm in an attempt to block the blow. When the chair hit his arm, both broke with simultaneous cracks. LaRossa dropped as if he had been poleaxed.

"My arm!" he groaned. "My arm! You *pistolino*, you broke my fucking arm!"

"Serves you right, you bastard. You shouldn't have been fucking with my woman."

"What do you mean, 'your woman'? I don't see your name tattooed on her."

Venezia picked up a piece of the broken chair and raised it over his head, intending to hit LaRossa again.

"That's enough!" Dobbs bellowed, pushing his way through the crowd.

A large corporal who Dobbs knew as Sean Flannery, a barrel-chested Irishman he had once treated for a smashed nose suffered in a barracks room brawl, beat him there. Moving with amazing speed for a man his size, Flannery approached Venezia from the rear. Wrapping his long arms around Venezia's body he kept him from carrying on the attack. "Just calm down," he said soothingly in the little Italian's ear. "If you don't I may have to bust your ass myself."

"He took my woman!" Venezia said angrily. "He knew I was coming down here but he got here first and paid her for the whole night."

"A whore ain't worth gettin' yourself kilt for," Flannery said in a reasonable tone. "There's plenty of women here."

"Not like Mary Jane there ain't," the new man argued. "That fucking dago stabbed me in the back."

"Who you calling a dago?" LaRossa wheezed, clutching his arm, which was bent in a broad U between the elbow and the wrist. "You goddamned spaghetti bender. Mary Jane gives the best blow jobs this side of Brooklyn and I just aimed to take advantage of it."

"She does not!" piped in a girl named Hannah, a plump, buxom, dark-haired refugee from Cincinnati. "I do."

"She's right about that," chuckled a private whose name Dobbs couldn't remember. "She'll flat suck your eyes out through your willy."

"Who you saying's better at sucking," an angry Mary Jane screamed, lowering her head and charging at Hannah, her arms flailing.

"Whoa," said the private whose name Dobbs could not recall, grabbing Mary Jane around the waist and yanking her to a halt.

"That bitch said she had more talent," Mary Jane protested.

"And it's the truth," said Hannah. "You think the only thing your mouth's good for is saying dirty words. Your tongue's as limp as an old man's pecker."

"Ladies! Ladies!" Dobbs called loudly. "Ladies *and* gentlemen," he added, turning an icy stare on Venezia and LaRossa. "The fun's over for the night. Save your fighting spirit for the renegades. Let's all take it easy. Come on," he said, waving a long skinny arm. "Up to the bar. The drinks are on me."

"Hurrah! Hurrah!" the men in the room yelled. "The Lieutenant's a jolly good fellow."

"Right now," Dobbs muttered under his breath, "I don't feel so goddamned jolly. Let me take a look," he said, stooping over LaRossa, who was rising unsteadily to his feet.

"I'm okay, Lieutenant," LaRossa said in a shaky voice. "I been hurt worse by a kicking mule."

"I daresay you have," Dobbs said absentmindedly, lifting the private's damaged arm.

"Oh, Jesus, that hurts!" LaRossa said, swaying.

"Sit down here," Dobbs said, pulling up an unbroken chair. "Let me get a better look."

"It's plumb broke, ain't it?"

Dobbs raised his eyes. "I think that's a massive understatement. The only good thing is the bone didn't come through the skin."

"That's good? Christ, do you have to push so hard?" he groaned.

"Have to find out how bad the break is," Dobbs said unsympathetically.

"Well, how bad is it?"

"I've seen worse. Does this hurt?"

LaRossa paled, leaned forward from the waist and vomited.

"I guess that answers my question. Can you walk?"

"I think so," LaRossa said in a shaky voice. "Where we going?"

"To get my medical kit so I can wrap this. Tomorrow, first thing, I'll put it in a cast."

"Cast, huh?" LaRossa said, color returning to his cheeks. "That means I can get out of wood cutting detail?"

"Not goddamned likely." Dobbs sighed. "You can drive the wagon."

"Just my fuckin' luck. I'll bet if he'd whacked me on th' head, I'd qualify for sick leave."

"If he'd whacked you on the head you might have qualified for burial detail," Dobbs replied. "Come on," he added, grabbing LaRossa by his good arm and lifting him out of the chair.

LaRossa looked wistfully toward the bar. "An' miss my free drink?"

"Bring it with you." Dobbs sighed. "You're probably going to need it."

"That was quite a night, wasn't it?" Biv said as he and Dobbs guided their horses north toward Fort Laramie. Although stars still dotted the sky, they would disappear before they reached the post. Since it was almost the summer solstice, the sun was scheduled to one of its earliest appearances of the year.

"Yeah," Dobbs grumbled. "Some night. I swear, I'm getting too old for this."

"Why do you do it then? Go to the Hog Ranch, that is?"

"Part of my job. As medical officer I have to inspect the girls for venereal disease or anything else they might pass on to the troops."

"Is that the only reason? You can do that during the day?"

Dobbs grinned sheepishly. "No," he confessed. "I also go because of Ellen. Otherwise I'd be in my quarters sleeping soundly with nothing to disturb me until reveille."

"You like her a lot, don't you?"

Dobbs glanced at him out of the corner of his eye, trying to see if he was being facetious. "Yeah," he replied when he decided that Biv was serious. "I like her a lot."

"Then why don't you marry her?"

Dobbs reigned his horse to a halt. "That's pretty goddamn personal."

"Don't get mad," Biv said calmly. "I'm just a straightforward person. I say what I think."

"And what do you think?"

"I think you two make a right handsome couple. She's a widow, right?"

"Yep."

"And you're a widower?"

"Yep," Dobbs said, urging his horse forward.

"Then why does it seem strange that I ask why you two don't get married."

"Because it isn't that simple," Dobbs said.

"What's complicated about it?"

"The Army for one thing. An officer on the frontier can't just get married because his dick gets hard."

"That seems like a pretty good reason to me."

"That's because you aren't a soldier. Regulations say I have to get permission from Colonel Kemp before I can take a wife."

"Do you think he'd refuse? If you want, I can talk to Uncle Al? He might . . ."

"No," Dobbs said quickly. "Thanks just the same. The problem isn't with the colonel. It's with me."

"I don't understand."

Dobbs exhaled loudly. "I'm a career soldier. I've been in the Army almost longer than I can remember. It's my life. I don't know what I'd do if I wasn't in the military."

"Have you thought about private practice?"

"Not more than a couple of million times. But I know myself. I'm afraid I'd be bored silly. I'd turn to drink or," he paused, remembering his earlier addiction to laudanum, "something worse."

"Well, why can't you be a *married* surgeon? There's no regulation against that, is there?"

"Because of what Ellen is," Dobbs said glumly.

"You mean it bothers you that she's a madam?"

"Not me it doesn't. But the Army doesn't take a positive view of its officers marrying operators of whorehouses."

"You afraid of the ridicule?"

"Goddamn, this is getting serious," Dobbs said. "Let's talk about something else."

"I'm just trying to help," said Biv. "It's one of my better traits. I'm a hell of a portrait painter first and a hell of a counselor second."

"I don't know if I want any counseling."

Biv looked at his companion. "Okay," he said finally. "Have it your own way. I won't mention it again."

For the next half hour they rode in silence. They were almost to the fort when the sun peeked over the eastern bluffs, bathing the Plains in a soft golden light and shining like a spotlight on snowcapped Laramie Peak.

"That's just about the most beautiful sight I've ever seen," exclaimed Biv, reining in his horse. "Look at those colors. Absolutely goddamn magnificent. People Back East have no idea of just how gorgeous it is out here."

Dobbs, who had seen the sight almost every day for going on four years, ignored the sunrise. "It's because of Ellen," he said softly.

"Huh?" Biv asked, puzzled.

"We can't get married because the officers would treat her like shit. I can put up with it, but I'm afraid it would be too much for her. She has no idea how cruel those bastards can be."

"Ummm," Biv said. "I can see your point. But," he added, brightening, "have you asked her? How she feels about it, I mean?"

"Sort of," Dobbs said. "We talked about it once and she said she was willing to take the chance."

"Well, there you have it," said Biv. "What the hell do you need a counselor for? If she's willing and she's the one who's going to have to put up with most of the guff, how come you aren't willing to try? Seems to me that you're the one with cold feet."

Dobbs straightened his back. "You know." he said, grinning. "You may have a point. I've been very selfish about this whole thing. Maybe we *do* need to talk about it some more."

"Makes sense to me," said Biv. "What's that?" He pointed toward the northeast. "Looks like a rider. Who the hell else would be out this time of day?"

Dobbs cupped his hands over his eyes to shield them from the sun. "By Good God this is your lucky day," he said cheerily. "That's 'tienne."

"Who?" Biv asked, puzzled.

"Etienne Legendre. Remember I told you about him? He's the one with the ties to the Cheyenne. If anybody can grease your way into the tribe, it's him."

"Well, what the hell are we waiting for," Biv said, digging his spurs into his horse's ribs. "Let's go talk to him."

"There's no hurry," Dobbs replied. "No one's going anywhere just yet. Just . . ." he started to add when he realized he was speaking to an empty space; Biv was already a hundred yards down the trail.

— 4 —

Less than three hours after Dobbs returned to the fort, a rider galloped in, heading straight for Old Bedlam. Twenty minutes later, Kemp called the officers together and told them that Colonel Sumner and his troops would be marching in before the day was over.

"They're going to be tired and footsore," Kemp explained. "It's been a hard march from Kearny and they had a rough crossing across the Platte. According to the rider, they lost the hospital wagon. They'll be here a few days while the men rest and reprovision. But before the end of the week, they'll be heading south to meet Sedgwick and go after the Cheyenne."

"Have you decided yet, sir, which of our troops will be joining the expedition?" Grant asked apprehensively.

Kemp allowed himself a small smile. "Yes, lieutenant. You're going to get your wish. Companies D, C, and G will be going with Colonel Sumner while E Company will remain on post."

Grant beamed and let out a small whoop.

"Don't be so anxious, lieutenant," Kemp said sharply. "You're going to get your chance to get shot at soon enough."

Benoit turned to Dobbs. "I'll bet Inge isn't going to be real happy about this. She was hoping I'd get to sit one out."

"Fortunes of war," whispered Harrigan, who had overheard the comment. "You accept the money, you take the duty."

"The three companies," Kemp continued, ignoring the by-play, "will, of course, be under Sumner's command. But, for organizational simplicity, I'm naming Lieutenant Adamson as commander of the Fort Laramie contingent."

"Congratulations, Zack," Benoit whispered. "You'll do a good job."

"Since Adamson will have enough on his hands, I'm going to take some of the load off by appointing an acting commander for his company. Benoit, you think you can handle it?"

Benoit's head jerked up. "Me, sir?" he asked in surprise.

"Dammit, Benoit, are you asleep? I asked a simple question: You think you can handle the job of company commander for a couple of months."

"Well, sir, I, uh, this is quite a shock . . ."

"For Christ's sake, Jean, tell him yes," Dobbs said angrily under his breath.

"Well!" Kemp demanded.

"Yes, *sir*!" Benoit replied sharply. "I appreciate the opportunity, sir. It's a great honor . . ."

"Don't overdo it, Jean," Dobbs said quietly. "Just shut up."

"If Benoit's going to C Company, who'll be my second in command?" Grant interrupted, much to Benoit's relief.

"Take Kohl. Since E Company is staying behind they can get by with one officer until you get back."

"Since I'm not formally assigned to any company, who will I be marching with?" Dobbs asked.

"You won't," Kemp said. "You're not going."

Dobbs's jaw dropped. "I beg your pardon, sir. Did I hear you say I wasn't going?"

"That's right," Kemp said. "Captain Harrigan and I decided you should stay behind."

"But, sir," Dobbs protested, his color rising, "I thought you said that Colonel Sumner lost his hospital wagon . . ."

"You heard correctly. He lost the *wagon*, not the medical officer. He'll draw from your stores."

"Begging your pardon, colonel," Dobbs continued. "But those are my men going off to do battle with the Cheyenne. I can't let them go without me."

"Oh yes you can, lieutenant. And you will. Colonel Sumner and Major Sedgwick both have surgeons. You'd be one more mouth to feed. You're needed here."

"Sir," Dobbs persisted, "I don't think . . ."

"This isn't a subject for debate, Lieutenant. Let me make it clear: I'm *ordering* you to stay here. Understood?"

"Yes, sir," Dobbs mumbled.

"It's okay, Jace." Benoit whispered. "The colonel has a point. We won't need *three* surgeons on the expedition. Besides—," he winked, "—somebody has to watch after the women."

Dobbs looked at him without replying. Swiveling his gaze to Harrigan he was surprised to see him smiling. What the hell is going on here? he asked himself.

At midafternoon, to the accompaniment of the First Cavalry Regimental Band's spirited rendition of *Sweet Betsey From Pike* and *Joe Bowers*, Colonel Sumner and the four companies under his command marched into Fort Laramie, tired, dusty, and looking wilted in the June heat.

Leading the column, directly behind the band, was Bull of the Woods himself and the ninety-eight men of A

Company, each of them astride a large, fat sorrel. Behind them was B Company, whose members were mounted on grays.

"Would you looka that," whispered LaRossa, his voice sounding as if it were being squeezed out of his thin chest. "They got different colored horses?"

"That's so they can tell each other apart in a fight, stupid," replied Venezia.

"What about them privates on white horses?"

"Them's the buglers. They ride white horses so the officers can find 'em easy if they need 'em. Don't you know nothing?"

"Know more'n you, you ignorant guinea."

"Knock it off back there," Flannery said without turning his head. "Silence in the ranks."

"Fuck you!" LaRossa said quietly, sending Venezia into a spasm of smothered giggles.

"How's your arm, paisan?" he murmured.

LaRossa looked down and studied his lower arm, which was encased from knuckle to elbow in a dun-colored ball of dried mud the same consistency and hardness as an adobe brick. "Not bad, considering."

"Will you two shut up," Flannery hissed. "You'll get all our asses in trouble."

"I purely like them uniforms," Venezia said, ignoring the corporal. "You think I could work a transfer?"

"Maybe if you could ride a horse," LaRossa replied. "But all you can mount is a broke down whore."

Although dragoons—the west's light cavalry who fought from horseback—had been part of the Army since 1833, and mounted riflemen—intended as horse-transported infantry—since 1846, the country's first two cavalry regiments were little more than a year old. As a result, many of those at Fort Laramie had never seen the cocky horse soldiers.

"Look at them hats, would you?" Venezia said, awestruck. "That's what I call right handsome."

In the cavalry, both officers and enlisted men—unlike in the infantry where caps were mandatory—wore jaunty, broad-brimmed, black felt hats whose high crown was encircled with cord—gold for officers, worsted yellow for enlisted men—that dangled down in front with braided tips. The right side of the brim, which was wide enough to comfortably shade the horseman's eyes, was looped up and held in place with a shiny brass eagle pendant. On the opposite side, enlisted men wore a single black feather while officers had two or three depending on rank. At the front of the enlisted men's hat was a large brass company letter while the officers hats had a number signifying their regiment.

"You think they got enough weapons?" LaRossa asked sarcastically.

Around his waist, each cavalryman wore a brightly tasseled saber dangling from a black leather strap that extended across his right shoulder. At each man's side was a polished U.S. Model 1854 .58 caliber carbine. In addition, the officers carried Colt Model 1851 .36 caliber navy revolvers slung on the right hip with the butt pointing forward so it could be comfortably drawn with the left hand if the right was occupied with the saber.

"Don't they make a pretty sight," whispered Venezia.

"Pretty don't make them fighters," answered LaRossa. "From what I know 'bout the Cheyenne, they'll take one look at these dandies and roll on the ground laughing."

Much to the surprise of most of the Fort Laramie troops, Sumner's men did not stop on the sprawling parade ground, but continued southward until they reached the Laramie River, where they turned upstream and headed westward, toward Laramie Peak.

"Where in hell they going?" LaRossa asked disbelievingly.

"Ain't enough room for 'em here, I reckon," replied Venezia. "I heered they're gonna camp upstream 'bout a mile an' a half."

"Guess that means they ain't going to be buying the drinks at the Hog Ranch tonight," LaRossa said, sounding displeased.

"That ain't gonna disappoint me none." Venezia laughed. "I truly hate to share my Mary Jane."

"What you mean *your* Mary Jane?" LaRossa said angrily.

"This is the last goddamn warning," Flannery whispered hoarsely. "Any more talk outta you two and you'll both be cleaning outhouses."

Venezia and LaRossa looked at each other, rolling their eyes. "Guess he wants us to be quiet and watch the parade," LaRossa muttered.

Following the two cavalry companies were the two companies of dragoons, spiffy looking in their own right in their high-crowned caps with a welt of orange cord around the bottom and the orange pompon on top. Instead of .58 caliber carbines, the dragoons carried U.S. Model 1842 muzzle-loading musketoons and Colt's dragoon revolvers rather than the newer model navy Colts.

"Rumor is, the dragoons ain't going on the expedition," said Venezia.

"Why in hell not? They come this far?"

"I heered it from Bianchi who helped the rider get a fresh horse that the dragoons been ordered to chaperone some of them handcarters to Utah."

"Huh!" LaRossa spat. "Better them than me. I ain't got much patience for them Bible-thumpers."

"And I ain't got no more patience for you, neither,"

Flannery said, turning to them angrily. His face was bright red and for a moment both Venezia and LaRossa feared he was going to break ranks and assault them.

Realizing they had pushed their luck almost to its limits, they nodded quietly. "Yes, corporal," they muttered in unison.

Following the dragoons were five Pawnee scouts enlisted by Sumner to help fight against their traditional enemies, the Cheyenne; the hundred marching recruits who would fill empty slots at Fort Laramie; two fearsome looking prairie howitzers pulled by four-mule teams; a long string of fifty supply wagons, each pulled by six mules; a remuda made up of extra horses and mules; a herd of depressed-looking steers who seemed to be aware of their destiny to fill the expedition's frying pans before the mission was completed; and a small, parched-looking rear guard. By the time the mile-long line had passed, the Fort Laramie troopers, who had done nothing but stand idly by while the procession progressed in front of them, looked as dusty and trail worn as the men who had just marched more than three hundred miles in less than three weeks.

Kemp lifted the fine crystal snifter, taking secret delight in the sparks, not unlike miniature lightning bolts, that spun outward when he tilted it to catch the candlelight.

"To the old days," he said, watching over the rim as Sumner returned the toast. "You know," he said ruminatively, "except for the gray you haven't changed a bit since Mexico."

"That's nice of you to say, Al," Sumner replied. "It isn't easy watching your hair and beard turn white, but I don't feel any older."

"Have to say," added Kemp, "the white makes you look distinguished."

"Elizabeth likes it. She figures it keeps the young women away."

"As if there were anything we could do if they were pounding on our door." Kemp cackled.

"That's for fucking sure," Sumner said, joining in the merriment. "Here's to you, too," he said.

For several minutes neither man spoke, enjoying the camaraderie shared by two old soldiers whose paths crossed at long, infrequent intervals.

"God, that's good stuff," Sumner said, taking a small sip. "How in hell did you manage that out here in the middle of nowhere?"

Kemp chuckled. "Remember that *finca* we occupied outside Tehuacán?"

"The one where that sloe-eyed señora with the long braids and the low-cut dress got down on her knees and begged us to leave her house alone? My what a temptation that was to see just how badly she wanted to protect her husband's property. But if I remember correctly, MacGregor complied with her requests."

"Weeelllll." Kemp smiled.

Sumner laughed explosively. "You sly old dog. You mean you didn't listen to your captain's orders?"

"Not entirely. I mean, no one in the family came to any harm but there was no sense in just ignoring the fact that she had a whole cellar full of prime Spanish wine. I doubt if she even missed the couple of cases of brandy."

"And you've been toting it around ever since?" Sumner asked, his dark eyes sparkling.

"Only two more bottles left after this one."

"Then I'm honored to be sharing your limited supply," Sumner said with a slight bow.

"Hell, Ed, we go back a long way. You can't imagine I'd invite any of these young whippersnappers under my command to come in and help me polish off something as smooth as this?"

"That Captain Harrigan doesn't seem quite so young."

"Odd that you mentioned him," Kemp said, reaching forward to top off his guest's glass. "I'm a little worried about him. He's a real strange duck."

"Been that way all the time? I understand he graduated high in his class at the academy."

"Just in the last few months. 'Bout a year, I reckon."

"Frontier fever? You know the Plains do unusual things to people's minds. I've seen soldiers go plumb crazy just from listening to the wind howling across the desert day and night. And I mean shoot-up-the-barracks, bludgeon-your-best-friend kind of crazy."

"Oh, Harrigan isn't like that at all. He's very quiet, and that's part of what disturbs me. I don't know what the hell's going on in that head of his and there are times when I don't *want* to know."

"But you're leaving him in command while you're off partying in Washington?"

"I just wish it were a pleasure trip, Ed. But yes, I'm leaving him in charge. He's got the rank and I don't have anybody else. The rest of my officers are barely shaving.

"But what the hell, let's don't talk about personnel. That kind of crap never changes. Bring me up to date; tell me what's happening back in civilization."

"You think Kansas is civilization?" Sumner said bitterly. "If that's civilization, please Jesus, give me the wilderness. They don't call it Bleeding Kansas for nothing."

"That bad, huh?"

"Worse. You know, when we were down South fighting the Messicans, that was one thing. They were just a bunch of foreigners. Besides, we were at war. But Kansas ain't at all like that. Back there you got white people fighting white people over a bunch of black people."

"Aren't you oversimplifying just a bit?" Kemp asked, lifting his feet onto the ammunition box that served as a small table in his cramped quarters.

"Maybe, but not a lot. There were a lot of people who thought Buchanan was going to be the answer to all our problems—a Northerner who was sympathetic to the South but able to see both sides."

"You don't think that's going to prove true?"

"Who knows. He's only been in office three months. But I'll tell you one thing," Sumner said, helping himself to the brandy, "that decision from the Supreme Court may be a powder keg."

"You mean the Dred Scott case?"

"None other. When the court ruled that he wasn't a citizen because no state had Negro citizens at the time the Constitution was adopted, that effectively said that this country's basic document is intended only for white men. That flat sent the anti-slavery people up the wall."

"There are some who would say that's justifiable cause," Kemp replied.

"I'm not arguing the point," Sumner said sharply. "But it really confused the issue because it made the Missouri Compromise unconstitutional."

"Well, hell. It was effectively repealed three years ago anyway when Kansas was formed under the Kansas-Nebraska Act."

"I know. And that's what started all the trouble. Leaving the question of whether Kansas was going to be free or slave up to popular referendum opened the door for violence. It was the underlying cause of the Border Ruffian attack on Lawrence and the retaliatory massacre by men under John Brown. Before it was over, six people were dead."

"Considering all the fighting that's been going on in the Territory for the last three years, that ain't many."

"Hell, that's only scratching the surface. What scares me—and should scare you, too, since we both have seen enough of war to know how ugly it really is—is that this is just a preliminary event for all-out war between the states. Mark my words, that's going to be a real son of a bitch."

"Maybe we won't be around to see it." Kemp sighed.

"I only wish that were true, old friend. From Kansas I see it rushing upon us a lot faster than most people think. I predict five years at the outside."

"*Five years*," groaned Kemp. "Damn, that's just around the curve."

"Maybe not that long. Depends on how well the politicians can hold things together."

"But the way you see it, it's inevitable."

"Unfortunately, yes."

"What's the matter with these politicians?" Kemp said angrily, slamming his glass down on the ammunition box with such force that a chip cracked off the foot. Neither of the men noticed.

"That's the political way. At the risk of sounding cynical, it's the politicians that start the wars and us that has to fight 'em."

"I should be old enough by now when I don't get too excited about what politicians do," Kemp replied, "but it just gives me a major case of the reds to sit back and see what's happening. Like this expedition against the Cheyenne. I don't want to insult you, but I think it's goddamned foolish."

Sumner shrugged. "You aren't insulting me, Al. It wasn't my idea. I just do what I'm told. I take it you aren't in favor."

"That's the truth if it was ever spoken," Kemp replied. "The Cheyenne are good people. Proud people. They don't want to see their way of life turned upside down.

Can't say I blame 'em. If I was in their shoes, I'd be fighting, too."

"You didn't see Harney's report from Fort Pierre?"

"Not likely. Once that bastard left here, after that stupid, needless massacre of the Sioux at Blue Water, I never heard from him again."

"He wrote a report to Washington saying, basically, that he didn't feel the Cheyenne were sufficiently chastised by what had happened to the Sioux and they deserved some of the same treatment."

"Did he now? Knowing Harney, though, that doesn't surprise me."

"He wasn't the only one. McIntyre over at Kearny chimed in, calling the Cheyenne—and I quote—'an unruly race' who could be controlled only—and I quote again—'if they are kept in dread of immediate punishment.' "

"Damn nasty business if you ask me."

"I'm caught in the middle," Sumner said, shaking his head. "My duty is just to follow orders and I have to do it to the best of my ability. Can't let any personal feelings get in the way."

"Amen. Most times it sure isn't easy being a soldier."

"Nope. But I have to carry out my mission. To do that, I'd appreciate your help."

"My *help*?" Kemp asked, puzzled. "You mean beyond my troops?"

"Yep. I could use any material you have as well."

"Material?"

"You know. Maps. Intelligence reports. Testimony from people who've been with the Cheyenne recently. That sort of thing."

"You're welcome to whatever maps I have. Intelligence reports, too. But I have to warn you, we don't have much on the Cheyenne. After that incident at the Upper Platte Bridge about fifteen months ago, the Cheyenne haven't been around. As far as people who have been with them, the only one I can think of offhand is Etienne Legendre."

"Who's he?"

"A trapper who does some work for me from time to time. He has a young son—part Cheyenne—who lives with the tribe and he spends a lot of time with them himself. He just got in this morning, as a matter of fact."

"This must be my lucky day. When can I talk to him?"

"Tomorrow morning soon enough?"

"That would be perfect. Thanks, Al. You're a good soldier."

"I'm not sure that's a compliment any longer, but thanks for the sentiment. By the way, there's something else you should be aware of regarding the Cheyenne."

"Oh?" Sumner asked, raising an eyebrow. "What's that?"

"They have two white boys in camp. Sons of German emigrants killed in a raid three years ago. One of 'em would be seven or eight, the other five or six. Holz can give you the details."

"Holz?"

"Frau Schmidt. The woman who prepared your dinner this evening."

"And a damn good meal it was. What's her connection?"

"She was in the group with the young'uns. She's real fanatical about getting 'em back."

"Okay, I'll talk to her, too. By the way. I forgot to mention it earlier but there's a wagon train a week or so behind me. They were reprovisioning at Kearny when I left."

"That's not surprising. It's the time of year. Anything special about it?"

"Not exactly. This is a group from Arkansas and Missouri. Their leader is a man named Alexander Fancher.

He seems like a good man but I heard he has some trouble-makers in the train."

"Just what we need. Who's the wagon master?"

"Irascible old bastard named Stuart."

"*Alf* Stuart?"

"That's him. You know him?"

"He was the wagon master on the train when the kids were kidnapped. There wasn't enough evidence of negligence on his part to ever bring charges against him but there are a lot of people who feel he was responsible for the attack."

"That sounds pretty serious."

"Well, what he did was push on and leave three wagons of emigrants to fend for themselves while they fixed one of the wagons that had broken down. In Stuart's favor, there was no reason why he shouldn't have. He had a whole train to shepherd and he was behind schedule. Worried he was going to be caught by the snow. There had been no trouble with the Indians at that time and no reason to suspect an attack might be forthcoming."

"Savages are always unpredictable."

"Well, we learned later it was a freak incident—the attack was led by a group of renegades."

"Still. People got killed."

"I know. I'll have Harrigan keep a close watch on Stuart this time. Another fuckup on his part and I'll have him thrown in the stockade. How long you planning to be here?"

"Just long enough to replace my supplies. Figure to be marching out in two, maybe three days."

"Okay, I'll have Legendre in the officer's mess right after adjutant's call. That okay with you?"

"Yep. Sounds perfect."

"Know you're exhausted. Let's call it a night. Why don't you take the rest of this bottle back to your quarters? Something to keep you warm till morning."

"That's mighty generous of you, Al. Course, if I had my druthers I'd rather have that little Messican woman you took it from."

"Wouldn't we all, Ed." Kemp chuckled. "Wouldn't we all."

Jean Benoit had everything spread out on the table in front of him, each item in its place.

"Pretend this is a surgery," he said patiently to Dobbs, "and you have all your equipment . . ."

"Instruments," Dobbs interrupted.

"Instruments. Equipment. Whatever. You have everything you need right here so you don't have to stop and go looking for it. Are you with me?"

"Jesus, Jean. I'm not an idiot."

"About this you are. Why, after three years, you can't learn to make a decent cup of coffee . . ."

"French coffee."

Benoit raised an eyebrow. "Is there any other kind?"

"No." Dobbs laughed. "I guess not."

"Okay. Now repeat after me. This is a bag of coffee beans . . .

"Well," he added when Dobbs did not respond. "I'm serious."

Dobbs rolled his eyes. "Beans."

"Good. Now this is a coffee mill."

"Mill."

"Very good. Iron skillet."

"Skillet."

"Coffeepot," Benoit said, pointing to a long-necked vessel.

"*Cafetière*."

Benoit grinned. "*Mais* yeah. *Gamelle*."

"Kettle."

"Now this is what you do. Watch me carefully. Hopefully for the last time. When I get back I expect you to be making coffee like you've lived in Louisiana all your life."

"That'll be the day. Swamps. Red bugs. Mosquitoes. Rains all the time . . ."

"But the food! Ah, the food!"

"Okay. The food *is* good."

"But right now we're talking about coffee. First you pour some water in the skillet. A half inch will be plenty. Then you put it on the stove to start heating."

"Okay. I've got that."

"Sure you don't want to take notes?"

"Don't get nasty."

Benoit laughed. "Then you put some beans in the mill and you grind them. Not too fine but better fine than coarse. Then you put them in the top of the pot. Right here," he said, lifting the small lid. "Am I going too fast for you?"

"Goddamnit . . ."

"Just pulling your leg. While the water's heating in the skillet, the kettle is also going. But—and this is important—you don't pour the water from the kettle into the pot."

"Right. You use the water from the skillet."

"Excellent. You spoon it over the grounds and let it drip slowly."

"What you end up with is a thick, dark liquid."

"Precisely. Then you pour a little—just about this much," Benoit said, making a space of about an inch and a half between his thumb and forefinger, "into the demitasse . . ."

"And then you fill the cup with hot water from the kettle."

"So why haven't you been able to learn that over all these years?"

"Just a mental block, I reckon. Where's Inge?"

"Over at Old Bedlam helping her mother. The colonel wants to put on a real good feed for Sumner tomorrow night and they have a lot of preparation to do."

"You know, I still can't figure out why Kemp ordered me to stay here. It makes me angry."

"It shouldn't," said Benoit. "Kemp's reason makes sense. Sumner already has two surgeons on the expedition."

"I guess so. But there's something that just doesn't feel right. I don't like the way Harrigan looked at me. Like there was a private joke between us except I don't know what the hell's supposed to be funny."

"He's been acting strange lately. I'll give you that. Maybe the pressure is getting to him."

"He was hanging around Ellen's office the other evening when I took Biv down to introduce him to the Hog Ranch. I don't know what happened but I could see where Ellen was really damn put out. As soon as I got there, he ran off like a cat with a scalded butt. Didn't even say hidy."

"That *is* strange. Ellen didn't say what it was about?"

"She didn't offer and I figured it was none of my business. If she wanted to tell me, she would."

"That sounds sensible. Seems like you two get along pretty well."

"You know, Jean, that's the truth. We've been, uh, *seeing each other*, for a couple of years . . ."

"I'll bet she could tell you down to the day."

"Maybe." Dobbs grinned. "Anyway, I've decided I'm not getting any younger. Or any less lonely . . ."

"You're finally going to ask her to marry you."

"I've been thinking about it."

"That means you are! God, Inge will be happy. Seems that nothing delights a woman more than seeing another woman get married."

"Well, I haven't asked her yet."

"You think she's going to say no. Who do you think you're kidding?"

"No," Dobbs chuckled. "Probably not."

"Do me a favor though," said Benoit.

"What's that?"

"Wait until I get back from this Cheyenne assignment."

"Oh hell yes. I have to wait anyway. You're going to be the best man."

"Well," Benoit said briskly, "now that's settled let's have some coffee. I think there's a little brandy around here somewhere. A celebratory drink."

"I'm not much of a drinker . . ." Dobbs demurred.

"Neither am I, but this is a special occasion. Just a nip. In honor of your forthcoming marriage."

"Why the hell not?"

Benoit and Inge lay close together on the hard, narrow bed that was little broader than a cot. Even though nights on the high plains tended to be chilly, they had the cabin's only window open as far as it would go. From the stables which were only a hundred yards to the north, they could hear the horses snorting and stomping restlessly as if they, too, knew something big was about to occur. The only light was from a three-quarters moon which beamed through the open window, imparting a silvery glow that seemed almost ecclesiastical.

"If I had a choice, I'd rather you weren't going on this mission," Inge said softly, speaking almost directly in Benoit's ear.

"I'd rather be here with you, too, Inge, but I don't have a choice. I'm a professional soldier. When my commanding officer says go, I have to pack my kit and saddle my horse."

"Well," she said, her voice going up an octave, "you don't have to sound happy about it."

"I'm not happy, honey. It's just that I'm accustomed to doing what I'm told without question."

"In that case," Inge said sweetly, "will you do what I say without question?"

Benoit pulled his head back and looked hard at his wife. Even in the faint light he could see a twinkle in her turquoise eyes. "I think I just put my foot in my big mouth," he said lamely.

"You certainly did. But you didn't answer my question."

"Well, I'd like to hear what you want me to do first."

"No," Inge said, smothering the temptation to laugh. "That's not the issue. You said you were used to doing what you were told *without question* . . ."

"But that's from a professional point of view . . ."

"Which means more to you? Your profession or your wife?"

"You do, of course. But . . ."

"No buts. Either you will or you won't."

"Well . . ."

"And no 'wells' either. Yes or no."

"God, Inge, you're a hard taskmaster."

"I am a *gut* German *hausfrau*. I have a very strong will . . ."

"You can say that again."

". . . and I expect my husband to make me happy."

"Okay, okay. What must I do to make you happy?"

"Write me while you're away."

"Write you? Is that all?"

"Yes." She paused. "Every day."

"Every day! God, Inge, have a heart. This isn't an excursion we're going on. It's a military expedition . . ."

"All right. Every other day."

"There's no mail service."

"Just save the letters and I'll read them all when you get back."

"That doesn't make much sense. When I get back I can just tell ..."

"*Nein, Nein, Nein,*" she said, pulling her hand from under the quilt and wagging a finger under his nose. "I want to know your impressions of things as they happen. I want to know what you think while the situation is still fresh."

"But we're going to be pushing hard ..."

"The letters don't have to be long. Just your thoughts."

"Like a journal? Like what Jace writes in?"

"*Ja. Wunderbar.* You would make me so happy."

Benoit said nothing for several moments. "Okay," he finally agreed. "I guess I can do that. If it will make you happy."

"It would make me *begeistert.*"

"What does that mean?"

"I'm not sure what the English word is." Inge giggled. "It means something like very happy."

Benoit pulled her closer, feeling her nipples turn hard as they pressed against his chest. As he leaned over to kiss her, he noticed her breath came in quick, warm bursts like tiny explosions of heat that escape when a log drops on the fire. Gazing on her face through half-closed eyes, he felt himself turn as solid as a fence post. Despite a complete absence of foreplay, he could feel her loins grow wet and he entered her easily, like a hot poker into a snowbank.

She clasped her legs around his back and squeezed.

"*Ja, ja,*" she said softly. Then, "*ja, JA, JA JA,*" each "yes" coming quicker and with more force than the one before.

"Oh my God, Inge," he panted. "I'm coming! I'm coming!"

"Me too!" she answered loudly, bucking like a colt which has never felt a saddle. "Me too!"

Ten minutes later, Benoit was almost asleep when Inge punched him gently in the ribs.

"Jean," she whispered.

"Not again, Inge. It's too soon."

"No, Jean. Not that. This is something else."

"Well, what is it?" he said sleepily.

"The letters."

"Letters?" he said, trying to collect his thoughts.

"Yes," she said perturbed, "The letters. The ones you are going to write me every other day while you are gone."

"Oh," he said, relieved. "*Those* letters. What about them?"

"I told you they didn't have to be long."

"I remember. Short letters. But frequent. Very frequent."

"I don't expect you to write a lot."

"Good. Short, frequent letters. Like journal entries."

"But," she said, pushing him harder. "When you write them . . ."

"Yes," he said, wishing she'd let him go to sleep.

"Don't forget to tell me you love me."

"Of course. I'll be sure to say I love you."

"And you miss me."

"And I miss you, too."

"Don't forget."

"I won't."

"You'd better not," she replied, but he didn't hear her. He was already snoring softly.

"Did you hear what happened?" Dobbs asked Benoit almost as soon as he sat down at the dinner table.

"No. I've been running like crazy all day," Benoit said, looking frazzled. "What happened?"

Dobbs cut into a juicy slice of elk, the last of the backstrap that Ashby and Erich had brought down from the mountains.

"Legendre ran away."

Benoit looked at his friend. "What do you mean, 'ran away'?"

"He left. Quickly and unexpectedly."

"There's nothing that says he can't come and go as he pleases. He's not a soldier."

"No. But this was cause and effect. It was military related."

"I don't follow you. What the hell are you talking about?"

Dobbs took a large bite. "God, this is good. Maybe I ought to ask for Frau Schmidt's hand instead of Ellen's."

"That's not funny, Jace. Will you quit trying to be a comedian and tell what's going on."

"It's this way," Dobbs, said, helping himself to more mashed potatoes. "Harrigan called 'tienne in this morning and asked him to help Colonel Sumner . . ."

"How could he help Colonel Sumner?"

"I'm about to tell you if you'll let me."

"Sorry. Go ahead."

"Harrigan told him, meaning 'tienne, that he, meaning Sumner, needed some up-to-date information on the Cheyenne. Where they were. What they're up to. Are they expecting a battle? That sort of thing."

"Uh-oh," Benoit said. "I'll bet 'tienne didn't take kindly to that."

"You're a born gambler. He certainly did not. The best we could understand, through 'tienne's torrent of French and English, was that the military was a bunch of whoremongers who wanted to use its people so it could take retribution against others. Said he would see Harrigan *and* Colonel Sumner in hell before he'd betray his family. That's not a literal translation of course, but you get the idea."

Benoit whistled softly through his teeth. "Wrong approach with a tough old trapper."

"Even I could have told Harrigan that, but he didn't ask. Not that he would have listened anyway."

"Where was Kemp?"

"In his office. Said he had a huge stack of paperwork that he had to complete before he left for Washington. Guess he figured Harrigan could handle something relatively simple like that if he's going to be acting post commander."

"So what happened?"

"Harrigan threatened to throw 'tienne in the stockade if he didn't tell him what he wanted to know."

"*Sacre merde.* That's even worse."

" 'Tienne got a sly look on his face and asked for a couple of hours to think it over. Harrigan said okay. 'Tienne went straight to the stable, saddled his horse, and skedaddled."

"You figure he's running to the Cheyenne?"

"Has to be. Where else would he go?"

"Well, if the Cheyenne didn't know something was in the works before, they sure as hell will soon."

"There's more," Dobbs said, sipping from his glass of water.

"More? Jesus, what else could there be?"

Dobbs paused. "He took Biv with him."

—— *5* ——

Biv studied his traveling companion out of the corner of his eye, determining that he was one of the most frightening looking men he had ever seen. Etienne Legendre, he decided, was certainly not someone he wanted to cross. Unless, of course, he was bent on suicide.

Tall and dark with a deep, broad chest and thick, powerful shoulders, Legendre reminded Biv of a painting he had seen once at the William Walters Gallery back in Baltimore, a small oil that depicted a grizzly on the attack. In the likeness, the bear was standing erect and ferocious looking, arms outspread, claws hooked and menacing, with spittle flowing from its wide open mouth and dripping off its long, deadly fangs. Try as he might, Biv could not remember the artist because the painting had not been on display for very long. One of the gallery owners' best patrons, a wealthy heiress known for her less than robust sensibilities, complained that it gave her nightmares and asked Walters to remove it forthwith. Needless to say, since the woman— her name was MaryAnn Mason, Biv remembered, and her father had made a fortune in cotton—spent quite a bit of money on her constantly changing collection. The bear painting, as Biv thought of it, quickly disappeared from its place of prominence. Taking another sideways glance at Legendre, Biv chuckled to himself, thinking that if MaryAnn Mason could see his companion her nightmares would be a thing of the past because she probably would collapse on the spot with a heart attack.

There was no little amount of irony, Biv knew, in his comparing Legendre with a bear. Although he had been at Fort Laramie for only a few days, he had already heard the story about the trapper's encounter with a creature of the species he so resembled. The story, as it had been told to him, was that Legendre, a Canadian by birth, had been on the trail with his pregnant Cheyenne wife, White Woman, and their young son, David, known to his wife's people as Plays With His Toes, when they had been surprised by an early snowstorm. Seeking shelter, they had spotted a cave that looked like an ideal place to hole up, not realizing that it already was occupied by a grizzly who had staked it out for his winter den.

Uncharacteristically, probably because he was worried about the threatening storm, Legendre acted contrary to his instincts and training. Since the storm was almost upon them, he decided he needed to gather fuel to last them for the next few days. Sending White Woman into the grotto without checking it first, he took David to help him. They were picking up deadwood not far from the cave's mouth when he heard the bear roar, followed by White Woman's screams.

Shoving David up a nearby pine, Legendre, armed with nothing but his skinning knife since his wife had carried his rifle inside with their pack, charged into the cave. The first thing he saw was White Woman, who lay crumpled on the rough floor in a growing puddle of bright red blood amid the bear scat and a few old elk bones. She was, he could tell at a glance, already dead or dying.

When the bear rushed at him, Legendre sidestepped

slightly, then swung on the animal's back and began stab-
bing it frantically about the head, hoping to penetrate one
of its eyes and go directly to the brain. Eventually, he succeeded but at great cost. Luckily for Legendre, Ashby and
Erich had been passing nearby when they heard the commotion. When they reached the cave, Legendre was
sprawled on top of the bear, which was lying motionless
with Legendre's knife protruding out of its right eye.
Legendre himself was not much better off. The animal had
bitten off the tip of Legendre's nose as well as his left little
finger and most of the ring finger. His left ear was hanging by a thread. Later, when Ashby and Erich reached
Fort Laramie with the wounded trapper, Dobbs had no
choice but to remove it completely.

Although his wounds had long since healed,
Legendre's body was still crisscrossed with scars from the
encounter and he wore his hair long and flowing, rather
than braiding it Indian style, to cover the hole where his
ear used to be.

Despite his fearsome appearance, however, Legendre,
who was known among the Cheyenne as Buffalo
Shoulders because of his massive upper body, was a
genial if decidedly taciturn man with a ready smile and a
bountiful sense of humor. As evidenced by his refusal to
help the army in its campaign against the Cheyenne, he
also demonstrated a powerful loyalty that Biv found
admirable.

While Legendre spoke Cheyenne like he had been born
into the tribe, as well as Siouan and a smattering of
Arapaho in addition to his native French, his English left
something to be desired. Consequently, Biv found it a
challenge to communicate, especially since Legendre's
tendency was to respond to most attempts at conversation
with a simple but effective grunt.

"I'm grateful to you for agreeing to take me along with

you," Biv said brightly, shifting his weight. Because he
was so small, he found it much more convenient to use a
child's saddle rather than one designed for an adult.
Although it invariably resulted in quite a bit of ribbing,
Biv found that the benefits of a comfortable seat far out-
weighed the torment. Long ago, he had come to terms
with his diminutive stature, coming to realize that the
problem was with those who teased him rather than himself. "And I'm especially appreciative that you don't mind
this short detour," he added cheerfully.

Legendre responded with something that sounded like
"ugh."

"I want to assure you that I don't plan to dally at the
Hog Ranch."

"Um," said Legendre.

"I mean, I don't plan an, uh, liaison, or anything."

"*Très bien.*"

"I just want to explain to Narcissa why she won't be
seeing me for a while."

"*Naturellement.*"

"I know a little French, you know," he said optimistically.

Legendre nodded.

"I spent a summer in Paris three years ago studying the
Masters."

"Um."

"There was a fellow living in the next room. He was a
former legionnaire."

Legendre stroked his horse's neck.

"The Foreign Legion," Biv amplified. "*Le Légion
Etrangère.* You've heard of it?" Biv asked hopefully,
doubting that the trapper had even though the organization had been in existence for twenty-five years or more
and had an international reputation.

Legendre said nothing.

"I learned a lot from him." Biv said, glancing at his companion. *"Je veux du whisky sur la table,"* he added with a heavy American accent.

I guess he doesn't care if the whisky is on the table, he thought when Legendre didn't reply. *"Ou est mon cheval?"* he tried.

Legendre looked at him as if he were retarded.

I reckon he knows where my horse is, Biv said to himself. *"Donnez moi mon fuscil, couteau et pistolet."*

"Why do you want your weapons?" Legendre asked, giving him a strange look.

"I don't." Biv smiled. "I was just trying to prove to you that I knew some French."

"I think," Legendre said solemnly, "it is better we not talk too much."

Biv nodded. I wonder, he thought, if I acted too precipitously in asking Legendre to take me along with him to the Cheyenne camp. I'd be willing to bet no one in the tribe speaks English and if Legendre doesn't want to talk to me, it's going to be a terribly long few months.

For the next two hours they rode in silence. Finally, rounding a bend, the Hog Ranch came into view. To Biv, the ramshackle, sprawling building, a curious mixture of unpainted lumber and washed out adobe, looked like the gatehouse to heaven.

"My little angel!" Narcissa cried when Biv walked into the bar. "Come tell me hello," she said, throwing her arms wide.

"Narcissa, my vast dumpling," Biv hollered, running across the room, leaping into her arms like a cat climbing a tree. Locking his legs around her waist, he held on for dear life.

"It's so good to see you," she said, showering him with kisses. "But I didn't expect you back so soon. I reckon I made you happy."

"You certainly did," Biv said. "Actually, I just dropped in to say good-bye. I'm on my way to visit the Cheyenne . . ."

"Ain't them the ones the army's getting ready to fight?"

"Yes. But I won't be involved in any battles. I'm a painter, not a soldier. I'm just going to spend a few weeks with them and paint as many portraits as I can in the time available."

"You going by yerself?" Narcissa asked, giving him a worried look.

"Heavens, no. I have a guide. Monsieur Legendre from Fort Laramie."

"You be careful, you hear. I don't want you to lose your scalp. Or," she winked, "nothing else."

"Don't worry, my substantial sugar plum. I'll be back in a few weeks and I'll be as horny as a Texas steer. You'd better set aside a week for me. At least."

"You say the sweetest things." Narcissa blushed. "You leave them squaws alone, too," she said, nodding soberly. "I'd druther you plugged a sheep."

"Don't fret on that score, my lofty turtle dove. When I get back I'll be as pure as a prairie fire and twice as ravenous."

For the rest of that day and most of the next, Biv and Legendre traveled in almost total silence. Every few hours or so, just to reassure himself that his voice box had not atrophied, Biv initiated a short conversation with his horse, asking the animal who his favorite painters were, what he thought of the new president, Buchanan, and how, considering he was completely under his control, his opinions on the slavery issue.

After a dinner consisting of stringy buffalo jerky washed down with cold creek water, he and Legendre sat close around a small fire that the trapper consented to be built, showing he was no longer worried about Harrigan sending a detachment to bring him back.

"Do you have a wife?" Biv asked, not really expecting an answer.

"*Mais oui*," Legendre replied.

Biv was so surprised he stuttered. "I . . . is she a Ch . . . Cheyenne?"

Legendre smiled. "*Mais oui*."

"And what is her name? Her *nom*?"

"I savvy English," Legendre said in a heavily accented bass voice. "But I speak it very little."

"You mean you've understood everything I've been saying for the last two days."

"*Mais oui*," Legendre chuckled. "You talk very much."

"Tell me about your wife."

"In English, she is called Antelope Woman. She is a member, I do not know your word, of the *Issiometaniu*."

"I thought you said she was Cheyenne?"

"She is. Issiometaniu is, how you say, a band?"

"Band is correct. You have a son, is that right?"

"*Oui*. His French name is David," he said, pronouncing it Da-veed. "And Antelope Woman, she is, how you say?" He made a motion signifying a swollen belly.

"Pregnant."

"*Oui. Enceinte.*"

"A-ha," Biv said, recognition dawning. "That's one reason why you didn't want to tell Colonel Sumner anything about the Cheyenne. It could endanger your family."

Legendre nodded vigorously. "That's for fuckin' sure," he said, using one of the phrases he had picked up from the troopers.

"You even say that with a Brooklyn accent!" Biv laughed.

In his broken half-English, half-French, Legendre
launched into a long tale about the history of the conflicts
between the tribe and the whites, giving Biv a glimpse
into the Cheyenne view of the situation. It was as if a dam
had suddenly broken because of the flow of words from
the man that Biv once considered laconic beyond redemp-
tion. And the more Legendre talked, the more Biv realized
that every dispute has two sides.

A major cause of the long-running series of disputes,
Biv learned, had to do with the increasing white presence
on the Plains and what the Cheyenne perceived to be serious incursions into their territory and, by extension,
threats to their culture.

The troubles, just now building toward a climax,
stretched back at least two years, predating by many
months General Harney's massacre of the Lakotas at Blue
Water Creek.

One of the first hints of the gathering crisis came when
the Cheyenne discovered that the army was planning to
build a wagon road virtually through the heart of the
tribe's prime buffalo hunting ground, from Fort Riley
along the Solomon, Saline and Smoky Hill rivers and then
up the Pawnee Fork to Bent's New Fort on the Arkansas.
In its naiveté, the army had actually tried to hire
Cheyenne and Arapaho guides for the survey party—a
suggestion that met with flat, vocal rejection from the two
tribes. The army went ahead with its survey anyway and,
a year later, began building bridges along the route.

Next came Harney's attack on the peaceful encampment of Brulé and Miniconjou which, although it did not
directly affect the Cheyenne, gave them a glimpse of what
all of the Plains tribes could expect from the army.

In 1856, Legendre explained, Cheyenne hunters came
across another army survey party which apparently was
scoping out a second road that was to be built through

another chunk of Cheyenne territory, from Fort Riley to
Bridger's Pass, along the South Platte River and
Lodgepole Creek, with an alternate route running beside
the Republican River.

Up until then, there had been no major physical conflicts between the Cheyenne and the soldiers. However,
that changed abruptly in April 1856 when the two cultures collided at Renshaw's Bridge, a major emigrant
crossing on the North Platte not far from Fort Laramie.

Kemp had stationed a small detachment of troops at
the bridge to help facilitate emigrant passage. Since it was
a funnel for the Oregon Trail and a popular resting place
for emigrants, Indians bent on trade also were attracted to
the site. One day one of the emigrants complained to the
soldier in charge that there were some white men's horses
among the Cheyenne herd.

When questioned about the horses, a Cheyenne chief
named Long Chin said that the horses had been strays
which his people had gathered up and brought back to
their camp.

The man in charge, a sergeant named McIntyre,
ordered Long Chin to return the animals.

Dutifully, a small group of Cheyenne warriors—Bull
Shield, Two Tails, and Wolf Fire—brought three of the
animals into the soldiers' camp. But Two Tails refused to
return the fourth horse, claiming he had found it at a location far from the bridge and therefore it could not belong
to the group of emigrants then camped nearby.

In response, McIntyre ordered his men to take the three
Cheyenne warriors into custody and hold them as
hostages until the fourth animal was returned.

"The *Tsis-tsis-tas,*" Legendre explained, using the name
by which the Cheyenne referred to themselves, "do not
understand *arrêter*. They think it means, how you say, *met-
tre à mort?*"

Biv looked at him blankly. Then, understanding: "Oh, you mean they thought they would be executed?"

"*Oui. Oui.*" Legendre nodded vigorously. "They want *liberté.*"

The three warriors tried to escape. McIntyre ordered his men to open fire. Bull Shield was shot in the head and killed instantly. Two Tails, although wounded, managed to get away. The third man, Wolf Fire, was recaptured and taken to Fort Laramie in irons. Held in the stockade, his spirit died and the following spring, his body did as well.

Two Tails, Legendre said, made it back to the main Cheyenne camp. When he told his people what had happened, they ran away to the Black Hills, fearing a Harney-style attack. They left so hurriedly they virtually abandoned their camp. That was a good thing, Legendre said, because the soldiers came in soon afterwards, taking what items they could use and burning the rest, including the empty lodges.

As they were fleeing, the Cheyenne stumbled across an old trapper who had been working the area for years. Angry about how they had been treated by the soldiers, the Indians killed and scalped him. The fact that the victim had a Cheyenne wife did not deter them: *his* skin was white.

The tale of what had happened at Renshaw's Bridge spread among all the ten bands of the Cheyenne, from one end of the territory to the other. Hearing it, some of the younger warriors became incensed and demanded that the tribe go to war against the whites.

Older and wiser men among the tribe, Legendre said, suppressed the cries for instant retaliation, but a seed for hatred had been sown.

A few months later, a Cheyenne raiding party en route to the territory of their traditional enemies, the Pawnee, came across an emigrant train along the Little Blue River. Since the group was made up mainly of young men who still seethed about the bridge incident, they attacked the whites, killing one man.

A few days later, while the group was camped not far from Fort Kearny, soldiers tried to arrest six of them who they believed had played a major role in the attack against the wagon train. Three of them were captured but three others escaped. One was seriously wounded in the fracas.

Frustrated, the commanding officer at Fort Kearny sent a detachment to attack a different Cheyenne camp. Before they got there, the soldiers raided the Cheyenne horse herd. Warned by the move against their horses, the Cheyenne in the camp fled before the soldiers arrived at the camp proper.

Deep into the night, long after the small fire had burned to embers, Legendre continued his tale, giving Biv example after example of how the Cheyenne felt they had been betrayed and preyed upon by the soldiers. Attack led to counterattack, which led to counter-counterattack until the entire Cheyenne nation was inflamed over the white man's perceived aggression. Just, Biv thought, as Washington was inflamed by what the politicians considered as acts of open defiance by the Cheyenne.

The situation came to a head late the previous summer, Legendre explained, when forty-one soldiers from Fort Kearny raided a peaceful camp at Grand Island. The mounted soldiers swept down on the unsuspecting Cheyenne at the edge of a thick grove of trees, scattering the Indians and killing six of them.

That incident, Legendre felt, marked the true beginning of open warfare between the Cheyenne and the whites. It was at that point that wiser heads among the various bands felt control over the younger hotheads slipping. It had not yet disappeared entirely, but the call for war was growing stronger by the month. As a result, groups of warriors led by those seeking retaliation against the whites began a series of attacks against emigrant trains in the vicinity of Fort Kearny.

Biv nodded in comprehension. Before he left Baltimore, he told the trapper, he had read in the *Sun* about an attack on a group of Utah-bound travelers that included Almon W. Babbit, a newly elected congressman as well as the Territory's secretary. Although Babbit survived, two white men and one child were killed and one white woman—the mother of the dead child—was taken captive. Soon afterwards, she, too, was killed when she proved to be a hindrance to the fleeing warriors.

"*Oui.*" Legendre nodded. "That is true."

"But I thought Babbit had been killed," Biv said, searching his memory.

"That was later," Legendre said. Eight days after surviving the raid, Babbit and two other Mormons decided to make a dash across Cheyenne country from Fort Kearny to Fort Laramie. Traveling in a light carriage, which they felt would give them mobility and speed, they were carrying cash for the Territory's treasury and a valise full of important documents. They never made it. Their bodies were found at an impromptu campsite about halfway between the two posts three weeks later. The carriage had been burned and the money and documents were missing.

"What happened next?" Biv asked breathlessly, enthralled by Legendre's monologue. "Were there more attacks?"

"One more," said Legendre. Late in the month, a group of warriors, some of whom had survived the army's Grand Island raid, discovered still another survey party. While they were gathering for an attack, a military escort arrived. While the Cheyenne contemplated the wisdom of an attack against a well-armed adversary, the weather turned and a cold rain driven by high winds swept through the area. The warriors withdrew.

After that, said Legendre, as if by common agreement, Cheyenne all over the Plains began traveling toward their winter camps.

"Did that cool them down?" Biv wanted to know. "Did the elders regain control?"

"They try," Legendre explained. Some of the southern bands showed up at Bent's New Fort to collect their annuities. There was no trouble. Representatives from the northern bands also met with the new Indian agent at Fort Laramie, William "Will" Harrison, to give him the Cheyenne perspective.

From what he had heard, the trapper said, Harrison was sympathetic. In mid-October he met with forty-one chiefs from the northern bands to try to resolve the differences. Peace could be had, Harrison told them, if the Cheyenne agreed to four things: (1) They had to stop the attacks against the emigrants; (2) They had to agree to treat all whites traversing their territory as friends; (3) They had to make peace with their traditional enemies such as Pawnee and the Crow; and (4) They had to agree not to take any aggressive action that might be viewed with distaste Back East.

"The chiefs say yes," Legendre added.

Biv frowned. "If everything was settled, how come there's an army expedition moving against them?"

The agreement was reached, Legendre said, during the month that the Cheyenne called the Moon of Dust in the Face because winds usually blow exceptionally briskly then. For all of the next month, November—the Moon of the Hard Face—and the month after that—the Moon of the Big Hard Face—the groups stayed in their camps, passing the winter as they always have done, that is by hunkering down and trying to survive. But by March, called the

Moon When the Buffalo and Horse Begin to Fill Out, the young warriors were becoming restless again. They had spent the winter listening not only to the tribe's traditional tales but the newer stories detailing the attacks on their people by the white soldiers. As a result, when summer began, they were primed to renew the retaliatory raids despite the agreement their chiefs had reached the previous autumn.

Disquieting news came from the southern bands. They passed the word along when they arrived at Bent's New Fort to draw their annuities. The commander told them that even then a military expedition was being planned and a vast number of soldiers would attack them the following summer.

At that point, said Legendre, the elders were not sure what to do. They did not want war, but neither did they want to see their people slaughtered as the Miniconjou and Brulé had been by forces under General Harney. To them, it seemed as if it were the whites who wanted war. Why else, he asked, throwing his hands in the air, would they continue to provoke the Cheyenne by building more roads which would drive off the buffalo, and why were more and more whites coming into the country?

The younger warriors felt it was because the whites wanted to control *all* of their country and the only reasonable rejoinder was to declare war.

Which group has proved to be dominant? Biv wanted to know. The elders or the young warriors?

Legendre shrugged. At this point, he could not say. Two months before, when the entire tribe gathered for its second most sacred celebration, the Oxhehoem, which the whites called the Sun Dance, there was much talk about the situation. Although nothing was resolved, the scales seemed to be tipping in favor of war.

What the younger members wanted, Legendre said, was for the whites to withdraw peacefully and leave the Cheyenne alone to pursue their lives as they had always done. As a white man, he knew that was impossible; that things for the Cheyenne would never be the same again. Still, he hoped that war could be averted. One way or the other, he felt, something would happen soon.

For the first time since he left Fort Laramie, Biv was aware of the precariousness of his own position. As a white man who knew nothing about the Cheyenne and had no ties to them, was he tempting fate by venturing into their midst? Thinking about how he might be an easy target for revenge-bent Cheyenne warriors, Biv's mouth went dry and his hands began trembling.

"Am I in danger?" he asked Legendre nervously. "Are they going to try to scalp me?"

"*Non*," Legendre said earnestly. "You with me. You no soldier. You do not have," he could not resist smiling, "*fuscil, couteau et pistolet*." He paused. "*Excepté*," he warned, his smile withering, "you no bother the women!"

Biv sighed in relief. "Don't worry about that," he said, feeling his stomach turn over. "I have all I can handle with Narcissa."

"The Tsis-tsis-tas women are *tres honête*," Legendre said solemnly. "They no give themselves to everybody. Not like the *gens du corbeaux*," he added, putting an exclamation point on his opinion by spitting a large wad of phlegm into the almost-dead fire.

"The *who*?" Biv asked, puzzled.

Legendre scratched his chin, searching for the English word. "You call them Crow!" he said shortly, happy with his fluency.

Biv laughed. Even Back East he had heard tales about the Crow's notorious and blatant promiscuity. "I swear," he said, lifting his right hand, no larger than a ten year old's,

"that I will leave the women alone." Remembering
Narcissa's words, he added: "And the sheep too."

Legendre laughed heartily. "We sleep now," he said.
"Day after tomorrow we enter Cheyenne territory. Then,
two more days, the main camp. Antelope Woman will be
tres heureuse that I come back so soon. That's for fucking
sure."

Biv felt himself tremble, excited by the prospect of his
first adventure among the Indians. Worriedly, he looked
at the bundle that he had strapped behind his saddle, a
compact collection of sketch pads, chunks of charcoal, a
small watercolor kit, a few paints, and some tightly rolled
canvases. It wasn't all the equipment he would have liked
to bring along but it would have to suffice, considering
the circumstances and the fact that he had packed so
quickly. I'll make sketches, he thought, and use those
as models for larger canvases once I get back to Fort
Laramie.

Following Legendre's example, he scooped out a small
depression in the sand for his hips, then lay on his back
and pulled the blanket up to his chin. Sleep would be a
long time coming, he knew, since his mind was churning
in anticipation of the prospects that awaited him. Once he
had been assured by Legendre that the Cheyenne would
not harm him, despite the fact that they were about ready
to go to war with the soldiers, he banished thoughts of
physical danger. Instead, he focused on the professional
challenge ahead of him. Staring up at the sky, so filled
with stars that it looked like a shimmering white canopy,
he began imagining scenes he would capture once they
got among the Cheyenne. Dammit, he thought just before
he finally slipped into the dream world, I wish I had
brought more pads.

Benoit stretched in his saddle, massaging his aching back. We've only been gone two days, he told himself, and already I'm beginning to feel the effects. Either I'm out of practice on long marches or I'm getting old.

He was resting his horse along the edge of the trail, watching the men troop by. First it was infantry. As the slowest moving members of the column, the contingent from Fort Laramie led the way on the march. Then came the cavalry, which seemed impatient at the slow pace. And off in the distance he could see the cloud of dust which he knew marked the wagons, the remuda and the beef herd, which was necessary since they could not count on finding enough buffalo to feed the hungry soldiers.

They had pulled out of the post promptly at eight A.M. the previous day, marching almost due south toward the planned rendezvous with the men under Major Sedgwick. The initial line of march took them along what was called the Trappers Trail, which led from the Platte and Laramie river junction into New Mexico territory, eventually ending at Taos.

At first, they made good time. Then they had to climb a steep rocky hill, which was harder to get down than up. At the bottom was a large canyon called Goshen's Hole, which was dissected by a stream called Cherry Creek. They spent the first night there.

The next morning, activity began soon after sunup, which was very early indeed since this was the period of the year's longest days.

Although Benoit traveled everywhere by horse and his men, even though they were infantry, were often mounted, he had never before accompanied a unit whose whole lifestyle was molded around the horse. For him, it was a totally new and somewhat puzzling experience.

As on the infantry post, the day began with the bugler blowing reveille, but from there the routine differed considerably. Once the cavalrymen had roused themselves, the bugler sounded "stable call," which sent the troopers rushing for their horses with currycombs and brushes in hand. But first, the men lined up at the forage wagon for a ration of shelled corn. Lugging the feed to where their horses were picketed, they poured it on a blanket on the ground and groomed the animals while they ate.

After the horses, the men themselves ate. On the first two days, Benoit noticed, breakfast consisted of coffee—unfortunately not the Cajun style to which he was addicted—hardtack, and a small portion of tough, over-cooked beef.

Once breakfast was done, the bugler sounded "general call," which was the signal to break camp. In what seemed remarkably quick time to Benoit, the tents were struck and packed on a wagon.

Still another bugled message, "water call," was an order for the men to lead their horses to the stream. Minutes later, the bugler sounded "boots and saddles"—the signal to get the horses ready to march.

Once that was accomplished, the bugler blew "to horse," and the horses were led into line. "Prepare to mount," the sergeants barked, followed by "mount" and "form ranks." When everyone was ready to go, the bugler sounded "advance," and the column moved forward at a walk.

As he watched the column, Benoit saw a familiar face. His eyes lighting up in recognition, he urged his horse forward, yelling as he went.

"Jeb," he hollered. "Hey, Jeb. Is that you?"

Hearing his name, the first lieutenant reigned his horse to a stop.

"Is that you, Jeb?" Benoit asked happily.

"Sure is," the man replied. "James Ewell Brown Stuart

in person." recognizing Benoit, he broke into a huge grin. "By God, if it isn't t-Jean, the ol' Cajun himself. I haven't seen you since you graduated. What have you been doing with yourself?"

"I guess what every career officer does." Benoit shrugged. "Soldiering. Did a brief tour in Washington but I've been out here since '54. And you?"

"About the same. Started in artillery and moved into cavalry when the regiments were founded last year. I purely *love* being a horse soldier. Right now I'm acting commander of Company B."

"I'm acting commander, too," smiled Benoit. "Company C, Sixth Infantry."

"By God, it's good to see you," Stuart said, clapping Benoit on the shoulder. "Although you were in the class ahead of me, it's still great to see a friendly face."

"Since this is all new to me, would you be my guide?" Benoit asked. "I can see I have a hell of a lot to learn."

"My pleasure," Stuart replied. "I don't have a hell of a lot to do anyway. Not until we catch up to the Cheyenne. I'll start your education right now." Pointing to the troops, he said, "That's B Company, my group. Company A is the unit behind us. Tomorrow the order will be reversed."

"Why's that?" Benoit asked.

"Simple." Stuart grinned. "Nobody wants to be in the back every day. Too much dust. That's why we always rotate the company that will ride in the lead."

As the sun reached its high point, Benoit complained about his stomach grumbling. Stuart chuckled. "We seldom stop for a midday meal," he said. "You've seen how complicated it is to get a mounted troop on the move so we just don't bother. Oh, we'll pause in a bit to give the horses some water and we take periodic quick breaks to let the men tighten the girths, but the troopers themselves don't get the chance to relax until we get to the evening camp."

"How much distance do you usually cover a day?" Benoit asked curiously.

"It depends on the terrain, availability of water, access to grass for the horses, and the mission," Stuart said affably, "but I'd reckon we average fifteen to twenty miles. Keep in mind, though, that the time period is only about six or seven hours since it takes us so long to get going and there's so much we have to do when we get there. Plus we'll probably be moving a little slower because of your troops."

Benoit noticed that his conversations with Stuart were held mainly at top volume because a cavalry unit on the move generated quite a bit of interior noise, what with the creaking of the saddles, the weapons slapping against horse and rider, the animals themselves snorting and blowing, plus the racket they made as their shod hooves tramped over rock or ground grown as hard as rock by the lack of rain and a merciless sun. Immediately, Benoit could see the important role that buglers played in a cavalry unit and the reason why they were mounted on white horses.

At the end of the day, procedures were reversed. Once the preselected camping site was reached, the horses were wheeled into line and the bugler sounded a series of calls that commanded the men to dismount, unsaddle, water the horses, and secure them to a picket line.

The primary rule in the cavalry was simple: Horses took priority over men. Once the horses were taken care of, the men tended to their own needs. First they erected their tents—the conical shelters called Sibleys—each of which housed twelve to fifteen troopers. Then they went out to gather fuel, either wood or buffalo chips. Dinner, like breakfast, was a simple affair. Both nights it had been beef, beans, weak vegetable soup, and hardtack, all washed down with tasteless Yankee coffee.

After eating, the men had an hour or so to do nothing while guards were posted. Around sunset on the long days the bugler sounded "tattoo," which formally ended the day.

"I'm fascinated," Benoit confessed to Stuart as they sat sipping coffee. "This is all quite different from the infantry. Tell me, though, why is Sumner called Bull of the Woods?"

"That's an interesting story," Stuart said. "Started out as just plain Bull because, rumor has it, a Mexican musket ball bounced off his skull during the battle of Buena Vista. Men said he had a head as hard as a bull's. The 'woods' part was added later by his men in honor of his parade-ground voice. Said he could bellow like a moose."

"You like him?"

"Sure do," Stuart said enthusiastically. "For a Yankee, he's a good man. He whipped this regiment into top notch shape in very little time. He's brave. He's fair. He rides like an Indian. And he treats his men right. Couldn't ask much more."

"No negatives?"

"Not from me. The only thing that bothers me about serving under him is this may be a limited command."

"What do you mean?"

"I haven't said this to anyone else," Stuart confided, leaning forward to make sure he wasn't overheard, "but you're a fellow Southerner and I think you'll understand."

"Uh-oh," said Benoit. "I think I know what you're going to say."

"You probably do," Stuart acknowledged. "I imagine every soldier from the South is thinking it whether he admits it or not."

"You're considering resigning your commission and joining up with a Southern unit?"

"You, too?" Stuart asked, not surprised.

"I've had an offer to join the New Orleans militia. A fellow I grew up with is now a Congressman. Got a letter from him just a week ago telling me about a unit being formed and wanted to know if I was interested."

"What did you tell him?"

"Nothing yet. I need to think about it a bit. Quite a bit, as a matter of fact. When I left the academy I never even imagined that the day might come when I'd turn in my commission."

"I felt the same way," Stuart said. "I've had an offer that sounds much the same as yours except it's a militia group in Charleston. I guess similar organizations are being formed all across the South."

"You think it's going to come to war?"

"Unfortunately, yes." Stuart said. "I've been in Kansas for almost two years and I can see how the slavery issue is tearing the territory apart. There are some who argue that the main bone of contention is states rights, or that the whole argument is economically based, what with the North being an industrial area and the South agrarian. But from where I sit, it's slavery. I presume the same thing's happening everywhere to one degree or another."

"It isn't something I want to think too much about right yet," said Benoit. "I'm just getting to the point where I'm starting to get a little authority and I don't want to piss it away. Besides, I'm not sure how my wife would take it if I told her I wanted to leave."

"You're married, too?" Stuart said, his eyes sparkling.

"Since last October. Which reminds me, I have to go write her a note. She made me promise to write every other day during the march. Your wife tell you the same thing?"

"Naw," Stuart chuckled. "I've been married longer. Emily only expects a letter once a week."

Benoit squirmed against the saddle that he was using for a backrest, trying to get into position to take some of the strain off his still-aching back. That's better, he said to himself, stretching his feet toward the dying fire. Because of the summer solstice it was not yet dark even though it was nearing the time for the bugler to sound tattoo. Still enough light to write a few lines, he said, eyeing the western horizon.

Reaching into his saddlebag, he produced a new ledger that Inge had given him over breakfast the morning they left. Once she had secured his promise to write, she had scurried down to Sevier's store to purchase something for him to write in.

Benoit held it up to the dying light, admiring its unscarred cover and the way its unused pages still fit together compactly. Holding it close to his face, he inhaled, savoring the aroma of new leather. God, I love that smell, he said half-aloud.

Sighing, he reached for his bottle of ink and quill pen. Slowly, concentrating on what he was going to say, he opened the book and began writing in a fluid, legible hand:

21 June 57
Along the Bank of North Bear Creek

My Darling Inge,

True to my promise, it is the second night out and I am sitting by light of the campfire penning you these few words.

I made a most delightful discovery today, having found that an old acquaintance from

the academy, a fellow lieutenant named Jeb
Stuart, is marching with Sumner's men. We
had quite an interesting day together and both
of us are looking forward to several more
before this mission can be completed. As I, he
is acting commander of a company so we have
quite a bit in common besides the academy
and outside of the fact that we are both
Southerners, seeing as how he hails from
Virginia.

I am learning quite a bit about the cavalry
and something about my own men as well.
Had to discipline two privates this evening for
fighting. A man named LaRossa, who already
has his arm in a cast as a result of a brawl at
the Hog Ranch, got into a squabble with a fellow private named Venezia because of a
wager over an incredibly trivial subject. They
had placed a small bet on which horse would
defecate first. Venezia won. When LaRossa
confessed that he did not have the two bits to
pay him, Venezia clobbered him with his frying pan. LaRossa retaliated by striking him
with his cast, which shattered into a half
dozen pieces. Even though he was screaming
with pain, we had to drag him off to the surgeon at Company B, who resplinted the injury
and repacked it with fresh mud. I surely wish
Dobbs were here; it would have saved us a lot
of time and damage to our eardrums caused
by LaRossa's bawling.

We had a long day today, covering more
than seventeen miles. The word has come
down that another long day is in store tomorrow so I am going to call it a night by telling

you how much I love you. Please be safe and dream good dreams about me.

Your loving husband (how strange it seems to write that),

Jean

P.S. I miss you, too.

July 1857

Biv reckoned he'd never wanted a drink of water so badly in all his life. For three days, they had been traveling over an expanse as desolate as none the Back Easter had ever seen: a land without trees, greenery, or any indication that it was inhabited by a living thing, man or animal. Even worse was the heat. Although it cooled somewhat during the night, the temperature started rising again almost as soon as the sun topped the eastern horizon. By late afternoon, it was well above a hundred degrees. Occasionally, there was wind, usually from the southwest, but that only made things worse since it created a blast-furnace effect that made Biv feel as if his blood was starting to boil.

"I'm beginning to understand why they call this the Great American Desert," he croaked, more to hear himself talk than to initiate a conversation with Legendre, who seemed not at all discomfited.

After the night around the campfire when the trapper had been so talkative, he had relapsed into his usual laconism. However, compared to what he had been like at the beginning of the trip, he was practically loquacious. At Biv's urging, Legendre had taught him a few useful words of Cheyenne, some carefully selected nouns and phrases that Biv knew he would need to communicate when Legendre would not be around to translate. Other than that, he figured he could get by with improvised hand signals. After all, he asked himself, wasn't sign language the lingua franca of the Plains?

But by getting Legendre to talk to him Biv was accomplishing another purpose as well. The more he listened to the trapper the better feel he could get for his companion's speech patterns, which, in the long run, made it easier for him to understand the nuances of what Legendre was trying to say. It also helped him remember words of French he thought he had long ago forgotten. By the end of the fifth day, Biv felt he could carry on a spirited conversation with Legendre and each could understand the other almost as if they were speaking the same language.

Legendre halted his horse and raised himself in his saddle. Shielding his eyes with his hand, he stared into the distance. Biv wondered what he was looking for since as far as he could tell the terrain had not changed. No matter which way he looked, there was nothing but emptiness and a cloudless sky.

"We stop soon," Legendre said, urging his horse forward.

"I hope there's water there," Biv said hopefully. "I'm drier than an old maid's twat."

"Twat?" Legendre asked, raising an eyebrow. "What is that?"

Biv smiled, feeling his lips crack and wondering if they were bleeding, like his fingers which, to him, looked like desiccated talons. "It isn't important," he said. "By the way," he added, trying to change the subject, "what made you come back to Fort Laramie? You seem as if you've made a comfortable life for yourself with the Cheyenne."

"Money," Legendre said. "The army owes me twenty dollars."

"And you were willing to ride for a week in each direction, leaving a pregnant wife and young son, to collect twenty dollars?" Biv asked, astonished.

"*Mais* yeah," Legendre said, giving him a strange look. "It owed to me."

Oh, that explains it perfectly, Biv thought. "Did you get it?" he asked instead.

"*Non*. I leave too quick. Next time. Look," he said, pointing, "that is where we camp tonight."

Biv searched to find the spot but all he saw was more sand and low shrubs. Therefore, he was slightly surprised when, thirty minutes later, they came upon a small canyon that had been invisible from half a mile away. To the west, the canyon ended abruptly in the side of a steep cliff, but to the east it ran for more than a mile before trickling off to the level of the plain.

Biv looked downward, praying he would see water. Although there were a few small box elders, which also had been invisible from the direction they had come, and what seemed a good supply of bright green grass, there was only sand where a stream should have been.

"Son a bitch," he cursed. "Just our luck that the stream is dead."

"Not dead." Legendre smiled. "Only sleeping. Come, we make camp."

Guiding his horse down the precipitous bank, he led the way into the bottom of the canyon. Biv had no choice but to follow.

After unsaddling the animals, they turned them loose to graze. Although they chomped hungrily at the grass, they lacked the saliva to swallow. While Biv watched in astonishment, they gagged and spit out the grass.

"I'll be dipped," Biv whispered. "I've never seen anything like that before."

"Tonight," Legendre said, "when ground cools, water will come up out of the sand."

Biv looked at him as if he had said he could fly.

"I swear," Legendre said solemnly. "Wait and see."

Still unbelieving, Biv made himself a rough lean-to with his blanket and some branches broken off the nearby trees. It was only ten inches off the ground and Biv had to get on his stomach and crawl inside like an ant, but the small amount of shade provided pleasant relief. Even though the sun was fast disappearing over the canyon's far rim, the heat remained incredibly fierce.

Rolling onto his back, Biv stared at the loose weave of the gray, army-issue blanket only inches from his face. This is the end, he told himself. All my vital fluids have evaporated into the thin desert air. Tomorrow morning Legendre will find a husk where my body used to be. I'll look like a locust that leaves its shell on the side of a tree.

"Sleep," Legendre commanded. "I tell you when it is time."

Convinced he was going to die before sunrise, Biv lapsed into a troubled sleep. The next thing he knew, Legendre was roughly shaking his left leg.

"What's the matter?" he asked sleepily. From beneath his lean-to he looked out onto a surreal landscape made silvery and incredibly bright by a nearly full moon.

Legendre shook his head slowly. "The stream awakens," he said, pointing.

Biv stared and rubbed his eyes, sure he was hallucinating. The bottom of the canyon, which had been only dry sand when he went to sleep, was now a slowly moving stream about three inches deep. The horses were already standing in the water, lapping it up as quickly as they could swallow.

"Holy Jumping Jesus," he exclaimed, wiggling out of his lean-to and crawling toward the stream on his hands and knees. When he reached the water, he let himself collapse, falling face first into the blessedly cool stream. Splashing it over his head, he looked at Legendre and grinned. "By God, you were right," he said.

Making a cup with his hands, he bent to drink.

"Not too much," Legendre cautioned. "Drink quick and you get sick. Be slow. The stream will not go back to sleep for four more hours."

Unable to resist, Biv took three big swallows only to find that the water rose immediately back into his throat. Turning his head, he gagged and vomited all he had taken in.

"One swallow." Legendre laughed. "Then one more. No hurry."

"Okay," Biv said, wiping his chin. "I believe you now."

At midmorning the next day, Biv caught a welcome glimpse of green on the horizon. By noon, they were in the trees.

"Soon we see the camp," Legendre said, leading his horse to the edge of a small river that to Biv, remembering the recent crossing of the barren plain, looked as wide as the Mississippi.

"Cheyenne call this *Mahkineohe*," Legendre said.

"What does that mean?" Biv asked.

In reply, Legendre made the sound of the wild turkey.

"Oh." Biv smiled. "Turkey Creek."

Legendre nodded. "The *vehoe*," he said, using the Cheyenne word for white man, "call it Solomon River."

Biv looked around him. Compared to the landscape they had just traversed, it looked like paradise. The river flowed swift and clear and its banks were heavily timbered. Lush grass grew waist-high at the edge of the stream.

"Much game," said Legendre. "Deer. Turkey. Not far away, buffalo. Good place to hunt. Cheyenne stay here. Eat well and get fat."

While he was rhapsodizing about the benefits of the land, two Indians clad in breech clouts moved silently out of the forest and stopped, staring at them. Thinking they were about to be attacked, Biv fumbled for the old pistol he had bought in a pawn shop in Independence but had never learned to use. Figuring it might be just as effective to brandish the weapon as to use it, he was still digging in the bottom of his kit when Legendre let out a gleeful shout.

Leaping off his horse, the trapper rushed forward on foot. The two Indians also dismounted and ran to meet Legendre. Taking his hand, they slapped him on the shoulder and began talking to him in a language that Biv deduced was Cheyenne.

"They are from the camp," Legendre explained, turning. "This one," he said, pointing to the tall, thin man with a sharp chin that was on his left, "is Sliced Nose, a brave warrior who has many Pawnee scalps. The boy," he added, gesturing to the other, a youth Biv figured was about nineteen, "is One-Eyed Bear. One day he, too, will be a great warrior."

Swinging aboard his horse, Legendre motioned to Biv to follow. "Come," he said. "We go with them to the camp. They know since yesterday that we are coming and they prepare a feast. Tonight we eat and sleep well, forget the desert."

Benoit took up his quill and scribbled hurriedly in the leather-covered notebook.

8 July 57
On the North Bank of the South Platte River

My Dearest Inge,

I just learned that Sumner has ordered the wagons back to Fort Laramie early tomorrow so I want to tear these pages out and send them back with one of the troopers so you will know that I am well and thinking of you. His reasoning is that from now on the going gets very rough and the wagons would simply be a hindrance. I think secretly he would like to return the infantry companies as well because we move so slowly as well, but he dare not go that far since his orders explicitly include the infantry as part of the expedition.

We arrived here yesterday but have not been able to cross the river since it is swollen from recent rains. In its current state it is flowing swiftly, a half mile wide and four- to six-feet deep. A cavalry trooper drowned yesterday attempting to string a rope from one bank to another so we could rig a ferry. They have not yet recovered his body.

Other changes also have occurred. Sumner, using his prerogative as commander of the expedition, has named one of his men, a Captain Ketchum, as commander of the infantry units. This means that Zack, who was doing a remarkable job, has returned as commander of C Company and I will go back to my old job as assistant to Grant. The net result is I am somewhat at loose ends because the infantry officers have very little responsibility under the cavalry command and Harry is quite capable of handling it on his own. Looking at it optimistically, it gives me more time to roam with Jeb Stuart and learn more about the horse soldiers.

Although we have had our problems with heat and water—first not enough and now too much—things have gone exceptionally well. Two days ago we made contact, as planned, with Major Sedgwick's column, which has been marching up from the south. We have not yet physically linked up because Sedgwick's men are on one side of the South Platte while we are on the other. As soon as we can find a place to safely cross, we will join forces and head southeastward toward where the scouts tell us the Cheyenne are cowering in fear of our arrival.

The only problem I have had in C Company is with those two hardheaded privates, Venezia and LaRossa. Three days after I disciplined them for fighting, they were at it again. This time Venezia accused LaRossa of taking his last clean pair of socks and the two squared off in front of the whole company. Before anyone could break it up, LaRossa hit Venezia in the face with a piece of firewood and knocked out two of his teeth. An hour later, they had their arms around each other's shoulders and were talking about what they were going to do if they ever get back to civilization. I suggested to Zack that he might want to send LaRossa back with the wagons since, because of the cast on his arm, he is of limited use. But both LaRossa and Venezia pleaded so convincingly to remain unseparated that Zack agreed to give them one more chance.

I must go, my love, since the men are forming for another attempt at crossing the river. It would be disastrous if we came this far only to be stymied by a thunderstorm. I hope you, your mother, and Erich are well. Please give them my regards. I will write more within two days but you may not read it until I return.

Your loving husband,

Jean
P.S. I miss you.

Biv lay quietly on his pallet, savoring the early morning sounds that surrounded him. Even though the sun had been up for less than a half hour, Antelope Woman had risen much earlier. Since he was a light sleeper, Biv had awakened as well, content to lie under his robe and listen to Legendre's wife bustling around the lodge, performing her womanly chores, groaning occasionally when her swollen belly interfered with her tasks.

Although he had been in the camp for less than two weeks, Biv had already adjusted to its routine. Soon, he knew the camp crier would circulate among the five hundred or so lodges that stretched along the stream, informing them of the developments that affected all the Cheyenne. Always included among the items was a progress report on the advance of the *Notaxe-vehoe*, a term that Biv had come to learn meant white soldiers.

Legendre had explained to him that the Cheyenne were aware of their presence long before they ever entered their territory. Even before Colonel Sumner reached Fort Laramie, small groups of Lakotas moving down from the north arrived with tales of many white soldiers on the move. Similarly, Arapahoes came in from the south to tell of other soldiers coming from that direction.

There was never any doubt among the Cheyenne that they were the intended target. The Notaxe-vehoe had tipped their hand the previous autumn when the commander at Bent's New Fort had told the Cheyenne who had come to claim their annuities that an expedition was being formed against them to retaliate for the raids against whites near Fort Kearny.

Biv could see that developments were having a profound effect upon the Cheyenne. With each new report of the advance of the soldiers, the war-seeking members of the tribe gained more strength, and this was threatening to upset the balance of a community which before had always been ruled by its older, and presumably wiser, members. The fact that there were two large, heavily armed units approaching from opposite directions toward the Tsis-tsis-tas allowed the war faction to argue that, despite the promises made by the Indian agent to the chiefs the previous October, the whites really wanted war. As far as Biv was concerned, it was a claim that, given the evidence, was nearly impossible to refute. In fact, from what Biv had seen, the elders were no longer even trying very hard to discourage the younger men's arguments. Biv watched in silent fascination as the camp, urged on by fiery pro-war advocates like Sliced Nose and Kills in Their Sleep, slowly turned from a peaceful settlement into one in which battle preparations had become the top priority.

While the war chiefs held sway in the council, making the proper political moves, two of the tribe's most prominent shamans, a member of the *Iviststsinihpah* band named Cut Lip, and a *Hotamitaniu* called Dark worked on things from the religious end. Just yesterday, the two had built a new sweat lodge just east of the village to which they planned to retire until they were able to communicate with the spirits on a correct course of action against the Notaxe-vehoe.

Biv took full advantage of the situation. Convinced he could not have arrived at a better time, he spent every waking hour running from one end of the camp to the other, pad in hand, wildly sketching scenes depicting life as it was unfolding in front of his eyes. He was certain that the Western world had never seen anything like the finished works that he planned to produce once he got back to Fort Laramie.

Acting more in frenzy than according to a thought-out plan, Biv might spend one entire day drawing the women at work around the camp, then the next day sketching the men as they went out to hunt. Despite the certainty that war was coming—maybe even because of it since they would need extra rations—the Cheyenne hunted even more fervently than normal as the short Plains summer neared its peak.

A few days after he arrived, early in the month the Cheyenne called the Moon when the Buffalo Bulls are Rutting, the village moved fifteen miles to the north to a new site along a river they called *Shistotoiyhoe*, which Legendre told him meant "Cedar." There, they had more space since they could spread out in the bottom land that lay in a large bend of the stream, smack in the middle of an area known to be occupied by several large bands of antelope. Plus, it put them closer to the buffalo, which were farther to the east as the summer progressed.

But more elbow room and the increased availability of game were not the only reasons the village changed locations; it was also part of a plan to give the Cheyenne an advantage in the coming fight. The broad valley of the Mahkineohe was well-known to the Cheyenne; they knew every creek, trail, hillock, and hideaway. Since the Notaxe-vehoe would have the advantage in firepower and numbers, the Cheyenne wanted to be able to at least pick the place where the battle would be fought.

In the space allotted to him inside Legendre's lodge, which was where the trapper had insisted that he stay, Biv had piles of sketches of ordinary Cheyenne. There was Legendre, of course, along with his wife and Legendre's son, David, a bright-eyed bundle of energy that Biv had to catch on the fly because the boy was never still for very long. He also had two very nice drawings of David's favorite playmates, two blue-eyed, blond-haired boys named Puma and Magpie. One drawing of which Biv was particularly proud depicted the four-year-old Magpie leading his pet otter by a leather leash.

If it were not for the boys' undeniably Germanic features, Biv would have sworn they were Cheyenne. They made no attempt to speak English with him; in fact when he once tried to initiate a conversation in the language they looked at him blankly, then burst into giggling fits since they were sure he was making up a new dialect for their benefit.

He also had sketches of the boys' adopted parents: Short Hair and Red Berry Woman who were raising Puma, and Large-Footed Bull and Lightning Woman, who had taken Magpie into their tipi.

Once he heard the tale about how Red Berry Woman had insisted that she be allowed to accompany Short Hair on a revenge raid against the Pawnee—and returned with an enemy scalp of her own—Biv made additional drawings of the two.

In his collection, there also were likenesses of Long Chin, the village chief, Sliced Nose and, among the rarest of all, a portrait of Big Nose, a contrary who lived off by himself on the edge of the village in a red-painted lodge.

Big Nose's story had special fascination for Biv. Until
he arrived in the camp he had no idea that there lived
among the Plains Indians certain individuals, called con-
traries, who insisted on doing everything backward.
They said hello when they meant good-bye. They said
they were warm when in fact they were freezing. They
plunged their hands and arms into pots of boiling water
without the least ill effects. But even more interesting to
Biv was the fact that these men played specific roles in
the Plains Indian culture.

When they went on a war party they carried a special
whistle and an odd-looking weapon—which Biv had captured in still another sketch—called a *hohnukawo* or
Thunder Bow. To Biv, it looked like a cross between a
bow and a lance, except the bow part had two strings.

Under prodding from Biv, Legendre patiently
explained that only the contrary could touch the Thunder
Bow, and anyone who violated that prohibition had to be
purified by being rubbed down with white sage.

The contrary had strange and unusual power, Biv
learned. When he was with a group, he had to walk off to
the side because it was believed that if anyone stepped in
his tracks they would go lame. The tribe used this to their
advantage by having the contrary walk across the foot-
prints or hoof prints of their enemies in the belief that
they would be crippled or quickly become exhausted,
thereby becoming easy prey.

When he went into a fight, the contrary could move
forward or backward as long as he held the Thunder Bow
in his left hand. But if he gripped it in his right hand, blew
his whistle, and made the sound of a burrowing owl, he
was prohibited from retreating. From that critical point
on, he had to keep charging the enemy until he was either
victorious or killed.

Since the Cheyenne were making preparations for war

simultaneous to their attempts to keep life on a normal plane, Biv also had numerous sketches of arrow makers frantically trying to keep up with demand, of warriors testing their horses to see which would be the best to ride into battle, and of men repairing or replacing their bows so their weapons would not fail them in the moment of need. One thing Biv noted was that they had very few firearms. And those that they had were old and of inferior quality, mainly trade guns that the whites had been only too happy to give away: old-fashioned flintlocks, muzzle-loaders and smooth bores that were of use only if the owner was close enough to use one of them as a club. To Biv, the pistol owned by Short Hair was an excellent example.

Legendre, whose opinion on weapons Biv trusted, explained that the revolver was a six-shot, self-cocking Allen's—an inexpensive handgun that, even when it was new, was known to be undependable and inaccurate. It had been in the Cheyenne camp so long that it was in terrible shape, Legendre said, pointing out the rust spots that spread across its surface. Holding up the handful of rust-specked cartridges that Short Hair carried in a small pouch, Legendre shook his head sadly. "No good," he said. "That's for fucking sure."

But Short Hair was so proud of the weapon that Biv made a sketch of him holding the Allen's in one hand and his deadly looking war club in the other.

Biv had stretched out in the shade of a large cottonwood for a short midday nap when he was awakened by many of the tribespeople talking excitedly and gesturing toward the lodge where the council met. As Biv ran to the tipi to see what was going on, he arrived just in time to see Cut Lip and Dark disappear inside, apparently straight from their sweat lodge and communion with the gods.

Grabbing a pad, he squirmed inside, and found a place next to Legendre, who had beaten him there. Pulling out a chunk of charcoal, Biv began sketching furiously, intuitively aware that something important was happening.

Cut Lip, a slim, distinguished-looking man of early middle age with a firm jaw, long neck, and narrow shoulders, was earnestly explaining something to Long Chin. First, he rubbed his hands together in a washing motion, then turned and pointed over his shoulder toward the north. Dark, who was older and stouter with puffy lips and an incisor missing from his left upper row of teeth, nodded vigorously, obviously agreeing with his colleague.

Legendre leaned over to whisper to Biv that what the two had to say was exceptionally interesting. After fasting and sweating, he quoted them as saying, they had been visited by spirits who promised the warriors a great victory over the Notaxe-vehoe if they did what the shamans told them.

"And what was that?" Biv asked excitedly, sketching furiously.

Legendre replied that what the Cheyenne warriors had to do was wash themselves in a specific lake not far away immediately before the battle. That would give them special power over the soldiers, essentially making their superior guns useless. "Their bullets fall to the ground," Legendre quoted Dark as saying. "No kill anyone."

In addition, as a trump, the two shamans said they would prepare a magical powder which would be distributed to all the Cheyenne who owned weapons. If they poured some of it down the barrel before the battle it would carry their bullets home; the Cheyenne warriors would be unable to miss their targets.

While Long Chin and the other older members of the council accepted the claims of Dark and Cut Lip stoically,

the younger, war-seeking members of the tribe were
beside themselves. While they had already been confident
of a victory over the whites, the shamans' words were
added insurance. In a few days, they loudly predicted,
once the battle had been fought and won by the
Cheyenne, the whites would leave their territory forever,
abandoning plans for roads through the buffalo country,
and quit interfering in the affairs of the tribe, leaving the
Cheyenne to hunt, to roam at will, and to go to war
against the Pawnee, as the Wise One Above, Hemmawihio, intended.

Caught in an uncomfortable position and unable to
denounce two of the tribe's most respected shamans, Long
Chin called a great feast for that night, telling the women
to scour the camp for plump young puppies and to dig
into their store of fresh buffalo and antelope.

"What do you think?" Biv anxiously asked Legendre
once the meeting in Long Chin's lodge had broken up.

Legendre shook his head sadly. "These are my people,"
the trapper said, looking as if he were going to break into
tears, "but these shamans are wrong. They think they
have magic, but they do not. They will not be able to stop
the white soldiers' guns."

"Can't you tell them that?" Biv said worriedly. "Can't
you convince them?"

Legendre chuckled bitterly. *"Non,"* he said. "They have
their minds made up. If I try to tell them, they will accuse
me of siding with the whites and kill me. You, *aussi."*

Biv shuddered involuntarily. "I can see the predicament," he said.

"I think," Legendre said slowly, "that it is time for you
to leave. Before the battle. Afterward, they may be angry
at *all* whites and forget that you are a friend."

Biv said nothing, thinking about what Legendre had
said. Viewed logically, he knew the trapper was correct.

The shamans could talk of magical lakes and powders but he knew that would be useless against Colonel Sumner and his men. Of that Biv was certain. While he wanted to stay, to draw the Cheyenne as they made their final preparations for war, he knew it is was not a sensible thing to do. He had been with the tribe for almost two weeks and he had more than two dozen first-class sketches in the pile beside his pallet. I shouldn't be greedy, he told himself. Besides, if I tarry too long, it could be fatal. Although he thought his hair was too fine and a rather ordinary color, he did not want to think about it as dangling from Sliced Nose's lance.

"Unhappily, I agree," he reluctantly told Legendre. "When do you think I should leave? When is the fight expected?"

Legendre shrugged. "Who knows?" The latest reports placed the soldiers only three days away, but that was if they came directly to the camp. They didn't know where the camp was and it might take them several additional days to find it. "Their scouts dumb Pawnee. Can't find woman's most vital point without help." But, he added, the army also had several Delawares and they were very good.

"Why don't the Cheyenne attack?" Biv asked. "Catch them by surprise?"

Legendre laughed. "No surprise soldiers. Not now." Anyway, he added, the Cheyenne wanted to fight on their terms, on their battlefield. The war chiefs have advised that it is better to let the soldiers come to them.

"Can I have one more day?" Biv pleaded. "There are some sketches I want to finish."

Legendre nodded. Be ready to go the day after tomorrow, he told him. Early.

Biv nodded, and started to leave the lodge to go work on a sketch of Dark and White Wolf. There were some details he still wanted to fill in. He was halfway out the opening when he stopped. Turning, he came back inside and looked solemnly at Legendre.

"How in hell am I going to get back?" he asked, a concerned expression on his face.

Legendre laughed heartily. "I take you," he said.

Biv frowned. How could he do that, he wanted to know. "What about Antelope Woman and David?"

He would take them to the Arapaho camp, he said, and leave them there while he returned Biv to Fort Laramie. The Arapaho were allies of the Cheyenne and his family would be safe. If the battle against the whites went as badly as he expected it would, the Cheyenne might try to take revenge against his family as well. This was a situation, he said, where it is was best not to be too visible for a few weeks.

"But can you go back into Fort Laramie?" Biv asked. "Will you still be subject to arrest?"

For what? Legendre replied. By then all their questions about the Cheyenne will have been answered. And there was still the matter of twenty dollars he was owed.

11 July 57
At the Headwaters of Dog Creek

My dearest, darling Inge,

Tonight there is both good news and bad. Optimist that I am, I will tell you the good news first. Since the colonel appointed one of his men to command the Fort Laramie companies and I was shifted back under Grant's command, Harry and I have been at each other's throats almost constantly. I went to Jeb Stuart and asked him if he could arrange a temporary transfer to his unit. He went to Sumner who, to the surprise of both of us, approved, after checking with Harry, of course. The colonel told me he thought it would be a good idea for an infantry officer to work closely with the cavalry and therefore obtain a better understanding of what the new regiment was all about.

Harry wasn't disappointed at all in Sumner's decision and doesn't seem to be angry toward me. In fact, I think he is glad to get rid of me, at least for awhile. Mindful of the forthcoming battle, he doesn't want to have to worry about sharing any honors.

The bad news is, there may be very few honors for the infantry. Once Sumner sent the wagons back (I wonder if you have received my first few pages by now?), he moved the Fort Laramie units to the rear of the column, claiming that he was afraid of losing his chance to attack the Cheyenne if he had to stop and wait for the infantry. By marching in front of the column, we were slowing everyone down.

As a result, the six cavalry companies (including the four under Major Sedgwick), have become the spearhead of the operation and frequently leave the infantry, along with the equally slow-moving artillery, a half-day or so behind. Harry and the others from Fort Laramie fear that when the time to fight comes, it will be the cavalry that gets to do battle; that by the time they arrive everything will be all over.

Otherwise, the days pass monotonously,

each one seemingly like the last. Rise early, eat a tasteless, cheerless breakfast, and then head relentlessly into the direction in which the Cheyenne are believed to be waiting. Although he rotates the scouts so someone is always on the lookout, so far he has not cut the Cheyenne's trail. For the troops from Fort Laramie, already footsore and exhausted from trying to keep up with the cavalry, it has become a contest of endurance. It is not so bad for me because I have a horse to ride, but the pace is beginning to wear down the men and they are starting to show the strain, becoming short-tempered and fractious, both infantry and cavalry alike.

Last night there was a brawl among the members of Sedgwick's H Company. After their meager dinner of beans and beef, which was about as chewable as a piece cut from my saddle, they got into a political discussion. Some of them advanced pro-slavery issues and they immediately got into a heated argument with those who are anti-slavery. Before the officers could move in to break it up, a fight broke out and several men were injured but none seriously. Jeb says it just goes to show how close to the surface are the tensions that threaten to divide the entire country.

Harry has been at a loss about what to do with those exceedingly quarrelsome privates, Venezia and LaRossa. If we were back at Fort Laramie the solution would be simple: court-martial them. But on a march, resolutions are not so clear-cut. Yesterday, I understand on very good authority, LaRossa tripped Venezia and pushed him down the bank of a dry wash because the latter called him a "dumb dago." As a result, he has been banished to the mule corps. This means that for the rest of the mission LaRossa, who will not be hindered there by an arm in a cast, will be required to work with those unruly animals, inhaling the odors of mule sweat by day and mule shit by night.

Venezia, rather than being delighted, is sad and moans about missing his best friend. If this situation were not so serious, it would be terribly humorous.

I find nothing humorous, though, in my absence from you. I go to sleep each night thinking of your compliant, inviting body. My only consolation is in recalling our happy moments together and counting the days until we can resume them.

This is decidedly longer than the few lines I promised. I hope you won't complain about reading the ranting of a tired and homesick soldier. If you do, I will simply ask Colonel Kemp to send me into the field more often.

Your loving husband,

Jean

7

Biv was inside Legendre's lodge, carefully packing his sketches for the trip back to Fort Laramie, when David came rushing in. *"Ne-hoe!"* he said excitedly, tugging on Legendre's arm. "Father! You must come see."

"What is it?" Biv asked curiously, unable to follow David's torrent of French and Cheyenne.

"Two Lakota are coming," Legendre explained, trying to calm his son. "David says it is the man who has been looking for that renegade band and his companion. We go and listen to what they say."

Sensing a new development, Biv grabbed a pad and followed Legendre to the council lodge. When they slipped through the opening, Biv saw immediately that most of the camp's top warriors were already there. In the center was Long Chin, and on his left, in the place of honor, was Coyote Ear, a thick-chested man in his late thirties whose cheekbones were so high and wide they gave his face a diamond shape. Like many among the Tsis-tsis-tas, Coyote Ear was part Sioux, a condition so prevalent that the half bloods had split into their own band which was called the Cheyenne Sioux.

A scarred, hardened veteran of innumerable fights

with the Pawnee and the Crow, Coyote Ear was the chief of the tribe's most combative military society, the Dog Soldiers. This, Legendre had told Biv, was a very high honor and accounted for his position next to Long Chin in the camp circle.

Before a warrior could even be considered for a chief's position in one of the military groups, he had to have scalped at least four live foes. Also, since the chiefs were required to lead warriors into battle, they were continually at high risk. "A military society chief is expected to be killed," Legendre had explained.

This was particularly true among the Dog Soldiers, a legendary group famous for going into battle carrying a short piece of braided rawhide called a "dog rope." When it looked as if their comrades might be overrun, Dog Soldiers would anchor the rope to the ground like a leash, signifying they would not retreat. The pin holding the rope to the ground could be pulled only if the Cheyenne were victorious or a comrade yanked it out. Three times, Coyote Ear had done this and still lived to talk about it.

Although Dog Soldiers were known for their aggressiveness, Coyote Ear had been slow to encourage the Cheyenne to fight the soldiers. As a veteran warrior he had tremendous respect for the Notaxe-vehoes' advantages in arms and manpower, so much so that he initially counseled against it when the young hotheads first began screaming for soldiers' blood. The results, Coyote Ear had argued, would be inevitable: in the end the Notaxe-vehoe would win.

However, when the younger warriors began making veiled references questioning his bravery, he had discarded the anti-war mantle. The worst fate that could befall a warrior, Coyote Ear had proclaimed, was to die of old age. So if there was to be fighting against the whites no matter what he said, it would be much better to be killed in battle than to be thought a coward.

Sitting next to Coyote Ear was the contrary, Big Nose, wearing his distinctive red paint. Glancing around the group, Biv noted that others present included Carries the Otter, an impetuous youth of about nineteen who liked to brag about his prowess with the knife; his best friend, One-Eyed Bear; Rock Forehead, the tribe's arrow keeper; Kills in Their Sleep; Large-footed Bull; Short Hair, the hero of a recent major fight with the Pawnee in which the Cheyenne and the Arapaho joined forces, and, on Long Chin's right, Sliced Nose.

When Biv and Legendre slipped into the lodge, the village chief was solemnly packing a pipe with a mixture of white man's tobacco and red willow bark, called *kinnikinnik* by the Cheyenne and *shongasha* by the Lakotas, that was commonly smoked among all the Plains tribes.

Once the pipe was full, Long Chin turned it straight up so its mouthpiece was pointing at the ground. Passing his right hand and then his left hand twice down the stem, he then handed it to Coyote Ear, who repeated the movements and then returned it to Long Chin. Reaching forward, the chief took a coal from the fire and dropped it into the bowl. Taking a few puffs to make sure it was going, he passed it to Coyote Ear. Slowly it went around the circle, left to right, each man—the visitors included—taking one or two leisurely drags.

Since all conversation halted while the pipe was being passed, the ceremony gave Biv time to ready his pad and study the group. While they were smoking, Biv stared at the two newcomers, who were sitting across the fire which had burned to coals, directly in front of Long Chin.

According to Legendre, the older one, who was about Biv's age, was named Red Horse. Although the technicalities were lost on Biv, Legendre explained that he was a member of the Wazhazha band of the Brulé, which, in turn, was one of the seven groups of the Teton Sioux. The

Teton Sioux called themselves Lakotas to differentiate them from their eastern cousins, the Santees and the Yanktons, who called themselves Dakotas. The word Brulé, Legendre added, meant the Burnt Thighs People. Red Horse's companion was a youth of about eighteen named Sad Bear.

"Is he also a Brulé?" Biv asked to show he was paying attention.

"*Non*," said Legendre. "He is a Miniconjou—Those Who Plant Near the Water People. They also are Lakotas and very close to the Brulé."

Legendre looked up. The pipe had come back to Long Chin, who placed it reverently on the ground in front of him and cleared his throat.

"The talk begins," Legendre whispered. "I tell you later about Red Horse and Sad Bear."

Since he had a surplus of sketches of the Cheyenne, Biv concentrated on the two visitors. While far from being an expert, he could tell at a glance that they were not Cheyenne. For one thing, he noted, they dressed differently. While the Cheyenne were wearing what they usually did when they were in the camp—plain breech clouts looped through their legs and held in place by a thong belt, Red Horse and Sad Bear were dressed for travel. Each wore buffalo hide leggins designed to help protect their legs from branches and brambles. The fact that they were unadorned indicated they were utilitarian, not ceremonial. The two Lakotas also wore plain elk skin or deerskin shirts. In camp, the Cheyenne rarely bothered with shirts but they put them on when they traveled to prevent sunburn or to keep themselves warm. On their feet, Red Horse and Sad Bear wore moccasins with just a touch of beading around the edges while the Cheyenne everyday footwear was low-cut and close-fitting with stiff rawhide soles. Finally, Biv noticed, the visitors had their hair braided with the twisted ends hanging over their shoulders and across their chests—another indication that they had been traveling. The Cheyenne, who did not have to worry that day about their hair being whipped into tangles on the trail, let theirs hang free.

As Biv began sketching, Red Horse, in response to a question from Long Chin, began talking in a mixture of Siouan and Cheyenne, punctuating his conversation with hand signs that moved too quickly for Biv to follow. His voice, Biv noticed, was slightly higher pitched than that of most of the Indians he had come into contact so far and he spoke in quick jerky sentences, the result perhaps, Biv reasoned, of trying to communicate in a different language.

"He is telling about how they see the white soldiers," Legendre whispered, providing a quick, rough translation. They had come from the northwest, more or less following the trail that Biv and Legendre had taken, except they had been ahead of, not behind, the soldiers. About three days ago, Red Horse said, they had spotted the huge dust column that trailed behind Sumner's expedition. Carefully working themselves closer, they spent most of one morning observing the troops, following them for several miles as they tramped across the plain.

All told, they estimated the approaching force at about five hundred men, slightly more than half of whom were mounted while the others marched doggedly along, sweating in the heat and coughing on the horses' dust. "Being one of those on foot must be a terrible punishment," added Red Horse, who could not conceive of how true warriors would not have their own horses. There also were four large guns—Legendre took that to mean artillery pieces—but the wagons they were mounted on moved even slower than the foot soldiers and probably would not play a part in forthcoming hostilities, provided the Cheyenne moved quickly.

While the Cheyenne questioned Red Horse about the Notaxe-vehoe, adding the information to that obtained by their own scouts who had been watching the soldiers for more than a week, Legendre filled Biv in on the two Lakotas.

Red Horse, he explained, was obsessed with finding a renegade Brulé named Blizzard who had murdered his brother, Badger. The killing, he had heard, was brutal and senseless, the act, in his opinion, of a deranged man since murder was extremely rare among members of a band and even rarer when there was no apparent motive. After Badger was killed, Red Horse did the proper thing by marrying his brother's widow and vowing to track Blizzard down and kill him.

"How interesting," Biv had exclaimed. "What has taken him so long?"

After Badger's murder, Legendre said, Blizzard fled into the Black Hills. Later, on a visit to the Miniconjou, he had been camped at Blue Water when Harney's men attacked. Although badly wounded in the fight, he had escaped with the help of a man called Crow Killer.

Embittered by the action of the white soldiers, the murderous Blizzard turned even more vicious, promising to lead a campaign against the whites to force them to retreat from the Plains. Hearing about his plans, anti-white warriors from several groups had sought him out, asking if they could join him.

"How many are there?" Biv asked, envisioning a small army.

As far as anyone could tell, Legendre said, the group, which called itself Blizzard's Pack because they hunted like wolves, numbered fewer than a dozen. Sad Bear himself, who had been orphaned when his entire family was wiped out in the Harney attack, had been among the group. But he left, Legendre had been told, when he correctly judged Blizzard as a cruel, needlessly violent man who sooner or later would meet his own violent end.

"But how did Sad Bear come to join Red Horse against his old leader?" Biv asked, temporarily forgetting his drawing.

What he had heard, Legendre said, was gossip, but it had the ring of truth about it. What he had heard was that Red Horse and his childhood companion, White Crane, had been on Blizzard's trail when they decided to split up to follow divergent reports. White Crane had come upon the pack before Red Horse could join him and was killed by Blizzard in hand-to-hand combat. Sad Bear witnessed the fight, which convinced him that Blizzard was an evil, heartless man. Abandoning the pack, he waited along the trail for Red Horse to show up for his rendezvous with White Crane. After explaining what had happened, Sad Bear had asked Red Horse if he could join him in his search since he thought Blizzard deserved to die.

Ever since then, Legendre said, the two have been moving among the tribes searching for Blizzard and his group. In fact, he added, nodding toward the circle, that is what Red Horse is asking now: Have any of the Cheyenne seen Blizzard or any of his cold-hearted companions.

"Have they?" Biv asked excitedly, hoping that he might be able to witness an Indian showdown.

Legendre shook his head. Long Chin was telling them that no one in the Cheyenne camp has seen Blizzard for two winters but they probably should go and ask the Arapahoes, who were camped farther to the north and therefore closer to the territory in which Blizzard usually roamed.

"That's where *we're* going, isn't it?" Biv asked. "To the Arapahoes, I mean?"

"*Oui*." Legendre nodded. "And we should get started very soon. The day is already half gone. We want to be well away from here by the time of the battle with the white soldiers."

"Can't I get you to change your mind about that? It would make some wonderful sketches."

"*Non*," Legendre said resolutely. "There is too much danger. If we don't get killed by the soldiers, we might by the Cheyenne."

"What about Red Horse and Sad Bear? Will they travel with us to the Arapaho camp?"

"I will ask," Legendre said.

After a short discussion with the two Lakotas, Legendre told Biv that they wanted to rest at least a night because they had been traveling long and hard. "I tell them we go and they come later."

"All right," Biv said, his voice heavy with disappointment. "Let me go finish gathering my material and say my good-byes. I'll be ready to leave within the hour."

19 July 57
On the South Fork of Sappa Creek

My Beloved Inge,

At last some good news. Last night, just as we were finishing another dinner of tough beef and tasteless beans, Sedgwick's Delaware scout, Fall Leaf, rode into camp saying he had found the site of the Cheyenne's Sun Dance village along a small river not more than a day's march from here.

This is encouraging because it indicates that the Cheyenne were all together (it being a strict tribal edict, I understand, that every able-bodied Cheyenne attend a Sun Dance) as recently as six weeks ago. Sumner, after consulting with Fall Leaf and the other scouts, feels that the Cheyenne have probably remained in at least one major group rather than breaking up into bands, especially if they know (and they must by now) that we are on the prowl for them.

Accordingly, Sumner has drawn up a plan of action for the next few days while the scouts spread out and see if they can pinpoint the tribe's location. He is afraid the Indians will run when they see how many men are in the expedition and the quality of our arms compared to their pitiful weapons. In preparation for this eventuality, he is going to put the cavalry in the front of the line of march and move them forward at a reasonable pace. This means, unfortunately for Harry, Zack, and Will Barnes, that their companies are going to be left even farther behind. The chances that they will get to take part in any of the fighting are getting slimmer by the hour. I know this is discouraging to them since they have walked all this way and now will have to turn around and walk back once the battle is over. But such are the fortunes of war.

Despite myself, I find I am getting excited by the prospect of a good scrap, if only as a relief to the boredom that has set in like a toothache. For more days than it seems we can remember we have been trudging over dry, dusty, featureless plains, fighting the heat, vicious thunderstorms, and persistent winds that leave us parched and exhausted. The strain is really beginning to show. There was

another fight the day before yesterday among
the men of Sedgwick's H Company over the
slavery issue, the second in the last eight days.
This time, even more men were involved and
one corporal was seriously hurt. I think a fight
with the Cheyenne will help relieve some of
the tension since the men will have someone
else to fight instead of attacking one another.

I still find my feelings mixed about the current situation. I continue to believe that the
army has no justification for an attack against
the Cheyenne other than a desire by those Back
East to erode the Indians' claim to the land. It is
no secret that this campaign is political, nothing more than an attempt to force the Indians
off land that powerful, rich businessmen want
to secure because it is one of the most likely
routes for a transcontinental railroad. The railroad interests were the main force behind the
move in Congress to create the Kansas and
Nebraska Territories since their leaders realized the value of being able to gain access to
the Plains. It is enough to make me nauseated.
Those numbskulls in Washington see only
money and power and have not the slightest
notion of what effect their greed is having on
the existence of an entire culture. I guess it's a
good thing I decided to be a soldier because I
would have made a truly bad politician.

On the other hand, the soldier part of me is
excited about the prospect of a battle; it is what
I have been trained to do. Still, I am not at all
comfortable with the idea of taking up arms
against the Cheyenne, who, from what I have
seen, are a very noble race. I have many very

fond memories of the days that Jace and I spent with the tribe two years ago when we visited them while chasing that elusive smallpox scare. The Cheyenne with whom we stayed, Short Hair and Red Berry Woman, were wonderful people, just like whites. Although it hurt in a way to see Werner and Wilhelm being raised like Indians, it gladdened my spirit to see them so happy and well cared for. I know your mother thinks otherwise, believing that it would be for their good if they would only come to her at Fort Laramie, I disagree. It was unfortunate enough that the boys' parents were killed but from what I observed each seems to have found a good home and they appeared to be much loved. My sincerest hope is that Short Hair and Wilhelm's new father, Large-footed Bull, have taken the children and separated from the main Cheyenne body. It would grieve me greatly to think that we might find them in our sights when the battle comes.

I consider myself very fortunate that my temporary assignment to Jeb's company continues. The colonel has said nothing about ordering me to return to Harry's command and I certainly do not plan to remind him. In fact, I try to keep out of his way as much as possible, figuring if he can't see me he won't remember that I don't belong.

The bugler has started to blow tattoo so I must close this. For the last several nights all bugle calls as well as campfires have been prohibited on grounds that the colonel did not want to give away our position. But Fall Leaf has told him that the Cheyenne are far from stupid, that their scouts have undoubtedly seen us—in fact have probably been keeping us under observation for longer than we know—so it is useless for us to try to hide.

I trust you are well and that I am as much in your heart as you are in mine. Give your mother a hug for me and pass my regards to Jace and all the others.

Your loving husband,

Jean

As the small group consisting of Biv, Legendre, Antelope Woman, and David progressed up the winding trail northward, Legendre explained the relationship that existed between the Cheyenne and the Arapahoes. Their languages were not very dissimilar, the trapper said, and often they found themselves cooperating on large-scale hunts as well as in joint efforts against their common enemies, the Pawnee and the Crow.

The Arapahoes and the Cheyenne, Legendre said, truly hate the Pawnee; they are always killing each other in intertribal battles and horse raids. "Remember Short Hair?" Legendre asked.

"Of course," said Biv. "I have some wonderful sketches of him as well as the white child he is raising as his own. What about him?"

He and his wife, Red Berry Woman, became heroes among their people a few years ago, Legendre said.

"I love a good story," Biv said encouragingly. "Tell me. It will give more life to my work if I paint Short Hair in oil."

"Why not," said Legendre. "We have time to kill. It

began when the Pawnee kidnapped Beaver Woman, the daughter of Short Hair and Red Berry Woman."

"*Kidnapped* her? Why would they do that?" Biv asked.

"The Pawnee wanted to use her as a human sacrifice in a ceremony honoring one of their favorite gods, Morning Star."

"Are you making this up?" Biv asked, giving Legendre a suspicious look.

"Of course not."

"I didn't think the Plains tribes used human sacrifices."

"It is an old, old custom among the Pawnee but it has been practiced only rarely in recent years. But, from what I have heard, one of the Pawnee had a vision in which Morning Star appeared, telling him to find a Cheyenne maiden to be his companion."

"So they picked the daughter of Short Hair and Red Berry Woman."

"Purely by coincidence, I'm certain. But they rode into the Cheyenne camp while the men were off hunting, entered Short Hair's lodge, and took the child."

"So Short Hair organized a revenge raid?"

"*Assurément*! He also sought—and received—the cooperation of the Arapahoes, which is the point of what I was saying."

"That they are strong allies, even to the point of going into war together."

"*Oui.*"

"Well, what happened? Did they rescue the girl?"

"No," Legendre said, shaking his head. "They did not even try. White Wolf—you know, the Cheyenne shaman?"

"Yes."

"He said the signs indicated that the Cheyenne should not try to interfere with the Pawnee religious ceremony."

"But I thought you said they hated . . ."

"They do, but religion is religion. They will kill each

other over honor and horses, but not because of spiritual beliefs."

"But they still attacked the Pawnee."

"Oh, yes. A very decisive battle. If I remember correctly nine or ten Pawnee were killed, including three by Red Berry Woman herself."

"You don't mean to tell me that she actually took part in the battle? Fought like a warrior."

"It is not unheard of at all among the Cheyenne. While it doesn't happen often, it is not at all unusual. But Red Berry Woman insisted that she be allowed to go along since it was her daughter that had been kidnapped."

"That is truly fascinating," Biv said half dreamily. "It is having information like that that gives true life to a drawing. The subjects cease to be merely objects and take on their own identities. In that way, a painter is not much different from a writer."

Legendre shrugged. "To me, it is an unimportant fact. I read very little, but I enjoy a nice painting as much as anyone. But, to return to what I was saying. It is because of the close ties between the Cheyenne and the Arapahoes that it is possible for me to leave Antelope Woman and David in their care while I deliver you to Fort Laramie."

"How far is it from the Arapaho village to the fort?" Biv asked.

"Four days. Perhaps three if we ride hard."

"Then let's ride hard," Biv said with a smile. "For your sake as well as mine. I'm anxious to get to work on these sketches and you want to get back to Antelope Woman before she gives birth."

"And you also want to see your woman?" Legendre grinned.

"That, too," Biv replied, laughing. "I hope we will not be staying long with the Arapahoes?"

"Tonight only," replied Legendre. "Long enough to eat some good dog stew. The Arapahoes, you know, love dog more than any of the Plains Indians. The other tribes call them the Dog Eaters."

"That's comforting to know," Biv said weakly, feeling his stomach turn over. While he could eat his weight in liver and even enjoy buffalo nose and tongue, the thought of dining on yet another fat puppy made his throat seize up.

By the time they reached the village, there was a small crowd waiting to meet them. Although Biv had not seen a single Arapaho until they rode into the camp he realized that they must have seen them much earlier.

"Long Leg is very clever," Legendre said. "Even I not detect him watching us."

Long Leg, Biv learned, was one of the village's permanent scouts, a wizened hermit who lived alone in the hills, celibate and antisocial. He and four others with similar tendencies lived an Arapaho tradition. Called Coyote Men because they wore white buffalo robes and kept their faces painted with white clay, they saw and reported everything that happened on the camp's outer boundaries but were seldom, if ever, seen by those on whom they were reporting.

Biv's eyes lit up. "Would it be possible for me to sketch one of them?" he asked enthusiastically. "I don't know of anyone who has ever done that."

"With good reason," Legendre said, chuckling. "No one can find them. You don't go to them; they come to you. They move like ghosts."

"It would be worth the effort," Biv persisted.

"Only if you have unlimited time. I thought you were in a hurry."

"I guess you're right," Biv said reluctantly. "I guess I can always come back."

An hour later, they were in Crooked Nose's lodge, watching as the chief prepared the customary pipe. After they had smoked and exchanged pleasantries, Crooked Nose looked at them solemnly.

"You must be careful after you leave here," he told Legendre, who translated for Biv. "Our Coyote Men have found tracks of a roving group of Indians who do their best from being seen by us. We think it is Blizzard and his men."

"Blizzard!" Legendre said in surprise. "I didn't think he would be this far south."

"I think he has been trailing the white soldiers, hoping perhaps to find a few off by themselves so he could slaughter them."

"That sounds like something he would do." Legendre nodded. "How recently were his tracks noticed?"

"Two days ago."

"And which direction were they going?"

"North."

Legendre calculated quickly. "By now, he's well across the North Platte and deep into Lakota country. I don't think we need to worry about him hanging around here. There's nothing to attract him."

"He is totally unpredictable," Crooked Nose cautioned.

"I agree. But my instincts tell me he has passed beyond our route of travel."

"In any case," Crooked Nose added, "be cautious. He is a very dangerous man and his followers are no better than cold-blooded murderers."

"Why don't they track Blizzard down and kill him themselves?" Biv whispered to Legendre.

"Blizzard and his followers are not a threat to the Arapahoes," the trapper explained. "They want to kill whites, not other Indians. If they made enemies of every tribe on the Plains they would not last very long. The

Arapahoes and other tribes believe in live and let live. As long as Blizzard is not a danger to them, they do not make themselves a danger to him."

"That's very convenient," Biv nodded, marveling at the logic.

Legendre turned to Crooked Nose, ready to ask if they would give them enough fresh meat to last for the trip to Fort Laramie since he didn't plan to take the time to stop and hunt, when a high voice piped in from the rear of the lodge.

"Maybe it would be a good idea if I went with them," the voice said.

Squinting in the uncertain light, Biv could see that the speaker had been a youth he estimated to be no more than seventeen.

"Is that you, Cut Neck?" Legendre asked. "You have grown so much since I was last here I am not sure I recognize you."

"You are correct," Cut Neck replied, blushing. "I'm flattered that you remember me."

"Oh, yes, I remember you," Legendre said lightly. "You almost drove me crazy last time I was here, begging to dog my footsteps."

"He has an unreasonable thirst for adventure," Crooked Nose said unhappily. "Even for a young warrior he has a need for danger. He cannot seem to get enough."

"Is that true?" asked Legendre. "Is that why you want to go with us? You think there might be danger."

"One never knows with Blizzard," Cut Neck said, his words, Biv thought, betraying a maturity beyond his years. "But maybe I want to go because I enjoy your company."

"You prankster," laughed Legendre. "You think that will convince me?"

"I was a good scout for White Crane when he was looking for Blizzard," Cut Neck argued.

"We're *not* looking for Blizzard," Legendre said. "We want nothing to do with him. Besides, look where your scouting got White Crane. Blizzard killed him."

"That wasn't my fault. If he had let me stay with him, it may not have happened. But he sent me back to the camp to wait for Red Horse so I could tell him where they had gone. We could have left signs along the trail. Red Horse would have found us. He is not dumb. In any case, I don't want to lead you to Blizzard; I want to lead you to Fort Laramie."

"Are you saying that I would be dumb if I did not say you could go with us?" Legendre teased.

"Oh, no," Cut Neck parried. "I think if you took me you would be very smart. I know some trails that even you are not familiar with. I can take you there in half the time. And I would be company for you on your return."

Legendre laughed heartily. "You make a very persuasive argument. If Crooked Nose has no objection, neither do I."

"Why would I object?" Crooked Nose said, picking up the pipe and the tobacco pouch. "Cut Neck is qualified to make his own decisions. Besides, I might have used the same argument myself years ago, but probably not as effectively."

"Very well," Legendre said, smiling at the youth. "But we will leave early."

"I will be up long before you," Cut Neck replied facilely. "In fact, I am so excited thinking about it, I may not sleep at all."

Biv nudged Legendre. "What was all that about?" he asked since the trapper had not paused to give him a running translation.

When Legendre explained, Biv looked sharply at Cut Neck. "He seems so young," he said. "Do you think this is the right thing to do?"

"He *is* young," admitted Legendre, "but as far as being the right thing, who knows. Indian boys become men quickly. Most of them are taken on horse-stealing raids by the time they are fourteen. By your standards, Cut Neck may be young but by the Arapaho calendar, he is well into adulthood."

"And you think it's all right?"

Legendre nodded. "I have heard Crooked Nose and others speak highly of him. I think he should be given the chance to try his wings."

"Even if it places him in danger?"

Legendre looked sharply at Biv. "Did I tell you that when you asked to accompany me on my journey to the Cheyenne?"

"But I'm not seventeen."

"No, but neither are you an Indian. Older doesn't make you smarter in the ways of the frontier. You may be ten years Cut Neck's elder, but he is vastly more knowledge-able about the situation we are facing."

"You're right," Biv said, embarrassed. "I apologize for questioning you."

"Don't give it a second thought." Legendre smiled.

21 July 57
On the South Bank of Bow Creek

My Cherished Inge,

When I left Fort Laramie I said that some of my entries might be short. This one will follow that pattern. We marched twenty miles yester-day, one of our largest treks so far considering the infantry, the artillery, the remuda, and the mule corps. Tonight everyone is exhausted (for

once no one has to worry about fights among
the men) but there will be few able to sleep.

Fall Leaf and his fellow scouts have found
the village we have been seeking. They report
that the Cheyenne are making preparations for
war, which is no surprise to Sumner. Based on
the scouting reports, the colonel estimates the
number of warriors, judging by the fact that it
is a very large encampment with five hundred
or so lodges, at about three hundred or more.
This will not be as many men as we can field,
even if Sumner decides to go into battle only
with the cavalry, but the Indians have the
advantage of fighting on their own territory.
Plus, they have more to gain. In their eyes we
are the invaders who need to be driven out.

Surprisingly, I am not as anxious as I
thought I would be. Although I was a little
nervous with Harney's men on the night
before that battle, I knew that the attack would
be catching the enemy by surprise; that they
would not be able to put up a sustained
defense. This situation is different. When we
take the field on the morn, we will be facing a
foe that is ready for us; one that has much to
gain by fighting us to a standstill.

Uncountable millions of soldiers before me
have written letters to their loved ones on the
eve of battle, expressing their love just in case
the unfortunate occurs and they are picked by
God to die on the field. But just because I cannot be unique in uttering these sentiments,
that does not mean that such thoughts are
alien to my being. Although I consider it
highly unlikely that such a fate will befall me

(Jace has always said, for example, that I am too mean to die) I want you to know that if God deems otherwise and, if by some fluke, I do not survive this battle that your face was my ultimate vision and that my last thought was of you.

Having said that, let me add that I am confident that one day soon we will read these words together and laugh at the overly dramatic tone. In the meantime, I must get my weapons ready. Sumner has again banned fires and bugle calls but that does not excuse us from giving the rifles one last swipe and from administering one more honing to the sabers.

I stare at the stars thinking wonderful thoughts about you.

Your loving husband,

Jean

8

5:26 A.M.

Benoit, his head on his saddle, arms resting lightly across his chest, stared upward into the cloudless sky, watching without seeing as it metamorphosed from star-studded black to a sparkling azure. I wonder if this is the last sunrise I'll ever see, he thought as the men around him began to stir. Since Sumner had again banned bugle calls, the order to rise and begin preparations for what everyone expected would be the final march before battle was passed down mouth-to-mouth, man-to-man. Rising into a sitting position, Benoit looked at the eager yet anxious faces that surrounded him and realized that he was not the only one who had spent a sleepless night; very few men in B Company had to be shaken awake by their comrades. Since no one had removed anything but his boots and all had kept their weapons at their sides in case of a preemptive attack by the Indians, all they had to do to get ready was roll up their blankets and stuff some beef jerky into their saddlebags to carry them through what was certain to be a long day.

Within an hour, with the sun already well above the horizon and starting to heat the ground, the men and animals of the Sumner expedition against the Cheyenne were on the march. Observing the same order established since they crossed the South Platte, the cavalry led the way, followed by the two artillery pieces, the infantry, the mule corps, and the driven stock consisting of extra horses and a few remaining steers. Turning in his saddle to look behind him, Benoit gazed at the tall column of dust the large force created as it moved across the dry, nearly treeless prairie and wondered if its presence alone was striking fear in the hearts of the unfortunate Cheyenne who must realize how outgunned and outmanned they were.

"By God, you can rightly *feel* the tension," said Jeb Stuart, shattering Benoit's philosophical mood. "It's like a lightning bolt passing through the column."

"I was with Harney's men at Blue Water and it wasn't at all like this," replied Benoit. "Most of the men who knew what was going on felt more dejected than excited. It was not an experience I'd like to repeat."

"That's a curious thing to say," Stuart remarked quietly. "How was it different?"

"With Harney, it was like spearing fish in a pond. He approached the Sioux camp stealthily, sending Cooke and his dragoons on an all-night march so they would be in position around the Lakota camp when the sun came up. The Brulé and Miniconjou didn't know we were coming; they had no reason to suspect an attack. They had been hunting buffalo, minding their own business, not preparing for battle."

"That's not the way we heard the story back in Kansas," said Stuart. "The reports we received said Harney was moving against a hostile force of bloodthirsty warriors who had wiped out an entire Army detachment."

"The wiping out part is accurate enough," Benoit said. "The Brulé and Miniconjou had killed Grattan and his men after they burst into the Indian camp looking for a fight. Grattan simply bit off more than he could chew and he paid the ultimate price."

"And that set the Indians off on a campaign to kill every white they could find?" asked Stuart. "Wasn't Harney sent to turn the tide?"

Benoit smiled. "I don't know who you've been talking to, Jeb, or what you've been reading, but that's all bullshit. After the Grattan incident, the Lakotas could have walked into Fort Laramie and taken it with only half an effort. Instead, they melted into the hills and settled in for the winter."

"You saying the Harney campaign was unnecessary?"

"Well," Benoit drawled, "maybe it was necessary for the politicians in Washington. They probably felt they had to show the Indians who was boss so it wouldn't slow down the emigration movement. But it sure as hell wasn't necessary to kill a whole hell of a lot of women and children."

"The newspapers made Harney a hero," Stuart said. "The war department proclaimed a great victory."

"Hero my ass," Benoit replied, making no attempt to hide the contempt he felt for the general and his tactics. "The chief of the Brulé camp begged Harney to negotiate a settlement and Harney refused, opening fire on the camp even before he could get back to his people. You want to know the truth, it was a goddamn massacre, pure and simple."

"That disturbs me considerably," Stuart confessed. "Another idol with feet made of clay."

"And a heart full of deceit," added Benoit.

"Certainly you don't think the situation is going to be the same here, do you?"

Benoit shrugged. "I don't know for sure, but I don't think so. From everything the scouts have told us the

Cheyenne know we're coming and they're ready for a fight. Do you think the colonel will try to negotiate first?"

Stuart chuckled. "My honest opinion? I don't think there's a chance in hell. The orders read that an attempt at conciliation will be made before a battle is joined, but I think that's just something those bleeding hearts in Washington stuck in at the last minute to ease their own consciences. The colonel will find some way to get around that. Tell me," he said, looking closely at Benoit. "Are you going to fight when the time comes?"

Benoit turned to him in surprise. "Of course I'm going to fight. Jesus Christ, what kind of question is that?"

"Just wondering. After what you said about Harney and the battle at Blue Water."

"That wasn't a battle; it was a slaughter. I'm a soldier not a paid murderer. As far as I'm concerned, I get my money to fight the enemies of the United States, but I'm not hired to shoot a bunch of women and children practically in their sleep."

"From what you're telling me I agree with you wholeheartedly. I just wanted to see where you stood."

Benoit grinned. "On the side of justice and equality, where else? Killing a Cheyenne who's trying to kill you is just and equal in my book." He paused, then added, "Speaking of books . . ."

"Books?" Stuart said in surprise. "What's this about books?"

Benoit looked embarrassed. "There's, uh, a book in my saddlebag," he said hesitantly. "Not a book, really, but a journal . . ."

Stuart looked at him without replying.

"It's, uh, a collection of letters to my wife," Benoit added, feeling his cheeks redden. "There are some really personal things in there. I just wanted to ask you, as a friend, if, uh, anything happens today . . ."

"You mean like you get killed?"

"Exactly," Benoit said in a rush. "If that happens will you see that the journal gets to Inge? I mean, will you deliver it personally?"

"Sure," Stuart said nodding. "By the way," he added, "feeling like that is completely natural. Coming to terms with the possibility of your mortality, that is. Facing the realities of the situation."

"You feel that way, too?" Benoit asked in surprise.

"Of course. I guess to a certain extent every soldier does when he's going into a battle. Just goes to show your mind isn't dead and you aren't bent on suicide."

Benoit sighed in relief. "Thanks for understanding, Jeb. As for the other, my mind may not be dead but my butt sure is. If a fight puts an end to this damnable, interminable march, I think we'll all be lucky."

5:42 A.M.

One-Eyed Bear stuck his head through the lodge flaps, calling excitedly to his friend, Carries the Otter. "It's time to get up," he said excitedly. "Today is the day we've been waiting for all summer."

"I don't have to get up," Carries the Otter replied, signaling One-Eyed Bear to enter. "I've been awake for hours. I don't see how you could have slept."

"I didn't," One-Eyed Bear confessed sheepishly. "I've been much too anxious."

"Is the whole camp awake?" Carries the Otter asked, offering his friend a bowl of boiled buffalo haunch.

One-Eyed Bear shook his head. "If I'm too nervous to sleep, you'd know I'm too nervous to eat."

Carries the Otter grinned. "You're not the only one. I was simply being polite. What's happening out there?"

"Dark and Cut Lip are circulating among the lodges,

reminding everyone that Hemmawihio is smiling on the Tsis-tsis-tas."

"Do *you* believe it?"

"Of *course* I believe it," One-Eyed Bear replied, giving his friend a strange look. "Why would the shamans tell us something that isn't true? Cut Lip and Dark have spoken to the gods and they predict an overwhelming victory."

"I hope they're right," Carries the Otter said, removing his knife from its sheath. Reaching behind him, he took a sharpening stone from a bundle that rested by his pile of sleeping robes and began to rhythmically stroke it backward and forward, honing the edge to a razor sharpness.

"You're going to grind that knife away to nothing," One-Eyed Bear said. "You won't have enough blade left to take all the scalps you're going to collect today."

"Don't worry about that." Carries the Otter laughed. "I have . . . what's that?" he asked, looking up at the sound of horses rapidly approaching.

"The scouts!" One-Eyed Bear cried animatedly. "They're bringing us word about the Notaxe-vehoe," he said, dashing for the opening.

"Wait for me," Carries the Otter replied, hurriedly jumping to his feet.

"There's no doubt they know where we are," Sliced Nose was telling the rapidly assembled members of the camp council when Carries the Otter and One-Eyed Bear joined the group. "They're heading straight in this direction."

"Are you sure?" Large-Footed Bull asked. A stoop-shouldered man in his early thirties with deep wrinkles in his face that gave him a perpetually sour look, Large-Footed Bull was known throughout the tribe as an overly cautious man but one who, once he was committed, proved to be as steadfast as any Tsis-tsis-tas warrior.

Sliced Nose nodded somberly, giving his questioner an

irritated look. "Their scouts have finally found the trail. Those Delaware are proficient; not like those useless *Honehe-taneo*," he added, referring to the hated Pawnee who also accompanied Sumner's troops. "They couldn't find a snowflake in a blizzard."

"Given their current rate of travel, when do you think they will be here?" Long Chin asked.

Sliced Nose paused, calculating. "Midday," he said. "Perhaps a little later."

"Then we should go to the lake," interjected Dark, "and make final preparations."

"Should we tell the women to pack the lodges?" asked Large-Footed Bull. "They can move the village and the children to a safer site."

"It won't be necessary," Cut Lip said confidently. "The soldiers will get no farther than the valley we have selected for the battleground. If I were you," he said, turning to Long Chin, "I would advise every warrior to take two horses so they will have a fresh mount available to pursue the Notaxe-vehoe once we have routed them."

"You are very certain it *will* be a rout?" Large-Footed Bull asked.

"The gods have told us so," broke in Dark. "Once the soldiers see that their guns are useless they will collapse like logs into the fire."

Long Chin threw back his shoulders. "Very well," he said emphatically. "Collect the horses," he said to the men around him. "We will follow Dark and Cut Lip to the sacred lake."

"I have dreamed of this day for a long time," Carries the Otter said to One-Eyed Bear as they hurried to their lodges to gather their weapons. "This time the Notaxe-vehoe aren't going to slip up on a sleeping camp."

"Yes!" One-Eyed Bear exclaimed. "This time *we* will be the victors."

"I'll wager my best war horse against yours that I take more scalps than you," Carries the Otter said with a laugh, ducking into his lodge.

"Ho-ho," One-Eyed Bear laughed, rushing past his friend. "I'm going to enjoy having *two* prime horses."

10:06 A.M.

Benoit dropped to his knees in the soft ground at the edge of the stream and scooped the cool, clear water into his hands, forming a rough drinking cup.

"Sure tastes good," he mumbled to Stuart.

"That's for sure," replied Stuart, dipping his hat into the water and emptying it over his head of thick, dark hair. "The horses think they've gone to heaven."

Almost a dozen miles from the previous night's camp, the column had unexpectedly come upon a fast-flowing stream that zigzagged through the rough, broken country toward its eventual junction with the river that showed on their maps as the Solomon. Deciding to take advantage of the opportunity, Sumner ordered a brief halt. The pause not only gave the horses a chance to refresh themselves slightly since they had not had a chance to graze the previous evening, but it provided time for the artillery and infantry to gain some ground. While the mounted troops had been moving at no more than a fast walk, it was still much too fast a pace for the foot soldiers and the clumsy howitzers.

Stuart nodded at Sumner, who was standing off to the side with the regimental adjutant, Second Lieutenant Albert Colburn.

"Ol' Bull is really full of beans," Stuart said softly to Benoit. "I've never seen him like this."

Although white-haired and well into his fifties, the colonel showed no effects of advancing age. Despite the long march that actually had begun more than two months before, Sumner still rode as erectly as any of the younger troopers under his command, giving no indication that he was suffering either mentally or physically from the strain of the campaign. While he must have been as tired as anyone in his command, his voice remained strong and vigorous, and his eyes glistened in anticipation of a showdown with the Cheyenne.

"They say that war is a tremendous energizer," Benoit whispered back. "Looking at the colonel, I'm beginning to believe it."

"Rider coming!" Sumner's interpreter, Josh Haskins, called loudly, interrupting all conversation.

Shading his eyes, Stuart stared in the direction the interpreter had pointed. "It's Shattered Lance," he said, referring to one of the expedition's Delaware scouts.

When the two columns—one led by Sumner, the other by Sedgwick—left Fort Leavenworth the previous May, each had been accompanied by five Indian scouts. Those traveling with Sedgwick were all Delawares and their leader was a loose-limbed, broad-shouldered warrior in his mid-twenties named Fall Leaf. The contingent with Sumner was composed entirely of Pawnee under a wiry, nervous looking warrior called Speck in the Eye. Sumner quickly determined that Fall Leaf and the Delawares were demonstrably superior to the Pawnee, who had proved to be lazy and only minimally competent. As the march progressed, the colonel began to rely increasingly on the Delawares and show growing contempt for the Pawnee.

Shattered Lance yanked his pony to a halt, speaking rapidly to Haskins but never taking his eyes off Sumner.

"He says Fall Leaf sent him back to say that they've spotted a party of a half dozen Cheyenne but they moved quickly away as soon as they saw the Delawares. Fall Leaf thinks they're retreating."

Sumner gazed into the distance, rubbing his chin. "Dammit all to hell," he cursed, speaking mostly to himself. "The Cheyenne are going to run. They'll be long gone by the time we get there if we don't hurry."

In a flash, he made his decision. Turning to the men, he summoned the thunderous parade ground voice for which he was famous. "Company commanders," he bellowed, surveying the troops, "see that your men are prepared for action."

Hearing those words, the men murmured excitedly among themselves, but again Sumner spoke, drowning out the chatter. "Tighten your saddle girths. See that you have a good supply of cartridges and are ready for a fight."

"What about the infantry and artillery, sir?" Colburn asked timidly.

"We can't wait for them," Sumner said briskly, swinging into his saddle. "They'll have to catch up the best they can. Bugler!" he commanded, turning to a pale-faced corporal who looked frightened enough to wet his pants. "Sound the advance."

As the notes echoed among the low hills, Sumner set off at a brisk walk, his eyes on the horizon, certain his men were only paces behind him.

10:48 A.M.

"I think this goddamn march is gonna be the end of us all," Private Salvatore Venezia complained to Private Len Bianchi as they plodded wearily down the rocky hillock, slipping and sliding on the loose shale. "If it ain't the fuckin' sun, it's the fuckin' rain. We're gonna kill ourselves chasing after a buncha goddamn savages that . . ."

"Who's that?" Bianchi interrupted, pointing behind them to a rapidly approaching rider.

"Some asshole on a mule, looks like," said Venezia. "Somebody musta put a bottle rocket up his butt."

"It's LaRossa!" Bianchi said, squinting. "What the fuck he think he's doing?"

"Carmine?" Venezia asked in surprise. "He musta gone plum fuckin' crazy."

"Look at them *succhiatores*," LaRossa called, yanking the mule to a halt.

"*Che cazzo stai dicendo*?" asked Venezia, wrinkling his brow.

"What am I talking about? Looka yonder, you dumb fuckin' wop. The cavalry's ridin' off and leavin' us to suck dust while they goes out and gets all the glory killin' injuns."

Venezia turned in the direction LaRossa was pointing. He and the other infantrymen had been so concerned with watching the ground in front of them they had not seen Sumner lead his men away at a lively pace which they could not hope to emulate.

"Sumbitch!" he said, slapping his cap against his thigh.

"You! LaRossa!" Corporal Flannery called from his position at the head of the squad. "What the hell are you doing here? You're supposed to be with the mules."

Extending his good arm toward Venezia, LaRossa urged him to hold on. "Swing aboard," he said, "we'll go get us some redskins, too."

Venezia grinned, accepting LaRossa's arm. He settled onto the mule's back behind LaRossa just as Flannery arrived at a trot.

"Halt!" Flannery yelled. "You're under arrest."

"*Vaffanculo!*" LaRossa yelled at the corporal, laughing as the mule kicked dirt in Flannery's face.

"And your mother, too," Venezia added as LaRossa pointed the wild-eyed mule in the direction of the rapidly disappearing cavalry troops.

"Halt or I'm going to fire!" Flannery bellowed, lifting his rifle. "Goddamn it, I said stop, you ignorant fuckin' dagos."

Venezia turned and made an obscene gesture.

"Okay you fuckers, I warned you," Flannery cursed, squeezing off a round.

The bullet made a sharp cracking sound as it zinged just inches over their heads. "Jesus, that was close." LaRossa gulped.

"We must be fuckin' insane," Venezia exclaimed. "We're going to get our asses court-martialed for sure. Maybe even shot."

"They ain't gonna punish a couple of heroes," LaRossa replied over his shoulder. "We didn't come all this way not to get our licks in against the injuns. But if you want, I can drop you off. You can say I made you do it."

"That's the dumbest fuckin' idea I've heard all day. You think I'm gonna let you get all the medals?"

"Shit," LaRossa replied. "We gonna get ourselves something better'n medals."

"Oh, yeah. What?"

"Scalps! Wouldn't you like to have an injun scalp to put in your kit? If we ever get back to civilization, I guarantee you that'll get you more pussy than you can even dream about."

"Hoo boy," Venezia yelled. "That makes me hard just thinking about it. Le's go get us some fuckin' injuns."

12:10 P.M.

"We waited until we were sure their scouts had seen us," Kills in Their Sleep told Long Chin, massaging the sweaty back of his panting pony. "Then we pretended to be running away."

"Do you think they believed the ruse?"

"Oh, yes." Kills in Their Sleep grinned. "We paused long enough to see one of the scouts go scurrying back to the main body to report what they had seen."

"Or thought they had seen," Long Chin replied. "You and your men did well," he added, clapping Kills in Their Sleep on the shoulder. "Now you and your men go and get yourselves fresh horses so you will be ready for the battle".

Turning to Large-Footed Bull, Long Chin smiled broadly. "Everything is going according to plan," he said happily.

"It would seem that way," Large-Footed Bull replied, nodding. "But I have been in situations before when defeat seemed impossible only to have everything go against us."

"Not this time," Long Chin said. "This is going to be one battle we are certain to win because of the magic woven by Dark and Cut Lip. The soldiers will be so shocked when they discover that their rifles are useless that we will only have to walk among them and chop them down like reeds."

"I wish I could be as confident as you," Large-Footed Bull said sadly.

"This time tomorrow you will feel quite differently." Long Chin laughed.

Earlier, when the Cheyenne warriors left the village, they followed Cut Lip and Dark to a small lake where each man dipped his hands into the water. Squatting along the shore, their faces alight with anticipation, they listened respectfully while Dark sang a song asking Hemmawihio's final blessing. "Remember," Dark intoned solemnly when he finished, "the white man's bullets will drop from their barrels like turds from a buffalo and you will be able to conquer them quickly with your bows and lances."

Following the brief ceremony, the warriors moved to a grove of trees at the eastern end of a narrow valley about three miles away. For almost three hours they lounged among the cottonwoods, nibbling on bits of dried meat and laughing quietly among themselves while their horses grazed on the tall grass.

"The Notaxe-vehoe will have to come this way," Long Chin had told them, pointing out how the valley was like a funnel leading straight to them. On one side was a steep bluff that effectively hid them from the soldiers until they were almost upon them. On the other side was the river, whose banks were lined with beds of quicksand that stood waiting to trap the fleeing Notaxe-vehoe.

After taking the report from Kills in Their Sleep, Long Chin gathered the warriors around him. "Put on your paint and your war shirts," he directed, speaking softly, in carefully measured tones. "Make your medicine. Prepare for the great battle that will make our land free once again. When you get your first sight of the enemy and your blood begins to run cold, do not lose heart," he cautioned. "There will be more white soldiers than any of us have ever seen, but," he said, spacing each word, "do . . . not . . . be . . . intimidated. Have no fear. Remember the power we hold over the Notaxe-vehoe, the great magic that Cut Lip and Dark have brought us.

"Before this day is over," he continued, his voice rising, "we will have won a great victory. Our success will be retold more times than you can count by our children and their children and *their* children. Our names will be invoked for years to come by Cheyenne warriors going into battle. You are warriors every bit the equal of the Notaxe-vehoe, and today you will prove it."

12:40 P.M.

Short Hair and Fat Bear stood their ground, waiting exposed on the rocky hillside until they were sure they had been seen by the army scouts.

"Very well!" Short Hair said in satisfaction when the scouts turned and galloped back toward the column. "Now we go tell Long Chin."

As they broke out onto the open floor of the valley, Short Hair whirled his horse in a series of tight circles as a signal to the waiting warriors that the army's approach was imminent.

"I thought they would never get here," One-Eyed Bear said excitedly, grabbing his saddle.

"Don't use a saddle," Carries the Otter advised. "Do as I do and ride bareback."

"Why is that?" One-Eyed Bear asked, puzzled.

"We want to be as light as raindrops when we ride to meet the enemy. Don't forget, their horses have come a long way and have been marching all morning. Every advantage we have, the better it will be."

"You're right," One-Eyed Bear said, throwing his saddle under a nearby cottonwood. "Don't forget," he said, as he vaulted onto his pony's back, "the one with the most scalps gets the other's best horse."

12:47 P.M.

From his position at the head of the column, Sumner could easily see Fall Leaf and the other Delawares as they moved steadily forward in the direction the retreating Cheyenne had taken. On Sumner's left, as the column moved southward, was a high bluff and on the right was the Solomon River. A few minutes earlier, in a last-minute check of the map, the colonel saw that the valley took an abrupt turn to the east, forming almost a right angle to the direction they currently were traveling. Until they got to that juncture, they could not see beyond the bend.

"Something's happening," he said excitedly as the Delawares reigned in their horses. As he watched, the scouts turned and headed back toward the column at a gallop.

"This looks like it," Sumner said to his officers, "the enemy, I believe, is at last in sight. I don't know how many Cheyenne are waiting for us around that bend but I want you to know that I have implicit confidence in you. If all of you obey orders promptly, and we all pull together, we can whip the whole tribe. Bugler!" he called, summoning the pale corporal. "Sound the advance."

As the notes sounded clearly in the quiet desert air, breaking the days-old prohibition against bugle calls, the men let loose a loud cheer.

12:59 P.M.

"Spread out," Long Chin told his warriors. "Make a long line from the hill to the river. Go slow. Make the soldiers ride hard to meet us so they will expend the last of their horses' strength."

1:03 P.M.

"Is that buffalo among the trees?" Benoit asked as they rounded the corner into the eastern end of the valley.

Stuart yanked a spyglass out of his saddlebag and turned it on the blurred forms. "Not hardly," he said, his voice rising excitedly. "Those are Cheyenne. They're mounted and heading straight at us."

At a sharp command from Sumner, the column halted,

then wheeled smoothly to the right as the colonel sang out
a new order: "Front into line!"

As the troopers began their maneuver, Sumner turned
and faced them. Although there were more than six hundred men under his command, about half of them were
infantry and artillery, and they were now so far behind
the cavalry as to be irrelevant to the forthcoming battle.
The force that he would lead against the Cheyenne in the
first major fight in the history of the west between Indians
and soldiers in which both were prepared for battle, was
slightly more than three hundred troopers.

As he watched them move into a formation that had
been practiced over and over again to the point of exhaustion at Fort Leavenworth—a configuration that would
bring them into a string six companies long and four men
deep—Sumner felt his battle-tested heart quicken in pride
and anticipation. The vast majority of them, he knew for a
fact, had never been shot at. But, despite their inexperi-
ence, they had performed admirably on the long march
and were behaving now as seasoned troopers. Smiling at
Colburn, he commented that they looked surprisingly
spiffy in their soiled and dusty but still presentable dark
blue jackets and jaunty Jeff Davis hats.

As the men moved into their predetermined positions,
they swiveled to look at Sumner, presenting him with a
sea of eager faces, each obviously impatient to join the
fight they had marched hundreds of miles to commence.
Even the horses felt the excitement, Sumner noted, smiling as he watched the troopers struggle to control the
massive, deep-chested animals.

Once they were in position, Sumner bellowed the command that would bring them another step closer to the
showdown. "Trot! March!" he commanded, anticipation
evident in his voice.

Benoit, so tense he thought he would faint from the

strain, looked soberly at Stuart. "Here we go," he croaked, his mouth feeling as dry as the prairie over which they had been marching. "Good hunting."

"And the same to you," Stuart replied with a smile.

1:05 P.M.

Long Chin gazed to the right, then to the left, beaming at the overall symmetry of the three hundred Cheyenne riding out to do battle with the Notaxe-vehoe. The warriors, like the troopers, were moving forward in a more or less orderly line, an unusual situation since all the tribes, the Cheyenne included, historically went into battle as individuals rather than as a unit. While the Plains warriors were brave, determined, and tireless fighters, the concept of battlefield discipline was totally foreign to them. Although they might join together to complete a common objective such as a raid against a group of traditional enemies, there was no overall commander and no overriding strategy. When they fought, it was almost always every man for himself. This time, however, Long Chin noted in surprise, they moved uniformly forward. In front, leading the way into battle, were the chiefs of the tribe's military societies: The Kit Fox, the Crooked Lance, the Red Shield, the Bow Strings, and the Dog Soldiers. Looking particularly splendid, Long Chin saw, was Coyote Ear, who was wearing a bonnet of eagle feathers that draped down his back and across his horse's flank. Since the Dog Soldiers were by far the most aggressive of the military societies they held the largest number of war honors, which entitled Coyote Ear to wear the magnificent headdress.

As they advanced, the men began singing their war and death songs, creating an eerie cacophony that Long Chin was certain was striking fear in the hearts of the

Notaxe-vehoe. Occasionally, one would lift his feather-bedecked lance and wave it at the soldiers, calling on Hemmawihio to protect him and bring him glory in the coming fight.

After they had gone a short way up the valley, a small group led by Coyote Ear split off and crossed to the south bank of the river before continuing westward toward the troops.

That sly fox, Long Chin said to himself, watching in admiration. He plans to try to get around the soldiers' right end and attack them from the rear.

Almost simultaneously, another group of men under Short Hair broke off from the right end of the Cheyenne line and began climbing the hill, intending to turn the soldiers' left flank.

As they got closer, the Cheyenne chanting changed from war and death songs to battle whoops, signifying they believed the fighting was soon to begin.

1:06 P.M.

Sumner watched calculatingly as the Cheyenne on each end of the opposing line started their flanking maneuvers.

"Lieutenant Stuart!" he barked over his left shoulder. "Take your company to the left. Don't let those Indians turn you. And you! Lieutenant Stockton!" he added, rotating to the right, "take your men over there. Don't let them turn that flank."

Directing his attention toward the front, Sumner and the entire command was surprised to see the Delaware scout, Fall Leaf, break out of the line and race toward the Cheyenne.

"What the hell is he doing?" Benoit asked.

"He must be suicidal," Stuart replied, watching in

fascination as the scout hurtled toward the steadily progressing warriors.

When Fall Leaf was about a quarter mile away, he reined his horse to a stop and lifted his rifle.

Seeing the puff of smoke and, almost immediately, hearing the report, Sumner turned to his adjutant. "Lieutenant Colburn," he said with a broad grin, "in case anyone ever asks if we tried to negotiate before the battle, bear witness that an Indian fired the first shot."

Colburn had to bite his lip to keep from laughing. It doesn't matter if the Indian was one of ours, he thought, as long as the colonel can say an Indian fired first.

After firing the single shot, which as far as Benoit could see had been totally ineffective, Fall Leaf reversed his direction and galloped back to the troops, yelling loudly in exultation.

1:08 P.M.

Although the gap was steadily closing between the opposing armies, neither side had yet committed to final closure. The troopers were still moving at a somewhat leisurely trot and the Cheyenne were advancing at a somewhat slower pace.

As they got within rifle range, Sumner cautioned the troopers not to be overanxious. "Steady, men," he roared, his voice clearly audible even over the noise of the horses. "Hold your fire! Keep your weapons at the ready until I give the command."

All along the line, men caressed their carbines, sure the order to begin firing was imminent. If Sumner followed the procedure in which they had been drilled so extensively before leaving Kansas, the colonel would soon call a halt, then order the men to fire a volley before replacing the rifles in their scabbards and charging with their pistols.

"What the hell's he waiting for?" Stuart asked nervously, urging his horse up the steep slope. "Why in hell doesn't he issue the order to fire?"

1:10 P.M.

"Can't you make this fuckin' mule go any faster?" Venezia yelled in LaRossa's ear. "We're gonna miss the fun."

"This ol' bag o' bones is about tuckered out," LaRossa replied, kicking the animal hard in the ribs yet again. "We're almost there. You got your rifle?"

"Ready and hungry for some injun blood," Venezia replied.

1:11 P.M.

"I think he's giving the command now," Benoit said to Stuart, watching as Sumner turned and spoke his to bugler. Seconds later, the notes of "Sling—carbines" blasted across the valley.

Stuart, who along with every other trooper in the six companies had been expecting Sumner to call a halt so they could fire their rifles, looked at Benoit in amazement. "What the hell? . . ."

As if he had heard the lieutenant, Sumner's thunderous voice swept across the line. "Draw—sabers!" he bellowed.

Benoit glanced at Stuart, noting that the cavalry officer's mouth had dropped open in shock.

"I d . . . d . . . don't believe it . . ." Stuart stammered. "He's gone crazy!"

Having been trained for months to obey orders no matter how illogical they sounded, the troopers, acting as one, reached across their bodies with their right hands and wrenched their short swords from their sheaths. Raising them over their heads, they then lowered them until the hilts were level with their eyes, a position known in the cavalry as tierce point.

Pausing dramatically, Sumner loudly added the final order committing the men to battle. After a terse exchange, the bugler sounded the stirring notes of "Charge!"

"Son of a *bitch*!" Benoit ejaculated, turning to Stuart. "I thought those sabers were only for decoration."

"So did I," Stuart laughed, spurring his horse. "So did I."

~9~

When he saw the sunlight flash off the soldiers' sabers, Long Chin tugged on his pony's reins, bringing the animal to an abrupt halt.

"What is this?" he yelled at Dark, who had been riding just to his rear.

"I don't know," the shaman spluttered, surprise evident in his voice. "The Notaxe-vehoe were supposed to draw their rifles, not their long knives."

"What does it mean?" Long Chin asked anxiously.

"I don't understand. I must talk to Cut Lip."

Long Chin looked around him. The tribe's bravest warriors were immobilized by the troopers' action. They had been expecting the Notaxe-vehoe to try to use their rifles, then panic when they saw they would not work. Dark and Cut Lip had told them they could then use this window of opportunity to ride among the troops and chop them to pieces. However, when the Cheyenne saw they were faced with the totally unexpected, they froze.

"We came to fight men with rifles," Fat Bear said in shock to Red Deer, the man riding beside him.

From man to man, the comments were almost identical.

Long Chin turned angrily to Dark. "There is no time to talk," he spat, noting that all along the line, the Cheyenne had stopped their chanting and yelling and were milling about in indecision as the soldiers rushed forward.

"Then we must retreat," Dark said hurriedly. "The medicine was effective against bullets, not knives. It can only mean that Hemmawihio does not want us to fight today, that we must disappear into the hills and come back to challenge the Notaxe-vehoe some other time."

As if in punctuation to his remark, some of the warriors regained enough of a sense of presence to loose a barrage of arrows at the onrushing troops. But even before the missiles reached the soldiers, a large number of warriors had turned their horses and were galloping back in the direction in which they had come.

1:14 P.M.

"Look!" Venezia screamed. "Them cowards is running away. Can't you hurry?"

"It might be faster if we got off and ran," LaRossa wailed, beating on the animal's shoulder with a closed fist.

The sentence was hardly out of his mouth when an arrow zinged by his head, nicking his left cheek.

"God, that was close," he said, turning to tell Venezia about the narrow escape. "What the fuck?" he added, seeing that the space behind him was empty.

Looking back, he saw a form on the ground twenty yards back. "Sal!" he called excitedly, trying to turn the mule.

Minutes later, he halted the animal and jumped to the ground, running to where his friend lay in a jumbled heap. "Sal!" he yelled, dropping to his knees. "Holy sweet Jesus," he gasped. A Cheyenne arrow was buried up to its feathers in Venezia's left eye socket. Its point and five inches of the shaft extended out the back of his friend's head, dripping blood and gray matter.

"Oh, shit," LaRossa said, turning his head and vomiting.

1:15 P.M.

"Why are they running?" Short Hair asked Kills in Their Sleep. "A fight is a fight, whether it's with bullets or knives." Lifting his bow, he began firing a string of arrows at a group of blue-clad soldiers working their way down the steep hill, their approach slowed by the incline.

Figuring since he had no saber he was free to use his rifle, Benoit fitted his weapon to his shoulder and took quick aim at one of the group of Indians that had tried to turn their left flank.

"Got him!" he yelled excitedly when he saw the man tumble off his horse.

Out of the corner of his eye, Short Hair saw a stream of blood erupt from Kills in Their Sleep's throat as the large-caliber slug from Benoit's rifle struck him in the hollow below the Adam's apple. With a scream that ended in a gurgle, the Cheyenne pitched to the ground and lay still.

"Where are you going?" Short Hair yelled angrily at Rock Forehead, who had turned his horse. "And you, Trembling Leaf," he hollered. "Come back and fight."

Realizing he was alone against the oncoming horsemen, Short Hair lifted his club and turned his horse in the soldiers' direction. Screaming his war cry he dug in his heels, thinking it was a beautiful day to die.

1:18 P.M.

Sumner's eyes flashed when he saw the Cheyenne line waver and then break. "We've got 'em on the run," he yelled in delight. "I'll be a son of a bitch, but we've got 'em on the run!"

Turning to the bugler he ordered him to blow the call known as "Charge as foragers," which meant that every man was free to act on his own in pursuing the retreating foe.

1:27 P.M.

Coyote Ear slid to the ground. Picking up a loose stone, he hammered the wooden stake attached to the end of his dog rope into the loose soil, signifying he would not voluntarily retreat. Once his dog rope was in place, Coyote Ear would stand his ground, fighting until the Cheyenne were victorious, he was killed, or another warrior removed the stake, thereby relieving him of his obligation. Laying his lance and his club at his feet, he notched a fresh arrow on his bow. "Who will stay with me?" he yelled over his shoulder to the men who had crossed the river with him.

"I will!" yelled Big Nose, blowing his special whistle and gripping his Thunder Bow tightly in his right hand.

"It's a foolish cause," replied a youth named Owl. "The medicine is not any good against the long knives. We must escape while we can so we can survive to fight another day."

"The boy is right," echoed Large-Footed Bull. "To go against such an enemy when Hemmawihio is not on our side is senseless."

"Then run like a woman," Coyote Ear called over his shoulder, fitting an arrow onto his bow string. "Big Nose and I prefer to fight like men."

"It isn't a question of being a coward," Large-Footed Bull replied. "We owe it to the Tsis-tsis-tas to fight another day."

Coyote Ear ignored him, concentrating on the oncoming cavalry.

"Come," Large-Footed Bull urged Owl. "We must hurry before it is too late."

As he turned, a soldier's bullet crashed into the small of Large-Footed Bull's back, pummeling him to the ground.

"I see you decided to stay after all," Coyote Ear said dryly. "Can you use your bow?"

"Yes," Large-Footed Bull replied, working himself up to one knee. "But my side feels as if it's on fire."

"You and Big Nose take those two soldiers to the left," Coyote Ear said. "I'll watch the ones on the right."

1:35 P.M.

"You rotten sons a bitches," LaRossa screamed, wiping the vomit off his chin. "You killed my best friend. I'll get your asses for this." Climbing on his mule he pointed the animal to the closest Indians he could see, three of them on the ground firing a steady stream of arrows at anyone within range.

Oblivious to the danger, LaRossa plunged forward.

The fact that he was riding a mule and not a horse caught Coyote Ear's attention. Notching another arrow, he aimed at the animal, then grunted with satisfaction when the missile slammed into the mule's chest, dropping it virtually in its tracks.

When his mount plunged to its knees, LaRossa flew over the animal's head and skidded headfirst across the ground, his head rebounding off a boulder. Only semiconscious, LaRossa rose into a sitting position and stared vaguely around, not sure where he was or what had happened to him. When he recovered his wits, he saw that the Indians were exactly where they had been before.

"I'll get you cocksuckers," he screamed, staggering to his feet. Drawing his pistol he wobbled unsteadily forward, trying to close the distance.

Coyote Ear noticed the movement out of the corner of his eye. Somewhat surprised to see him still alive, he grabbed another arrow from his quiver and fired it at LaRossa.

With a good bow and a strong arm, a Cheyenne warrior is capable of driving an arrow completely through a buffalo at ten feet. LaRossa's hide was not nearly as tough as a buffalo's. Coyote Ear's arrow struck the charging soldier just below the rib cage on his left side and exited out the rear, miraculously missing his spine and vital organs. The force of the blow, however, drove LaRossa back four feet and dumped him on his back.

He was trying to rise when he realized the extent of the wound. Clasping his hand over the entrance hole in an attempt to stop the flow of blood, LaRossa sagged back to the ground, his face falling into the dirt. "I think I'm done for," he mumbled weakly.

1:57 P.M.

"Everything is going wrong," One-Eyed Bear yelled to Carries the Otter, his horse turning wildly in tight circles. "I don't know what to do."

"Look!" Carries the Otter cried, pointing toward Coyote Ear, Big Nose, and Large-Footed Bull. "They are not afraid to lose their lives."

"We should go help them," One-Eyed Bear replied, urging his horse forward.

"This will surely be the death of us," Carries the Otter said, following his friend.

1:58 P.M.

"Over there!" bellowed Johann Swenson, a private in B Company.

Private Harry McDonald looked to where his friend

was pointing. "By God, I'd sure love to get me that bonnet," he said.

"Then let's go get the sumbitch." Swenson said, laughing. "All we gotta do is kill those three old fuckers first."

2:01 P.M.

One-Eyed Bear was on his feet even before his pony had come to a complete stop. Running forward, he yanked the stake that tethered Coyote Ear to the battlefield and threw it toward where LaRossa was lying inert in the dust.

"By doing this I'm absolving you of your obligation," he yelled. "Come with me. We must live to fight another day."

Coyote Ear looked over One-Eyed Bear's shoulder, noting that two troopers were rapidly approaching. They had put away their sabers and replaced them with firearms, one with his rifle, the other with his pistol. McDonald, the one with the carbine, halted his horse and lifted the weapon to his shoulder.

Coyote Ear saw the smoke erupt from the barrel and heard Big Nose grunt.

Turning, he saw the old contrary trying to keep his feet. The bullet had cut across Big Nose's stomach from side to side, slicing it open as if it had been cut with a knife. Big Nose stared downward, trying to shove his looping entrails back into the gash. Slowly, like snow slipping off an evergreen branch, he slid to the ground. His legs kicked three times involuntarily, then stilled.

Coyote Ear turned to One-Eyed Bear. "Get on your horse," he said calmly. "I'll slow these two down and then climb up behind you."

"Hurry!" One-Eyed Bear called anxiously, extending his hand.

"That will give them something to think about." Coyote Ear grunted in satisfaction as he watched his arrow bury itself into the thigh of the man who had killed Big Nose. The arrow went through the man's leg into the horse's side, sending the animal to its knees. When it fell, it landed atop the rider, crushing his uninjured leg and pinning him to the ground.

"Are you ready?" One-Eyed Bear called to Carries the Otter, who was helping the wounded Large-Footed Bull onto his horse's back.

"Yes," Carries the Otter replied, panting with the exertion. "You go and we'll follow."

One-Eyed Bear, with Coyote Ear holding on behind, urged his pony into the river, which was running low because it was the hottest part of the summer. Seconds later, the animal clambered up the opposite bank.

Twenty yards behind him, Carries the Otter, with Large-Footed Bull hanging on tightly around his waist, also plunged into the stream. But where One-Eyed Bear's pony had found firm footing, Carries the Otter's began sinking in one of the quicksand beds that lined the stream. Earlier, the Cheyenne had reckoned that the quicksand would trap the soldiers, not their own warriors.

"We're stuck!" Carries the Otter yelled as his pony thrashed about, its eyes flashing wildly in fear.

One-Eyed Bear turned his horse, intending to go back.

"No," Coyote Ear commanded. "We can't help them. The soldier is almost upon them."

One-Eyed Bear watched in horror as _____ the gap. Raising his revolver, Swenson _____ Otter between the eyes.

During the horse's struggle to fr_____ ing sand, Large-Footed Bull was _____ on his back in six inches of mud_____ pain in his side, he tried to w_____ position, his good leg sinking in the same sand that had trapped Carries the Otter's pony.

Laughing at the Indian's situation, Swenson holstered his pistol and pulled out his saber. Riding as close as he could to Large-Footed Bull without getting stuck in the quicksand, the big-shouldered, thick-necked farm boy from Minnesota lifted his saber above his head and brought it down with all his might, splitting Large-Footed Bull's skull like a melon.

2:34 P.M.

Once Sumner loosed his men to chase the Cheyenne, the battle lost all semblance of organization. Poised atop a stony hillock, the colonel watched as entranced as a child at a puppet as his troopers, most of them in groups of five or fewer, charged off in a hundred different directions after the rapidly disappearing Cheyenne. All around the narrow valley, too separated for any one officer to chronicle, soldiers and Indians fought in desperate struggles that often broke down into hand-to-hand combat.

Private Rollin B. Taylor of E Company fell behind his comrades when his horse got stuck in the quicksand. After about twenty minutes, the horse managed to free itself and Taylor guided the animal the rest of the way across the river. He had no sooner reached the other side that he saw a single Cheyenne scrambling up the bank, apparently searching for his horse that had escaped.

Taylor let his saber drop, trusting the bit of knotted cord that held it attached to his wrist. Waving his pistol, he gave a loud whoop and charged after the warrior.

When he heard the soldier yell, Sliced Nose spun and his bow, loosing an arrow in Taylor's direction.

the arrow could hit home, Taylor's horse ⸗rairie dog hole and Taylor went sailing to the ground, his pistol lost somewhere among the brush and rocks.

Grinning, Sliced Nose notched another arrow. And another. And still another, each of them narrowly missing the petrified private who was jumping about as if he were dancing on coals.

One of Sliced Nose's missiles went through the sleeve of Taylor's blouse, scraping his biceps. Another knocked his hat off his head and creased his scalp.

Looking around in panic for something with which to defend himself, Taylor spied a carbine that apparently had been dropped by one of the other troopers. With one eye on Sliced Nose and the other on the carbine, he hurried to retrieve the weapon, only to discover that it was empty.

Cursing in frustration, he heaved it at Sliced Nose, who jumped nimbly aside.

Picking it up, the Cheyenne threw it back at Taylor, also missing his target.

By then, Sliced Nose discovered he was out of arrows.

For several seconds, the two stood glaring at each other, panting and trying to catch their breath. Taylor still had his saber; Sliced Nose his bow but no arrows, and his knife.

Lifting his saber, Taylor let out another yell and charged.

Sliced Nose parried the blow with his bow, and took a sideways swing at Taylor with his knife.

For several minutes they danced around each other, Sliced Nose trying unsuccessfully to get within easy knife range while Taylor kept chopping at him with the saber.

Finally, the soldier had chopped Sliced Nose's bow to pieces and the Cheyenne was left with only his blade.

Taylor thrust and took a large chunk out of Sliced Nose's upper arm, rending the limb virtually useless.

Undeterred, Sliced Nose switched his knife to his other hand and charged.

Taylor sprang aside and Sliced Nose went rushing by, tripping over a stone and sprawling on his face. Rolling over quickly, he was trying to regain his feet when Taylor ran him through, pinning him to the ground.

Exhausted, Taylor sank to his knees and looked into Sliced Nose's eyes.

Aware that he was breathing his last, Sliced Nose looked at Taylor and, with hand gestures, asked the soldier if he intended to take his scalp.

When Taylor understood what Sliced Nose was trying to communicate, he shook his head emphatically. "No," he said, realizing that Sliced Nose would not understand his language. "You fought a damn good fight. You deserve to keep your hair."

Summoning a small smile, Sliced Nose's eyes rolled back in his head and he died.

Taylor was still hovering over the body when Dark Eagle, one of the Pawnee scouts, galloped up.

Hopping off his horse, he moved quickly to Sliced Nose's body. Grabbing his hair in one hand, he lifted his head and was about to scalp him when Taylor sent him reeling with a hard right to the jaw.

Dark Eagle jumped to his feet and advanced toward Taylor with his knife in front of him, as if he were preparing to attack. Taylor lifted his saber and glared at the Pawnee. "If you come another step closer, you redskinned savage, I'm gonna chop your fuckin' head off."

Even if he didn't understand the language, Dark Eagle correctly read the gesture. Looking at Taylor as if he were insane, he remounted his pony and rode away, searching for another scalp, Taylor figured.

What Taylor did not know and Dark Eagle lacked the linguistic ability to tell him was that the Pawnee had recognized Sliced Nose from an earlier fight with the Cheyenne. When Short Hair and his wife, Red Berry Woman, led the revenge raid against the Pawnee to retaliate for their daughter's kidnapping, Sliced Nose had been Short Hair's lieutenant. When the warriors from the two tribes clashed along the South Loup River more than two years before, Dark Eagle's best friend, Leading Elk, had been killed and scalped by Sliced Nose.

2:46 P.M.

Captain William Beall of A Company flogged his mare, urging her to use her last bit of strength to overtake the Indian fifty yards ahead of him. A heavy-set man with a thick, wild-looking beard, Beall had spooked the Cheyenne out of the timber that grew along the south bank of the Solomon while searching for retreating Cheyenne. Although he caught only a fleeting glance of his foe as the Indian darted out of the trees like a flushed quail, Beall was sure the Indian was a mere youth, probably no more than fourteen or fifteen. He's probably an inexperienced rider so that should give me an advantage, he said to himself, while giving chase. And once I catch him, I'll make mincemeat out of him.

But that had been almost twenty minutes ago and Beall still had not been able to significantly close the gap. In addition, he had used all his ammunition by firing wildly on the run and as far as he could tell none of his shots had ever even come close.

Although Beall's mare, Marybelle, was tired as a result of the long march and inadequate feed for the last few days, it was a larger, sturdier animal than the Indian pony and the captain hoped he would be able to wear his prey down. In fact, in the last few minutes he seemed to have gained a little ground.

"Just a little more Marybelle honey," Beall pleaded. "Give me some extra juice and I'll promise you a lifetime of apples and sugar cubes. Just catch that little bastard."

Owl, hunched down over his pony's neck to present as small a target as possible, looked over his shoulder. The soldier was still there, he noted, maybe even closer. Since there had been no more shots fired at him for several minutes, he correctly figured his pursuer had run out of bullets.

Displaying wisdom beyond his years, Owl began calculating his odds and what he would have to do to survive. He knew that his pony was fast and comparatively fresh but the big, heavily-muscled mare the soldier was riding had a lot of heart. If he didn't do something soon, he felt, the soldier might ride him down.

Owl's ambition ever since he had become old enough to begin thinking seriously about his future had been to join the Dog Soldiers. His hero was Coyote Ear. In fact, he would have followed the old warrior earlier if somehow he had not become separated in the confusion that accompanied the beginning of the march against the Notaxevehoe. Once they left their sanctuary in the trees and began the trek up the valley, Owl found himself on the opposite side of the group from Coyote Ear. From his point of view, however, it was not an unfavorable position. Since he respected Short Hair almost as much as he did Coyote Ear, he had eagerly gone along when Short Hair and a few others broke off from the main group to try to outflank the soldiers.

Up until the time the soldiers drew their sabers instead of using their rifles, Owl had felt comfortable with the role fate had assigned him, even when he considered the possibility that he might be killed. If the situation had developed as Dark and Cut Lip had predicted, Owl was certain he would have waded into the midst of the soldiers without giving it a second thought. But when he saw the sabers his blood ran cold. When the sun flashed off the long knives, Owl panicked. Staring transfixed at the shiny blades instead of down the muzzles of rifles, the only thing he could think of was getting away, even if it meant abandoning Short Hair.

By the time he reached the river, he knew he had made a mistake. When he saw Coyote Ear standing with his dog rope pinned to the ground, he was ready to go join him but Carries the Otter and One-Eyed Bear got there first. He was pausing in the trees, waiting for his horse to catch its breath after fighting through the quicksand, when the soldier surprised him and he had to run for his life.

He's definitely gaining, Owl thought, looking over his shoulder one more time. I must do something to tip the odds in my favor. If I were Coyote Ear, he told himself, what would I do? As if by magic, the solution came to him. Lifting his left arm while keeping a tight grip on his lance with his right, Owl tossed his bow and quiver of arrows onto the ground.

"What the fuck is he doing, Marybelle?" Beall said aloud.

After divesting himself of his bow, Owl made a smooth little leap backward, hopping out of his saddle and onto his pony's back. While clutching his lance and the reins in left hand, he used the right to ease his knife from the sheath at his waist. Being careful to maintain his balance, he squeezed his knees against his pony's back and leaned forward. Reaching as far under his pony's belly as he could, he sawed away at the girth. Once he had cut it, he returned the knife to its sheath, then used that hand to lift the saddle off his horse's back. With a grunt, he threw it over his shoulder, adding the blanket several seconds later.

"You smart little son of a bitch," Beall said, comprehending. "You're trying to make the load lighter."

Just as smoothly as he had hopped out of the saddle, Owl hopped back into his customary position, smiling as his pony seemed to understand. "It's up to you now," he whispered in the pony's ear. "Use your speed."

As if there was a direct line of communication between horse and rider, the pony snorted and doubled its efforts.

Owl grinned, feeling the new power beneath his legs. Lifting his lance, he twirled it over his head twice in what Beall sadly interpreted to be a victory salute. Letting out three loud whoops, Owl left the captain as if he had been standing still.

"Whoa, Marybelle! Whoa," Beall said, pulling steadily on the mare's reins. "You did your best, old girl, but that young pup flat outrode us. I thought I was a pretty good horseman but I reckon he showed me a spectacular new trick. As far as I'm concerned," he said to his sweating, panting mare, "he deserves to get away."

2:57 P.M.

After leaving Short Hair alone to face the soldiers, Rock Forehead and Trembling Leaf followed other Cheyenne who were dashing across the river. But once they were on the other side, Rock Forehead began having second thoughts.

"Stop!" he yelled to Trembling Leaf, who swirled around, reining in his own pony.

"What is it?" Trembling Leaf asked, looking anxiously behind them to see if they were being pursued.

"We should go back and fight," Rock Forehead said. "We should not be fleeing like children from a porcupine."

"It is no use trying to fight," Trembling Leaf argued. "Hemmawihio has indicated his displeasure by withdrawing the magic he had promised. He wants us to leave the battlefield as quickly as possible and come back some other time to fight the Notaxe-vehoe."

"All the same," Rock Forehead replied stubbornly, "I am going back to help Short Hair. Will you come with me?"

Trembling Leaf looked anxiously at his friend. "No," he said, shaking his head. "I will not go against Hemmawihio's wishes."

"Very well," said Rock Forehead, unperturbed. The Tsis-tsis-tas believed that every man had to make his own decisions and it was not up to others to judge him for following his instincts. Rock Forehead, before he had become the band's arrow keeper, had been on enough raids with Trembling Leaf to know that he was not a coward. He decided to retreat, Rock Forehead knew, because he truly believed that it would be an insult to Hemmawihio, who knew *everything* and thus had his own reasons for suddenly withdrawing his promise of an easy victory.

"In case I do not get back to the village, please see that Blue Woman is taken care of," Rock Forehead said. "She has relatives with the *Ohktouna*."

Trembling Leaf nodded solemnly but did not reply.

No more words were spoken. The men turned their horses and rapidly rode away in opposite directions.

3:17 P.M.

Jeb Stuart raised his head cautiously, lifting it out of the dirt just far enough to take a quick peek to make sure the Indian was still there.

"That's one tough son of a bitch," he commented to Benoit, turning his head to the side when he spoke to keep from getting a mouthful of sand.

Benoit couldn't resist stealing a glimpse himself, bobbing his head up and down in a quick motion that reminded Stuart of a chicken pecking at grain.

"Can't see anything but a couple feathers sticking up on the other side of that dead horse," Benoit mumbled. "You think he's still alive?"

"Dunno," said Stuart. "But I'm not anxious to wind up like Rogers."

Corporal Ike Rogers, a grizzled veteran who would have been a sergeant except for his tendency to drink too much, had made the mistake of underestimating the Cheyenne's skill with a bow. The corporal's previous battle experience had been against terrified, hastily recruited *muchachos* the Mexican officers had used as cannon fodder at Buena Vista—boys of eleven and twelve who had never held a rifle until one was shoved into their hands as the American troops approached—and he figured the Cheyenne represented the same class of opposition.

Anxious to add an Indian scalp to his collection of war souvenirs, Rogers had eagerly charged as soon as he saw the lone Cheyenne. While a wild shot with his carbine succeeded in killing the Indian's pony, the Cheyenne himself survived unscathed. Rogers discovered this seconds later when one of the Cheyenne's arrows thudded into his side just above his appendix.

The three remaining soldiers in the group that had found the Indian—Stuart, Benoit and a sergeant named Sean O'Leary—took what cover they could find, deciding that caution was the better part of valor and it might be conducive to their longevity to wait until the opportunity presented itself to make a final assault. For a few minutes they debated making a united horseback charge against the Indian, but Stuart pointed out that at least one of them would be hit before they could overpower the enemy. They decided to proceed on foot instead when no one seemed anxious to commit what seemed certain suicide.

For the moment, though, there was nothing they could do. Sumner's command freeing the men to go off on their own in search of the enemy resulted in the rest of the company tearing off in hot pursuit, abandoning the four to try to subdue the Indian on their own. After all, four against one had seemed pretty good odds at the time. The four, however, had shortly been reduced to three; Rogers was lying in a puddle of blood, obviously in great pain, alternately cursing and crying help from anyone, from God to his mother.

"Can you see O'Leary?" Benoit asked quietly.

Stuart swiveled his head the other way. "His boots and his butt. He's still crawling away from us so I don't guess he feels he's gone far enough yet."

Ten minutes before, the sergeant had volunteered to try to crawl around to the Indian's side. From there, he reckoned, he might be able to get a clear shot or at least distract the Cheyenne while Benoit and Stuart attacked from the front.

The sergeant was almost in position when the three soldiers heard a horse approaching at a gallop. Turning quickly in the direction of the hoofbeats, they saw another Cheyenne heading straight at them, leaning over his horse's neck so he would present little if any target.

"Son of a bitch!" screamed O'Leary, who was directly in the rider's path.

The Indian was not interested in the sergeant, however. He was aiming for his tribesman who was hunkered down behind the dead pony.

When he got within shouting distance, the rider called out loudly in Cheyenne. "It is Rock Forehead!" he screamed. " I've come to rescue you. When I get close, take my arm and swing up behind me."

O'Leary, thinking he was the target, doubled into a ball and covered his head. When the rider's horse leaped over him and continued on, he looked up in surprise. While Rock Forehead was not a target when he was riding at

O'Leary, once he passed him his back was exposed to the
soldier.

Taking advantage of the situation, O'Leary threw his
carbine to his shoulder and squeezed off a round. At only
thirty yards, the sergeant's aim was true. The bullet struck
Rock Forehead in the spine four inches above his waist
just as he was leaning forward to scoop up his trapped
comrade. He fell to the ground at the other Indian's feet
while his horse galloped on, moving out of reach before
the trapped Cheyenne could grab the reins.

"I got the fucker!" O'Leary yelled excitedly, jumping to
his feet and running toward the two Indians, forgetting
that one was still alive and dangerous.

Too late he realized his mistake. He had taken no more
than two steps when the Cheyenne fired an arrow that
struck O'Leary in the upper right part of the chest just
below the shoulder. The impact spun him around and
sent him toppling to the ground.

O'Leary's move, however, proved to be the distraction
that Stuart and Benoit were waiting for. While the
Cheyenne was concentrating on O'Leary, they leaped forward. Stuart was quicker. Drawing his pistol, he fired at
the Cheyenne, hitting him in the thigh.

Stuart was aiming for a second shot when Benoit
grabbed his arm.

"Don't!" he yelled excitedly, pushing until Stuart's pistol was aimed at the ground. "I know that man. Don't
shoot him!"

As soon as he got an unobstructed look at the Indian
that had been holding them off, Benoit was amazed to see
that it was Short Hair. Recognition immediately changed
his perspective; a single thought popped into his head,
burning through his brain like a red-hot poker: If I kill
Short Hair, Frau Schmidt will never forgive me; she'll
never get Werner and Wilhelm back.

"That's Short Hair!" he said quickly to Stuart, who was looking at him as if he had suddenly gone insane. "I was a guest in his lodge. I can talk to him."

When he was shot by Stuart, Short Hair lost his bow; it lay on the ground several feet away. While Benoit was arguing for his life, he was crawling toward his weapon.

"Give me a chance!" Benoit pleaded with Stuart.

Stuart nodded, and Benoit trotted toward the Cheyenne. "It's me!" he called. "Remember me and Lieutenant Dobbs?"

He knew the Cheyenne would not understand English, but he was counting on being recognized. "Put down your weapons," he said beseechingly. "You don't have to die."

Short Hair, crazed by pain and the intensity of the battle, was beyond being able to make any sense out of what was happening. In his mind, there were only Notaxevehoe and Tsis-tsis-tas; if you were not a Cheyenne, you were an enemy. When Benoit came rushing up, Short Hair did not see the man with whom he had shared his food and hospitality, but only a soldier who he assumed was trying to kill him.

Realizing he could not reach his bow in time, Short Hair fumbled at his waist, drawing the old Allen revolver he had decided to carry with him for use in an emergency. Since this certainly classified as an emergency, he leveled the pistol at Benoit.

"Oh God, no!" Benoit screamed just as Short Hair pulled the trigger.

Benoit felt a heavy blow to his chest, like being kicked by a horse. Surprised more than hurt, he wondered why he could no longer see Short Hair but only a clear, light blue sky.

In one quick motion, Short Hair turned to Stuart and pulled the trigger a second time. He was as dumbfounded as Stuart when the old revolver failed to fire.

Before he could try again, Stuart raised his own pistol and shot Short Hair in the face. The bullet entered just below the tip of his nose and exited out the back, creating a small cloud of blood and pieces of skull. The force of the bullet picked him up and knocked him two feet backward, where he landed on his back and lay still.

Sighing heavily, Stuart lowered his pistol and turned to Benoit, who also was sprawled on his back, his eyes closed, a serene expression on his face, looking, Stuart thought, as peaceful as if he had just stretched out for a nap. The impression was destroyed, however, when his eyes moved downward to the blood stain that was spreading across the front of Benoit's blouse. Rushing to his side, Stuart saw that he was still breathing. His fingers shaking in fear for what he might find, Stuart ripped off Benoit's buttons, exposing his chest. "Shit!" he exclaimed, staring at a red wound the size of his thumbnail squarely in the center of Benoit's chest. "Jesus H. Christ," he swore, slamming his fist on his thigh.

From Benoit, Stuart's gaze drifted to Short Hair and Rock Forehead, to Rogers, who had quit kicking and moaning and was staring at the sky with sightless eyes, to O'Leary, who was trying to stand up while grabbing at the arrow protruding from his shoulder and cursing.

"What a right fucking mess this has turned into," he mumbled despondently, barely conscious of the fact that the bugler was blowing "Recall."

10

Waving down a group of soldiers who were returning to the command in response to Sumner's bugled order calling off the chase, Stuart directed them to improvise a shelter using blankets for a roof and sabers rammed into the ground as the corner supports. They then carried the unconscious Benoit and the still-cursing O'Leary into the shade, trying to provide them with some relief from the scorching sun which was burning its way toward the hottest part of the day.

"Go find the ambulance and the surgeon, Harrison," Stuart crisply directed one of the privates. "And don't come back until you do."

While he waited, he made the others dig shallow graves for Short Hair and Rock Forehead. Rogers's body would be carried back to the command where it would be buried after brief services, but the Cheyenne, since they were heathens, did not need praying over.

Two privates were piling rocks onto the single grave in which both Short Hair and Rock Forehead were buried when Captain Wilson, one of the two regimental surgeons traveling with the expedition, arrived with the ambulance, a make-do rig consisting of a cushioned platform mounted on two wheels and pulled by two mules.

Without ceremony, Wilson hurried to the shelter, going first to Benoit who seemed the more seriously wounded.

"How bad is it, captain?" Stuart asked anxiously, hovering over the surgeon's shoulder.

"Can't rightly tell, lieutenant. You're casting a shadow over the man. Either move to the side or, better yet, back off and I'll let you know in a few minutes."

Chastised, Stuart walked away about ten feet. Plopping onto the ground, he was dejectedly flipping pebbles at a nearby ant hill when the surgeon called him.

"Lieutenant," Wilson said briskly. "Come over here. I want you to see this."

Scrambling to his feet, Stuart was at his side in two long strides.

"You aren't going to believe this, lieutenant," the surgeon said, "but look here."

Fearing the worst, Stuart nervously peeked over his shoulder. The physician had wiped most of the blood off Benoit's chest, leaving the raw wound as the focal point. As Stuart leaned over, the bullet hole stared wetly back at him, looking to Stuart like the ultimate bloodshot eye.

"See," Wilson pointed with his finger, "this is where the bullet went in. Do you know what kind of weapon he was shot with?"

Stuart nodded. "It was an old Allen. A rusty piece of crap. One of the privates kept it for a souvenir."

"That explains it," Wilson said sagely.

"Explains what?" Stuart asked, sounding sharper than he intended.

"Why the wound didn't kill him, you dunderhead," Wilson replied, not accustomed to being spoken to in that tone of voice.

"Sorry, sir," Stuart said quickly. "He's my friend. I'm just anxious, that's all. Is going to live?"

Wilson nodded. "Probably no more than another fifty years or so provided he can stay the hell away from the wrong side of pistols. Damned lucky man, this," he said, thumping Benoit's shoulder.

"How's that, sir?" Stuart asked, puzzled.

"See," he pointed again, "this is the entrance wound . . ."

"Where's the exit wound?" Stuart interrupted.

"Lieutenant, please be quiet and let me finish explaining."

Stuart bobbed his head. "Yes sir," he mumbled sheepishly.

"There isn't any exit wound because the bullet's right here," he said, putting his finger on a spot about five inches from the entry wound. If there had been a compass on Benoit's chest, the place he indicated would have been to the south-southeast.

Looking closely, Stuart saw a prominent lump, a factor he had missed in his early quick examination.

"Way I figure it," Wilson went on, "that old revolver had a cartridge with a really weak charge. Wasn't enough powder to provide any force at all. It must have been in the pistol for a long time. As a result, the bullet, rather than continuing on through this man's heart, glanced off the breastbone and traveled downward, coming to rest right here, over this rib. Man's damn fortunate to be alive."

"What about the bullet?"

Wilson shrugged. "Get him back to headquarters and I'll take it out. Simple operation. Don't have to do much more than make an incision and it'll pop out of there like a seed out of a slice of watermelon."

"If he isn't wounded very bad, how come he's not conscious?" Stuart asked, biting his lip.

"Shock, I guess. No real medical reason. I imagine he'll come awake any minute now."

"What a relief." Stuart sighed, feeling his knees tremble. "What about the sergeant?"

"Same prognosis. Wound isn't serious but it's going to hurt like a son of a bitch for awhile, especially when we take the arrow out. But, barring an infection, he should be back on duty in a couple of days. He might be using only one arm for awhile, but it should heal nicely."

"Wish you could say the same for the corporal," Stuart added, nodding at Rogers's body, which had been covered with a blanket.

"Yep," Wilson said sadly. "Sure hate to see men killed but it's a by-product of the profession we're in. Can't make an omelet without breaking eggs."

Stuart looked at the surgeon out of the corner of his eye, wondering if he would ever be that cynical.

Wilson turned and started walking back toward the ambulance. "Oh, there's one other thing," he added.

Stuart looked up. Suddenly, with the crisis over, he felt more exhausted than at any time he could remember. All he wanted to do was lie down and sleep for fifteen or sixteen hours. "Sir?" he asked wearily.

"Tell that private, the one who took the pistol . . ."

"Yes, sir."

"Tell him not to try to use it in the next fight he's in or he'll be as dead as that poor, dumb fucking injun."

"Yes, sir." Stuart smiled. "I'll tell him."

Roy Biv lay shivering under the buffalo robe, his knees pulled up to his chest, his thumb in his mouth. Over and over in his head, he kept repeating the prayers of his youth: the Our Father, the Hail Mary, and—in desperation—the Act of Contrition. It was only a matter of time, he knew, and he, too, would be as dead as Legendre. The trapper had finally slipped away the night before, having withstood three days of brutal, inhumane torture. He himself, he knew, would never be as strong; he would never be able to stand up against the foul-smelling renegades the way Legendre had done. Even as they were slowly peeling strips of skin off Legendre's body like rind from an orange and burning him with hot knives, Legendre had been able to curse them and spit in their faces.

God, he had been brave, Biv thought. Even when he knew from the very beginning what was in store for them. What was it, he asked himself, trying to control his feverish thoughts, that Legendre had told him soon after they were captured? Biv concentrated, trying to recall the trapper's exact words. Finally, he had it: "These are truly bad men," the trapper had told him. "They intend to kill us as painfully and as slowly as they can. If you get the chance, kill yourself first."

I only wish I could, Biv said to himself. But I'm not made of the same stuff as Legendre. There's nothing I'd like better right now than being able to end it all quickly. But they had thought of that. That was why they kept his hands and feet bound tightly with strips of rawhide, why they made him sleep in their midst.

Sleep, he thought sardonically. What was that? He hadn't slept since the day they were captured. He was far too afraid. Maybe once in awhile, because of sheer exhaustion, he dozed off but it was certainly not into a state that could be called *sleep*. On the other hand, he reflected, *they* didn't have any trouble sleeping. After a hard day of torturing Legendre, they simply stretched out on their robes and before he could finish an Our Father they were snoring and farting and probably dreaming of what new ways they could find of inflicting pain and misery.

To Biv, it was a terrible, unbelievable nightmare. No, it

was worse than a nightmare. A nightmare ended with the sun. This had no ending. It would go on until he was dead, and then they would just ride off and leave his body, as they had done with Legendre's, unburied, unmourned, at a lonely campsite that no one would ever find.

Trying to keep from thinking about what lay ahead of him, Biv let his thoughts go back four days. Painstakingly, he tried to put together the series of events that had led him to his current predicament. It had begun innocently enough. He, Legendre, and the boy, Cut Neck, had left the Arapaho camp for Fort Laramie. According to their plan, they left Antelope Woman and David there. Legendre was going to take him to the fort, then return and pick up his wife and son. Then, presumably, the fighting would be over between the army and the Cheyenne and he could return to the Tsis-tsis-tas camp. If not, he would spend the rest of the summer hunting and preparing for winter. It wasn't as if he hadn't done it before. The whole plan was very uncomplicated. Cut Neck was going to guide them to the fort using trails that Legendre did not know. Although Legendre originally planned to head north until they hit the Platte, then turn westward and follow it to Fort Laramie, Cut Neck said he knew a shorter, quicker route. Legendre had acquiesced, which was why they headed almost due west out of the camp instead of north or northwest.

On the morning of the second day out of the Arapaho camp, they had come across a group of Oglala Sioux. They had been hunting buffalo and they had a large supply of fresh meat. But, looking for a change from the steady diet of buffalo, they had paused to hunt rattlesnakes on a rocky hillside. Biv had been fascinated when Legendre explained the process. The women, he said, pointing, moved among the rocks with forked poles. When they saw a rattler, they trapped its head in the fork, then quickly decapitated it before the snake could bite itself. If that happened, the trapper explained, the meat would be poisoned.

"Is rattlesnake good?" Biv had asked.

Legendre licked his lips. "Like chicken," he said.

At Biv's urging, they had paused long enough to let him make a couple of quick sketches of the snake hunt, one of which he traded to the Oglala in exchange for two heavy snakes that Legendre said he would prepare for dinner that night.

It was only a few hours after they left the Oglala behind that they were ambushed by the renegades. They were setting up that evening's camp along the banks of a small, fast-moving creek when the renegades suddenly appeared out of the bushes that grew along the edge of the stream. Before they could resist, they were already prisoners.

As they waited for the renegades to finish eating the snakes that were meant for their dinner, Legendre told him about the men who had taken them. Their leader was the Brulé outcast he had heard about earlier, the man named Blizzard. Just looking at him made Biv's bowels queasy. He was sure if he had food in his stomach, he would have defecated on himself. Biv's first thought, the first time he saw Blizzard in the day's fading light, was that he would make an ideal model for one of his sketches. Seen in profile against a darkening sky, Blizzard looked to be tall and broad-shouldered, with rippling muscles and a confident demeanor that exuded power. Soon afterward, Biv learned that it was not power he exuded, but evil. And, once he got a good look at his captor, he could see the consequence of a violent life.

Although he was trembling in fear, the capacities for observation that Biv had been honing ever since he knew he was going to be an artist took over. Looking at Blizzard more closely he saw not a Plains Indian ideal, but a man whose ravaged body was testimony to his cruel, ruthless mind. Indeed, Blizzard's physique was admirable, but, viewed in better light, Biv saw that it was marred from one end to the other by horrible, telltale scars. There was one, obviously left by a knife, that sliced across the upper left side of his chest from his collar bone to his sternum. Below that was a circular scar about the size of cherry. When Legendre asked about that, Blizzard said it was where he had been shot by a soldier with a small caliber pistol during the Harney raid at Blue Water. Turning, Blizzard proudly showed an almost identical scar on his back, explaining that was where the bullet had exited. He also had a much larger gunshot scar on his left thigh—a sunken, purplish mark as wide as Biv's hand. But Blizzard's most fearsome feature was his face.

God, Biv thought, twitching at the memory of his first glimpse, what a visage. Across Blizzard's right cheek, running from his eyebrow to his jawline, was the healed-over reminder of a saber slash. But a worse result of the sword attack was the fact that the blade had also removed Blizzard's left eye, plucking it out of its socket like a raisin from a bowl of pudding. The socket was empty now, covered loosely by a drooping lid. When Blizzard saw the look of terror that his appearance generated, he laughingly pushed his face close to Biv's and slowly lifted the lid, exposing the empty eye socket. Framed by campfire flames that jumped and danced just behind him, Biv stared into the hole and was convinced it was the entrance to hell.

Almost as soon as they had been captured, the renegades had released Cut Neck. "They have nothing to fear by doing that," Legendre had explained. Blizzard and his men enjoyed a live-and-let-live policy with the Plains tribes; they did not molest them if they in turn were not molested. They had no argument with other Indians; it was the whites Blizzard and his group were after. They knew that they were safe in turning Cut Neck loose; that even if he went running back to his people, the Arapaho village council would not risk an attack against them simply to save two white men.

That first night, Blizzard had been almost congenial, sitting around the campfire and chatting with Legendre in Siouan as if they were old friends. They had been visiting with the Oglalas, trading for tobacco and gunpowder, and were leaving the camp when Crow Killer, Blizzard's top lieutenant, spotted Biv sketching the women on the rattlesnake hunt. Even though they were outcasts in their own bands, they still maintained fragile relationships with other Lakotas, most of whom were too frightened to turn them away. To Blizzard, the appearance of the two white men was an answer to his prayer. They had been roaming the Plains for weeks, Legendre translated, looking unsuccessfully for stray whites. But the only ones they found had been traveling in groups that were too large for Blizzard and his half-dozen followers to attack. Then he and Legendre had come along. Biv could picture Blizzard smiling cruelly, deciding on the spot to capture them so he could have a few days' "entertainment," helping break up what had so far been a dull summer. The next morning, the torture had started.

They had picked Legendre to go first, apparently because they reckoned he would give the most sport and was the most likely to offer resistance if he was not dealt with immediately. Eventually though, after what seemed to Biv unimaginable tortures, Legendre had died. Now it was his turn.

Suddenly, he felt himself being hoisted out of his makeshift bed, literally lifted and carried as effortlessly as if he were an infant. Crow Killer, a Miniconjou who had proved himself just as sadistic as Blizzard, threw Biv over his shoulder and hauled him to the campfire, where he was unceremoniously dropped on the ground at Blizzard's feet.

While he quivered and shook, Blizzard pretended to ignore him, pretending to busy himself with preparing a bowl of boiled buffalo. When the bowl was half full of bite-sized chunks of meat, Blizzard turned to him for the first time. Making what he probably thought was a smile, the large Indian leaned over and extended the bowl to Biv, urging him with signs to eat.

They don't want me to starve to death before they can kill me, Biv thought. But he could not have eaten if he wanted to. The mere thought of food set the bile to stirring in his stomach and he almost gagged as it rose into his throat.

Blizzard made a noise that he took to be a low laugh, then laid the bowl gently on the ground. Looking up, he said something that Biv could not understand to Crow Killer. In response, the Miniconjou brought him Biv's saddlebags, which he laid on the ground next to the bowl of buffalo meat. Reaching inside, Blizzard brought out a handful of Biv's sketches, which he proceeded to examine with interest. Pulling one out of the stack, he showed it to Biv. It was a handsome rendering of the group around the Arapaho council fire. Locking his eye on Biv, Blizzard fed it into the fire.

Biv gasped. Staring at the paper that burned quickly to a cinder, he forgot his fear, which was replaced by a terrible anger. When he looked up at Blizzard and cursed, the Indian laughed. Waving another sketch under his nose, Blizzard dropped it into the fire as well. After he had burned a half dozen of Biv's drawings, Blizzard seemed to tire of the game.

With his right hand, he grabbed a log that was waiting to be added to the fire, a short length of aspen branch five or six inches in diameter. But, instead of placing it in the fire pit, he laid it on the ground, next to Biv's saddlebags.

Reaching out he took Biv's right hand, tugging only slightly, much as a man might take his lover's. Looking at it, noticing how it was shaking almost uncontrollably, Blizzard smiled and grunted in what Biv took to be almost sexual pleasure.

Gently, he laid Biv's hand across the log, carefully separating the fingers.

Fumbling at his waist, he drew his knife, a huge grotesque-looking instrument he had used to peel Legendre's skin. After each session with the trapper, Blizzard spent an hour or more honing the blade, crooning softly to himself and softly singing what Biv supposed was some kind of personal song.

Suddenly, Biv recognized what was about to happen. Frightened to the point of terror, he tried to retract his hand, only to find that Blizzard had tightened his grip. Biv's eyes widened in panic and he fought unsuccessfully to free his hand. The effort made Blizzard laugh even harder.

Feeling like a steer about to be slaughtered, Biv looked around in horror. What he saw was not encouraging. All the members of Blizzard's group—Crow Killer, Four Wolves, Broken Club, Open Wound, Red Chin and Elk Ear—were looking expectantly over their leader's shoulder. With a swiftness that amazed Biv, Blizzard brought the knife down in a sure, perfectly aimed blow. As he stared at his hand, he saw the knife lop off the end of his little finger at the second joint. Unable at first to believe that it was his finger, Biv stared in fascination as the severed digit rolled off the log and flopped in the dust, quivering slightly. Blood spurted from where the finger had been, making a small fountain that jumped the gap between the log and Blizzard, splashing against the Indian's left knee. Without thinking twice about it, Blizzard ran his own forefinger through the blood, then stuck it in his mouth and sucked it clean.

Biv knew he was screaming. He had to be; who else was making such a terrible racket. Halfway through his second yell, his eyes rolled back in his head and he fainted.

23 July 57
Along the Solomon River

My Adored Inge,

Unless something drastic and unexpected occurs, you will read this only when I return. While I could just as easily wait until then to tell you my news, I want to write down this information while the details are still fresh in my mind.

Yesterday, we went into battle against the Cheyenne. As just about everyone expected, it was a resounding victory for the cavalry. I stress cavalry because Sumner decided to leave the infantry behind. Feeling that the Indians would disappear before he could get a chance to engage them, he hurried the horse soldiers ahead and they quickly outdistanced the poor foot soldiers. Although I have not yet seen him, I suspect that Harry (as well as the other officers and men from the Sixth) are fit to be tied because they were left out of the action. I was lucky to be included since I was detached to Jeb's unit. For me, it was a particularly fateful day. But more about that later.

The fight itself was something. As you
know, this was the first time in the history of
the west that our troops have gone against a
more or less equal number of Indians who
showed a willingness to fight. All the other
times, the soldiers have attacked their camps
and caught them unprepared or greatly outnumbered. This time promised to be different.
As the cavalry marched eastward through this
very pretty little valley, the Indians were coming to meet us, bedecked in their finest battle
clothing (Would it be proper to call them uniforms, although there was no uniformity about
their costumes?). For a while it looked as if it
was going to be a textbook type of fight, three
hundred Indians against three hundred cavalrymen. But then something very strange happened. Colonel Sumner, apparently acting on
instinct, ordered the men to draw their sabers.
This was very unexpected, since all along they
had drilled to precede an attack with a volley
from their carbines. The Cheyenne, who seemed
all too willing to risk death in a fight against our
guns, panicked at the sight of the sabers and
took to their heels, retreating ever so much more
rapidly than they advanced.

Probably no one will ever know why
Sumner gave the "draw sabers" order. If
asked, he likely would not be able to explain it
himself. But thanks to some very astute men
from H Company, we are at least able to
understand the Cheyenne response.

After the Indians fled in confusion, we
chased them across the plain, killing at least
seven of them, if we can use the number of

bodies recovered as an accurate account. There
is some feeling among the officers that many
more than that were actually killed but their
bodies were carried off by their comrades. But
that is all speculation. What is not speculation
is that one Indian was captured alive.

According to Sumner, who informed the
troops about the action over a cold supper last
evening, the captured Cheyenne was none
other than Cut Lip, one the tribe's most
respected shamans. While being questioned
extensively by the colonel's interpreter, Cut
Lip revealed that he and another shaman had
felt that the Cheyenne chief god (a deity
whose name I cannot even hope to render) had
promised them a decisive victory if only they
would do as the two medicine men said. Their
instruction to the warriors was to wash themselves in sacred water, thereby assuring them
immunity from our bullets. In other words,
they were prepared for an attack from our
rifles, but when they saw the men draw their
swords that put a new complexion on everything. They were literally shocked into impo-
tency. At least most of them were. Several of
them put up very vigorous defenses. As a
result, four soldiers were killed and another
four wounded.

This is probably a good time to tell you
(since I hope to be reclining next to you in bed
when you read this and you will be able to see
for yourself) that I was among the wounded.
As it turned out, it was no more than a scratch.
Nevertheless, it has left me very sore, too sore
to ride a horse for a few days so I will be toted,

like a sack of grain, on a wagon for at least part of our trip back home. Among the more seriously wounded was Private LaRossa, the Sixth's very own incorrigible brawler. It is too long a story to recount here, but he and Private Venezia decided to abandon their posts and try to insinuate themselves into the battle. Venezia was killed and LaRossa suffered an arrow wound in his side. Believe it or not, the arrow passed completely through him, apparently causing no major damage. Captain Wilson, the surgeon, was amazed. Although he was in some of the thickest fighting in Mexico he had never seen an instance such as this. I know Jace will be thrilled to examine him once we return.

Although LaRossa occasionally spits up a glob of blood, he seems no worse for wear and has refused to be treated. Not that it makes much difference, since he will be court-martialed as soon as we return. My guess is he will be spending a goodly number of his remaining years in a Fort Leavenworth stockade making small rocks out of big ones. Of course, that will be for the board to decide but I am confident that will be the outcome.

Now for the sad news. Among the Cheyenne dead was Short Hair, the man who was raising Werner, and, as luck would have it, Large-Footed Bull, who was raising Wilhelm. What the odds are of both of them being killed I have no idea. But I would guess they are astronomical. The two boys, of course, were nowhere near the battle site. Colonel Sumner and most of his cavalry pushed off early this morning in pursuit of the Cheyenne. If by chance they are able to recover Werner and Wilhelm, your mother will be overjoyed. I caution, however, that the odds are very much against it. I would imagine that the Cheyenne have split up into small groups and are fleeing in a dozen different directions. I would not wager my next month's salary that the troopers will luck upon the boys. Unhappily, I predict that your mother will again be disappointed.

Since Sumner was able to go into battle very successfully with only the cavalry he has decided it does not make good sense to continue ahead with the infantry, which would only slow down the chase and consume more of their rapidly dwindling rations. Jeb, who was a temporary quartermaster at Fort Leavenworth and has a keen understanding of military logistics, is very worried about extending this campaign further. Unless they are extremely fortunate and run across a buffalo herd in the next week or two, they are going to be dining almost exclusively on pack mule steak. Zack, as commander of our companies, also is worried about what we will be eating on the return trip. On the bright side, our chances of finding buffalo and other large game are much greater.

This had turned into a very long missive. I guess I'm still running on nervous energy. We will be leaving early on the morrow. Captain Wilson has made it clear to Zack that I am not to attempt to ride a horse for several days because of my inconsequential wound and it makes me feel like I'm an invalid. It has been a great adventure, my darling wife, but I am so looking forward to being back in your arms. You have no idea how much I have missed you and everyone else (well, maybe not Harrigan so much), and I am counting the days until we return. If all goes well, I will be back in our bed within a week. In the meantime, I will be dreaming about you.

Your loving husband,

Jean

Long Leg looked around nervously, obviously uncomfortable inside the council lodge. Crooked Nose noted the coyote man's unease and smiled to himself. He's worse than a bear in a trap, he thought. Long Leg had come into the camp an hour earlier, making one of his rare visits to renew his supply of tobacco, one of the few luxuries he and the other coyote men allowed themselves. As part of the visit, Long Leg felt compelled to meet with Crooked Nose and bring him up to date on events transpiring on the Arapaho boundaries. For one thing, he said, a group of Oglalas had been loitering in the west. The village chief shrugged off the report since various groups were always in motion on the Plains, especially during the summer when they needed to kill enough buffalo and other game to last them through the coming winter. He was much more interested when Long Leg told him he had also seen a group of thirty soldiers from Fort Laramie about a day's ride away. They appeared to be on a routine patrol, Long Leg said, perhaps waiting for a new group of emigrants moving westward on the white man's trail. But whatever they were doing there, they did not appear to be a threat. They made no attempts to conceal their presence and did not seem to be preparing for battle.

When Sad Bear and Red Horse showed up two days later and asked which groups had been seen in the area, Crooked Nose told them about the soldiers. When he learned how many troopers there were, Red Horse lost interest. "Blizzard may be mad, but he is not stupid enough to try to attack an overwhelming number of armed troopers," Red Horse said, sounding despondent.

It was then, almost offhandedly, that Crooked Nose mentioned the Oglalas. When he did, Sad Bear and Red Horse looked at each other and began laughing.

"This may be our lucky day," Sad Bear said excitedly, slapping Red Horse on the shoulder.

"What can you tell us more about the Oglala?" Red Horse asked Crooked Nose. "This could be important."

Crooked Nose told them what he had heard from Long Leg: where the Oglala had last been seen, how many there were, which direction they were heading, and what they seemed to be doing. "But explain to me why you're so interested," Crooked Nose added. "I fail to see the significance."

"It's very clear," Sad Bear broke in. "All of Blizzard's men except Elk Ear are Lakota. They work hard at maintaining a good relationship with the bands, especially the Oglala. If the renegades are likely to approach any group, it would be them."

Red Horse walked over to the lodge flap and looked outside. "We still have three hours of daylight left," he said when he rejoined the group. "Come, Sad Bear, we need to be on the trail. Maybe if we travel through the night, we can catch up with the Oglala by midday tomorrow. Crooked Nose," he added, turning to the chief, "may we get fresh horses from you? We'll return them in good shape."

"Of course," Crooked Nose replied. "But you can do something for me if you will."

"Gladly. What is it."

"If you have a confrontation with the renegades and you get the chance, will you kill Elk Ear as well?"

Red Horse raised an eyebrow. "Why is that?"

"He is from this village," Crooked Nose replied, "and a real troublemaker. I don't want him returning and making our lives more difficult. If he comes back, he will draw the soldiers here like carrion to a kill. I would just as soon that not happen."

Red Horse nodded solemnly. "We will do what we can," he promised.

The sun was just disappearing over the horizon when Sad Bear stopped his horse and squinted into the distance.

"Red Horse," he said, reaching out and pushing his friend's shoulder.

"What is it?" Red Horse asked, coming instantly alert. For the last five miles he had been riding with his head sunk on his chest, three-fourths of the way asleep.

"A rider," Sad Bear pointed. "An Indian. And he seems to be alone."

Slowly, warily, they moved their horses forward slowly, separating slightly so when they met they would bracket the stranger.

"It's just an Arapaho boy," Sad Bear said when they got closer. "And he looks exhausted."

Red Horse stared. "I know him," he said. "His name is Cut Neck."

Thirty minutes later, the three of them were sitting around a hastily built fire while Sad Bear roasted a chunk of buffalo haunch they had brought with them from the Arapaho camp.

"This is delicious," Cut Neck said, eating ravenously. "I haven't eaten for three days."

"Then don't eat so quickly," Red Horse cautioned. "You'll only make yourself sick. But why haven't you eaten?" he asked curiously. "Is there no game?"

"I've been traveling hard," Cut Neck said, his mouth full of half-cooked buffalo.

"You act as if someone were pursuing you. Are you in trouble?"

"I hope not," Cut Neck said nervously, looking back in the direction from which he had come.

Immediately sensing that Cut Neck might have information they were looking for, Red Horse began gently interrogating the youth. Gradually, the story of being ambushed by Blizzard and his men came out.

Red Horse looked conspiratorially at Sad Bear. "This is what we have been searching for," he said. "We must strike while we have the opportunity."

"What can you do?" Cut Neck asked. "There are only two of you and seven of them. They are very careful; they watch the trail closely to see if anyone is approaching. And they are cruel beyond description."

"What do you mean?" Red Horse asked.

"After they told me I could go, I didn't immediately leave the area. The next day I crept back to see what they wanted with the two white men."

"And what did you see?" Red Horse asked carefully.

"I couldn't get close enough to see. But I could hear the screams. They were torturing them."

Red Horse sat silent, idly poking the coals with a slender branch. "Would you come with us?" he asked Cut Neck.

The boy shook his head violently. "I cannot," he said.

"If I did, they might retaliate against my village and I am afraid to take that much responsibility upon myself."

"I think he's right," Sad Bear said. "If Blizzard knew that Cut Neck helped us find him, it could go very badly for his people."

Again, the group fell silent, each thinking of what could be done.

"I have it!" Red Horse said excitedly, throwing the branch into the coals.

"And what is that?" Cut Neck asked, misgiving evident in his voice.

"Remember that Crooked Nose mentioned there was a group of soldiers in the area . . ."

"Of course," Sad Bear said, breaking into a huge grin. "The soldiers themselves have been looking for Blizzard. And when they learn that he has two white men as captives . . ."

"Hurry," said Red Horse, springing to his feet. "We need to go find the soldiers before Blizzard has time to disappear. Cut Neck," he added, turning to the youth, "you have been most helpful. But we need one more thing from you."

"And what is that?" Cut Neck asked, relieved to have been let off the hook.

"Tell us exactly where you last saw Blizzard."

"That's easy." Cut Neck smiled. Picking up a twig, he quickly sketched a map for them in the dirt. "You should be able to find them without any problem," he said when he had finished. "But I caution you to be careful. They are very dangerous men."

Red Horse nodded solemnly. "No one knows that better than I."

The fire had long since burned down to coals and to see by its light Biv had to crawl very close. It was not something he wanted to do, but he felt he must. Gradually, by slithering along the ground like a snake, he edged closer to the pit. Slowly, he pushed his bound hands closer to the coals, turning them slightly so he could see the damaged right one. Although the light was very poor, it proved sufficient. Biv took a close look and thought he was going to vomit.

A little at a time, Blizzard had been chopping away at his hand, removing a joint in the morning and another in the afternoon. Fingers, Biv had come to learn, are very strange appendages. One can be removed and, while there is copious bleeding initially, the flow stops quickly. At first, when Blizzard lopped off his right pinky, he thought that surely he would bleed to death in a matter of minutes. He could hardly believe it when the flow stopped almost as quickly as it started. The same was true as Blizzard continued the amputation process. Now the thumb was the only remaining digit on his right hand and he had not, as far as he knew, even come close to dying from loss of blood.

Swallowing the bitter liquid that rose in his throat when he caught the day's first glimpse of his hand, Biv forced himself to look more closely. The stump of his pinky was horribly swollen and oozed a thick, greenish white material that exuded a sickening odor. The other fingers were not yet infected, but the stumps were all red and swollen. Through the scab on what little remained of the middle finger, Biv could see a thin white splinter projecting outward, a piece of bone, he presumed.

Surprisingly, after that first morning, his terror had gradually dissipated. All that remained was a horrible pain that engulfed first his right arm, then his entire body. Now, Biv felt, it was penetrating his mind as well. He no longer feared death; he welcomed it. If it would bring him relief from the suffering, it would be a blessing.

He looked up and noticed that the sky in the east had lightened considerably. Soon the sun would be coming over the horizon and another day would begin—another day of unbearable torture.

One thing he couldn't understand was why Blizzard had left him alive so long. He had finished off Legendre in a mere three days. Today would be the fourth day for him and Blizzard had shown no indication of wanting the routine to end. Doesn't he have somewhere to go? Biv asked himself. Doesn't he want to kill me and get along with his business? Apparently not, he thought, answering his own question. In which case I should do what I can about taking care of it myself.

Craftily, he began looking around him. Blizzard and his men were careful to make sure there was nothing around that Biv could use as a lethal weapon. The area's clean, he thought dejectedly. Even the firewood has been moved well beyond my reach. They must be afraid I might take a branch and use it as a makeshift club to batter myself to death, if such a thing is possible.

He studied the rocks that encircled the fire pit. Maybe he could bash his head against one of them. He considered the possibility, then discarded it. I can't get enough leverage to do any good.

The sky was getting lighter. In a few minutes Broken Club would rouse and walk off into the trees to relieve himself. He must have a weak bladder, Biv thought. He's always the first one up. Desperately, he let his eyes sweep the area one more time.

At first, he didn't believe what he was seeing. I must be hallucinating he thought. It's one of the results of my torture. To test himself, he glanced away, then back, just to see if what he thought he saw was still there. It was.

The night before, he had been tossing fitfully in pain, trying to force himself to sleep in the hope that it would give him some relief from his agony. He recalled waking and looking at the fire, where the men were sitting and laughing, probably telling stories about other people they have tortured, Biv thought. One of them, the man whose name Biv thought was Red Chin, had been working on his arrows. Maybe he was going out to get them fresh meat. Biv looked to where Red Chin or whatever his name was had been sitting. Lying on the ground, half buried in the dust, was an arrow he apparently had discarded as inferior. Perhaps its shaft was too crooked or maybe its point needed sharpening, or its feathers had to be replaced. But it was there. To Biv, it looked like a fist-sized nugget in the bottom of a gold miner's pan . . . a fat wallet lying uncollected on a city street.

He felt lightheaded with joy; it was his ticket out of the suffering. He remembered Legendre telling him how aged Cheyenne warriors, when their days were numbered and they didn't wish to be a burden to their families, would sometimes stick an arrow down their throats. That was exactly what Biv planned to do.

Carefully, mindful of the fast-approaching dawn, Biv inched closer to the arrow. When he thought he was close enough, he moved his hands forward slowly. I can grip it in my good hand, he thought, and use the pressure from both to ram it home.

His left hand was just closing about the shaft when he heard Broken Club bellow. Before he knew it, the Indian was upon him, lifting him three feet in the air and snatching the arrow out of his fist. Angrily, Broken Club tossed him on the ground and yelled to the others to rise and see what great act he had accomplished.

Biv drew his body into the fetal position and began sobbing as if his heart would break. Never had he felt so disheartened. Cringing in anticipation of only God knew what punishment would be meted out, he heard himself expel a loud, keening noise that sounded like the January wind. To him, it sounded like the noise made by a dog being beaten.

Broken Club thought that was hilarious. Gleefully, he slapped his thigh. Tossing his head back, he roared loud enough to wake any sleeping creature within a half mile.

He was still laughing when there was a loud explosion, close enough that Biv wondered if it came from inside his head. When he looked to where Broken Club had been, he saw that he was no longer standing. He was sprawled on his back and his heels were pounding on the ground. Half his face was missing, replaced by a bright red pulpy mass.

While he stared unbelievingly at Broken Club, the forest around him seemed to erupt in gunfire. All around him, the men who had watched happily while Blizzard and Crow Killer tortured first Legendre and then him, were running in confusion, trying to find their weapons. Red Chin, the one who had been working on the arrows the night before, had scooped up his lance and had turned toward the trees when three slugs ripped into his body at once, picking him up and throwing him for at least six feet. Biv had just swung his head to the right when Four Wolves dropped to his knees, gripping his stomach. As Biv watched, a gusher of bloody vomit erupted from the Indian's mouth.

Praying fiercely, Biv tried to make himself inconspicuous, covering his head and trying to burrow into the dirt.

As quickly as it began, the shooting stopped and a silence descended upon the campsite. For several seconds, the only sounds Biv heard were moans and Four Wolves vomiting. Then, as if out of a dream, a voice spoke to him in English.

"Don't worry, sir," it said. "My name is Lieutenant Hopkins, F Company, Sixth Infantry. Me and my men have everything under control. You're in safe hands."

Biv was trying to say thanks when he passed out.

11

Jason Dobbs shook his head slowly and made a quiet clucking noise with his tongue, reminding Benoit of a tactics professor at the Academy who made the same kind of sound whenever he graded his test papers.

"You can put your blouse back on," Dobbs said, rolling down his sleeves.

"Well, what's the prognosis?"

"Prognosis hell," Dobbs sighed. "You don't need a medical opinion, you need a long black robe and a crucifix."

"What the hell is that supposed to mean?"

"What it means," Dobbs smiled, "is that you are qualified to start your own religion because the fact that you survived at all, much less in relatively good shape, is just short of miraculous."

"Well, Sumner's surgeon said I was a lucky son of a bitch."

"Lucky is not the right word. You may never appreciate just how fortunate you were, but if that cartridge had been loaded with fresh powder or if the slug had hit a half inch lower you'd be fertilizing the Solomon River Valley right now."

Benoit whistled softly. "That close, huh?"

"Yeah. That close. Fact is, I've never seen one closer and I've been a practicing army surgeon for a decade."

"That means I have a clean bill of health? I can resume my duties?"

Dobbs grinned. "You mean professional or personal?"

"I guess both," Benoit said, blushing.

"You've been back for almost twenty-four hours now. As far as I know you haven't attempted the former, but if you haven't resumed the latter you can hook me up to a wagon and I'll pull the damn thing all the way to Oregon."

"You're a crude bastard, you know that?" Benoit laughed.

"Why don't you say 'outspoken'? It sounds so much nicer."

"Well, what's the verdict? Can I go back to work?"

"I think so. On a limited basis."

Benoit raised an eyebrow. "How limited?"

"I think for another few weeks you ought to stick close to the post. No more missions for at least a month."

Benoit smiled. "I don't think Inge would have any problem with that."

"I figured not," Dobbs replied, returning the smile.

"Jace," Benoit said soberly, clapping his friend on the shoulder. "You don't know how good it is to be back."

"I may not be the most tactful person you've ever met, but I know what you mean."

Benoit busied himself with his buttons, looking embarrassed about openly expressing his affection for the cynical surgeon. "So tell me what's been happening," he added briskly, anxious to change the subject. "What's happened while I've been gone."

Dobbs chuckled, recognizing his friend's discomfort. "Well, I guess you heard about Ashby and Holz. I'm sure Inge had *some* conversation with you during the night."

"Yes, goddamnit, she told me about the forthcoming marriage. She's tickled to death."

"What did he say?"

"He told me to do whatever I wanted with any of them. He never wanted to see them again."

"Ugh," Benoit mumbled. "That doesn't sound good."

"It isn't. But it isn't necessarily permanent. He may change his mind and decide to pick up where he left off. Bad things happen in life all the time and he has to see if he can get through it. I'm no expert on art, but I'd be willing to bet that he wouldn't be the first one-handed painter that ever lived."

"What about the renegades?" Benoit asked. "Did Hopkins and his men kill all those bastards?"

"Its strange that you ask that. One of them got away."

"Oh no!" Benoit exclaimed. "Don't tell me. Let me guess."

"You'd be right," Dobbs said grimly. "Blizzard. Don't know how that slimy son of a bitch survived, much less escaped. But when they started counting the bodies, his wasn't there."

"Jesus! Talk about a cat with nine lives."

"Maybe not." Dobbs smiled. "Red Horse and his right-hand man, I forget his name, took off after him. I figure they'll catch up with him. It's just a matter of time."

"Something Bear, I seem to recollect. But that's too bad about Legendre. I liked that crusty old guy. Wonder what'll happen to his son, David," he said, pronouncing it Da-veed. "He seemed like a good kid."

Dobbs laughed. "Legendre wasn't *old*, Jean. He just seemed that way. He'd had a hard life. I imagine David . . . oops Da-veed . . . will grow up as a proper little Cheyenne. Just like Werner and Wilhelm. Speaking of the Cheyenne . . ."

Dobbs stopped, turning at the sound of banging on his door. "Come in!"

"Sorry to interrupt you, sir," Sean Flannery said, sticking his head in.

"That's all right, Corporal. What is it?"

"Captain Harrigan asked me to come get you, sir. And you, too, I guess, Lieutenant Benoit. He wants all the officers in the dining room right away. He says something's come up."

Dobbs sighed. "Okay, Corporal. Thanks. We'll be right there."

"I hope this isn't a real emergency," Dobbs said softly to Benoit after Flannery closed the door. "It isn't something Harrigan needs right now."

"Well, I guess we won't know until we go see. After you, sir," Benoit said, making a sweeping gesture with his right arm. "Oh, Jesus God," he said, gripping his chest in pain. "I forgot about that goddamn wound."

"I *told* you to take it easy." Dobbs laughed. "That'll be with you for a couple of weeks. No sudden, grand gestures. Unless you're addicted to pain, that is. Now, after *you*," he said with a mock bow.

Benoit took one look at Harrigan and turned to Dobbs. "He looks like death warmed over," he whispered. "His cheeks are all sunken in and his eyes look like he's been in a hell of a fight. I've never seen such dark, deep circles."

"Stress," Dobbs whispered back. "It's a killer."

"I'm delighted you could make it, Dobbs," Harrigan said sarcastically. "And you, too, Ben-oight," he added, looking Benoit up and down. "I gather you're getting around pretty good now."

"I manage, sir," Benoit mumbled. "Thankful to be alive."

Harrigan abruptly shifted his attention, glancing at some papers in front of him.

"I guess you're all wondering why I asked for this assembly," he said in an attempt at lightheartedness. No one laughed.

"In that case," he said, clearing his throat. "I'll get right down to business. Do any of you remember Private Amos Henderson? A.k.a. 'Notch?' "

"Who?" asked Ahearn.

"Before your time," Harry Grant interjected. "I remember him. He and a group of other deserters made off with that payroll money, about $10,000 if I remember correctly."

"And took Congressman Couvillion as a hostage," added Benoit.

"But they were all killed by those renegades, weren't they?" asked Barnes.

"Not Henderson," said Benoit. "He escaped with the money."

"That's right." Harrigan nodded.

"What about him, captain?" Benoit asked.

"He's back. Or at least he was."

Dobbs shook his head. "Sorry, captain, I don't understand. What do you mean he's back? You have him in the stockade?"

"I wish to hell I did. He was here and he slipped through our grasp."

Dobbs shook his head. "Wait a minute. Who says he was here? Who says he slipped through our grasp?"

"Private Harrison of G Company says so," Harrigan replied. "And he says it under oath in this statement," he added, waving the papers he had been studying.

"Harrison's a bit of a slacker," Barnes interrupted. "I've had to discipline him several times."

"But is he a liar?" Harrigan asked.

"Not that I know of," Barnes admitted. "Lazy maybe, but I've never caught him lying."

"According to him," Harrigan continued, "Henderson came through in late June with a wagon train heading for California."

"That must have been right after we left with Sumner," Benoit whispered. "I remember hearing that a train was due."

"Shhh," Dobbs said, waving his hand distractedly. "When that private says Henderson was here, does he mean on the post?" he asked Harrigan.

"Not exactly. Harrison says he stayed out at the emigrant campground and never came on the post itself. Guess he's not *that* stupid. Let me read the private's statement," Harrigan added, turning to the papers. "That should clear it up. By the way, this statement was dictated to Sergeant Johansen, the clerk from E Company, who read it back to him afterward. It has Harrison's mark." Harrigan cleared his throat again and began reading:

> I was minding my own business one evening
> in June, I think it was the twenty-fourth or
> twenty-fifth, it was a Sunday anyways, when
> this woman come up to the barracks asking
> for me. I took quite a bit of ribbing about that,
> I'll tell you, because it weren't no girl from the
> Hog Ranch, but some woman from the emi-
> grant train. She weren't bad looking neither.
> Nice titties. Anyways, she was all mysterious.
> Said she wanted me to come back with her to
> the campground. There was someone there
> who wanted to see me. Wouldn't tell me who
> it was until we was halfway there. Then when
> she told me, I could of fallen on the ground.
> She said it was Notch, old Notch Henderson
> hisself. Me and him used to be real good pals
> but after he deserted and got mixed up in that

robbery and kidnapping and all that shit, then disappeared, I figured I'd never see him or hear from him again. I asked this woman, her name was Naomi, a right pretty name, you ask me. I asked Naomi to fill me in, tell me how she got to know Notch and what she was doing with him and all that. She said she met Notch about eighteen months ago in St. Louis. After they got kind of cozy, Notch said he had a deal for her. He wanted her to pose as his wife so they could join an emigrant group and get to Californy. She asked him why he felt he needed to do this and he told her he had gotten blamed for something he didn't do in the army and he had to leave in a hurry. He said they was still looking for him so he had to pretend to be someone else, at least until they got themselves to San Fran. He told her if she would do that, he'd pay her five hundred dollars, half when they left and the other half when they got there. She said that sounded pretty good to her because she was getting sick of that bawdy house she was working in anyhow and she heard a nice looking girl could make a fair bit of money out west. I know I'd a paid her four bits for an all-nighter if she had the time but she just looked at me like I was crazy. When I asked her why Notch wanted to see me, she said she thought it was just for old times sake, since we used to be friends and all. Anyways, I hardly recognized him when I seed him. He had a big, black beard and he had let his hair grow long, down to his shoulders. Plus, he had put on about twenty pounds, most of it under his belt. Sure didn't look anything like the Notch I used to know. I wouldn't have recognized him if he'd come right up to me. When I got out to the campground, Notch had a bottle he had Naomi buy for him at Sevier's and we got right drunk. Had a real good time, just like the old days almost. Notch asked me if I wanted to desert and come out to Californy. Said a couple of smart, tough men like us could make a tidy fortune. He told me he had already made a little money with that payroll theft but now that he had a taste of what it was like to be flush he wanted more. But he needed a partner and I fit the bill. I told him I wanted to think about it. He gave me a really hard look and asked if I was thinking of turning him in since there's bound to be a reward on his head. I told him I had no such thoughts, that I'd never do that to an old friend. He just laughed and said I'd better be careful because it'd be the last thing I ever did. He said even if he went to prison he had enough money hid away to hire somebody to come kill me. I believed him, too. Notch is that kind of man. Real mean son of a bitch. Anyways, he told me to think about it and if I wanted to come to San Fran, I'd be welcome. He warned me not to tell nobody that I seed him or that would rightly get him riled. The more I got to thinking about it, the more I decided I didn't want to go to Californy and be no outlaw. So that's why I'm telling you all this. I want to know if there is a reward for him and how much it might be. I could sure use a little nest egg when I get out of the

army. If this helps you catch him, I think I
deserve any reward that might be out. Signed
Private George Washington Harrison, August
13th, 1857.

"Phew," Dobbs exhaled. "That's quite a tale. Are you
going after him?"

"Not me," Harrigan said caustically. "But someone
from Fort Laramie is. Do I have any volunteers?"

"I'll go, sir," Grant said quickly.

Harrigan looked at him coolly. "You just got back.
What's the matter? Wasn't the Cheyenne Expedition exciting enough for you?"

"It was far from exciting, captain. All we did was
march our asses off and then the cavalry got to see all the
action. We didn't do anything but eat dust almost the
whole damn trip."

"Still, you had your chance. Anyone else want to go
fetch Notch?"

When no one responded, Harrigan slammed his fist
down on the table.

"Goddamnit," he screamed, his face turning scarlet.
"That's not the kind of response I expect from you men. I
want one of you to volunteer to take a detachment of six
men and go after this son of a bitch Henderson. Six men
against one ought to be pretty fair odds. Does anyone
have any problem with that?"

"Six men sounds like more than enough to me, sir,"
Grant said when no one else indicated an interest.

Harrigan rubbed his chin. "Okay, Grant. I reckon
you're it. You ought to be able to handle it. You pick the
men you want. And take Ashby, too. Ashby and his
puppy, the German kid. You think that'll be enough?"

"Yes, sir!" Grant said enthusiastically. "More than
enough. Where do you think we might find him?"

"That's a good question. The train he was with was going through Utah. Salt Lake City's five hundred miles. At their rate of travel, I figure they're about to Salt Lake City now. You'll have to hustle to catch up."

"That's okay, sir," Grant said, grinning. "At least this time we'll be riding. We were on our way to the Solomon when the train got here. What can you tell me about it?"

Harrigan scratched his head. "There were about a hundred and twenty, hundred and thirty people, most of them from Arkansas. The leader was a guy named Fancher. Don't remember his first name."

"Who was the wagon master?" asked Dobbs.

Harrigan looked puzzled. "Damned if I know. I never met any of 'em. I was too busy taking care of the paperwork that the colonel left piled on his desk."

"It was a foul-tempered old man named Alf Stuart," said Ahearn. "My company escorted them for a few days, then they decided they didn't need us any more. We sure didn't know anything about a deserter, though."

"Don't guess he came up and introduced himself," Dobbs said dryly. "Sir!" he said, speaking to Harrigan. "The army's relations with the Mormons aren't very good right now. You think it's wise sending a small detachment like that?"

"I don't want your opinion, Dobbs. I'm commanding here. If I think it's safe, it's safe. The ultimate responsibility is mine. Do I make myself clear?"

"Yes, sir." Dobbs shrugged.

"Good. I'm glad you agree. Lieutenant Grant, be ready to go tomorrow. Dismiss. Everybody get back to work."

Grant hurried to catch up with Dobbs. "Wait, Jace," he said, calling after him.

Dobbs turned. "Come on in my surgery. Benoit is going to make a fresh pot of coffee."

"What's all this about problems with the Mormons?" Grant asked while Benoit got the material together for the coffee. "Don't forget, I've been out of touch for awhile. And I'm not too big on politics anyway. Or history. I don't even know what the hell those people are doing in Utah. Figured if anybody around here could explain it to me, it'd be you."

Benoit glanced at him over his shoulder. Not big on politics, huh? he thought. Unlike Uncle Ulysses.

Dobbs pulled up a chair. "Okay, Harry," he sighed. "Let me give you a quick lesson in history. Do you know *anything* about the Mormons?"

"I know they're trying to cross the Plains with *handcarts*, for shit's sake. And they have a lot of wives. Oh," he added as an afterthought, "I understand a lot of people don't like them but I'm not sure why."

Dobbs rolled his eyes. "Why me, Lord?" he said to the ceiling. Leaning forward, he placed his elbows on his bony knees and looked steadily at Grant.

"Here's the situation," he said, sounding more than ever to Benoit like a professor. "I'll begin at the beginning. First of all, 'Mormons' is only a nickname. Technically, they're members of the Church of Jesus Christ of Latter-Day Saints . . ."

"How come they're called Mormons then?"

"That's because the founder of the sect, a man named Joseph Smith, claimed he was visited by an angel called Moroni. According to Smith, this angel showed him tablets covered with writing. He transcribed the tablets and called them the Book of Mormon. You with me?"

"Yep," Harry said, bobbing his head.

"Coffee?" asked Benoit, handing a demitasse to Dobbs.

"Yeah, sure, thanks. But can I have a whole cup?"

Benoit looked at Dobbs, who was trying to smother a laugh.

"You were saying about Jones . . ."

"Smith."

"Oh, yeah. Smith. So he saw this angel. Where was that?"

At the time, this was about thirty-five, thirty-seven years ago, Smith was living in a place called Palmyra. It's in New York."

"Never been there."

"Me either, but that doesn't matter. I won't go into a lot of details about the sect's doctrine. It isn't important to you. Let me just say that a lot of people who call themselves Christians disagreed with a lot of things that Smith preached. Smith moved from New York to Ohio. From there—because of local opposition—they kept on the move, ending up in Illinois, where they lived in their own town called Nauvoo. At one point it was the biggest city in Illinois and all its residents were Mormons. All this time, Smith was getting more and more powerful. Finally, he got to the point where he thought he could do or say anything. That's when he issued a decree saying it was all right for Mormons to have more than one wife . . ."

"I remember now," Grant said brightly. That was one of Fremont's campaign planks in the last presidential election. He was against polygamy."

"That's right." Dobbs nodded. "But that was later. I'm still talking about what happened a dozen years ago."

"How come you know all this stuff?" Grant asked, impressed.

"I read a lot. Anyway, there were enough people mad at Smith because of the polygamy decree that he and his brother, who was also prominent in the church, were put in jail for their own protection. Not that it did any good. A mob broke in and lynched 'em both. That's when the Mormons decided it was time to head west."

Dobbs paused, sipping Benoit's coffee and giving Grant time to digest what he had said.

"I don't guess you got any better with your coffee while I was gone, did you?" Benoit asked.

Dobbs smiled and shook his head. "Didn't really have time to practice. Hell, I knew you'd be back sooner or later."

Grant took a large swallow and made a face. "Holy Moses!" he exclaimed. "That's strong stuff. How do you guys drink it?"

"It's an acquired taste." Dobbs smiled. "Back to the Mormons."

"Jesus, Jace, I'm not writing a book. I just wanted you to explain what this is all about."

"I know that, Harry. But to do that I have to tell you what led up to it."

"Okay," he sighed. "But I don't have all day. I have a lot to do before tomorrow morning. Why didn't people like 'em, other than the polygamy thing that is?"

"They have their own ways of doing things," Dobbs said patiently. "And some of those ways go against accepted methods. Non-Mormons—the Mormons call them gentiles—think they're clannish and probably were plotting against the government, too. After the Smiths were hanged, a guy named Brigham Young became their leader . . ."

"That name I know."

"You should. He's been through here. Young decided he'd had enough of Illinois, the whole area as a matter of fact, so he took his followers west. They settled around the Great Salt Lake, in what is now called Salt Lake City. Ever since then, more and more Mormons have been flocking there. A lot of them couldn't afford proper wagons so they invented the handcart . . ."

Benoit began singing:

> "We say it is high time to start
> To cross the Plains with our handcarts . . ."

Dobbs chuckled, adding:

> "For some must push and some must pull
> As we go marching up the hill . . ."

Together, laughing, they finished:

> "So merrily on our way we go,
> Until we reach the valley-oh."

"That's not funny," Grant said righteously. "It ain't good to make fun of somebody's religion."

"We weren't making fun of the religion," Dobbs said, sobering. "The Mormons have done wonders, so I'm told, in that goddamn desert. Salt Lake City is the largest municipality between St. Louis and San Francisco with a population, last I heard, of some ten thousand people. It boasts a public library and two newspapers. The Mormons even have their own monetary system; they mint their own coins. The very fact that they've been so successful has made them despised. That and polygamy, which just won't go away as an issue."

"If it doesn't drive them crazy what's wrong with having more than one wife?" asked Grant.

"Ask those Blue Noses Back East," Dobbs laughed. "In any case, it doesn't mean much because Brigham Young and his top aides are about the only ones who can afford it. Still, it's got a lot of people in Washington upset. Some powerful politicians decided that Brigham Young shouldn't be governor of the territory, and President

Buchanan, bless his timid soul, went along. He named a
new governor, Alfred Cummings . . ."

"Never heard of him."

"It happened while you were off with Sumner.
General Johnston came through here in July with twenty-
five hundred men, headed for Utah to depose Brigham
Young . . ."

"You mean we might be going off right into the middle
of a *war*?"

"Ah hah," Benoit said. "*Now* he gets the point."

"That's exactly what I mean," said Dobbs. "But so far,
at least not that I've heard, there hasn't been any fighting.
But that doesn't mean there aren't a lot of hopping mad
people in Utah . . ."

"And that's where I'm going with a handful of men?
Right into the middle of a goddamn *uprising*? No wonder
Harrigan couldn't get any volunteers," Grant said ner-
vously.

"Well, just remember that you need to make it clear to
the Mormons that your visit has nothing to do with
Cummings or politics or any of that stuff," Dobbs said.
"Tell anyone who asks that you're just there to capture a
deserter and bring him back for trial. The fact that there
will be so few of you works in your favor. They aren't
likely to take you for invaders."

"Is that supposed to make me feel better?"

Dobbs shrugged. "You asked what the problem was
and I told you. Don't blame me for it. You can go to
Harrigan and tell him you've changed your mind."

Grant looked at him aghast. "Not a chance of *that*," he
said. "You know what Harrigan would say. He'd probably
throw me in the stockade for cowardice or something."

Dobbs nodded. "I think you're right. Best thing for you
now is to see it through. Just be wary. If anything happens, it's Harrigan's responsibility."

"If I'm dead in Utah, that's going to be a lot of consolation."

Dobbs looked at him steadily. "The moral, Harry, is not to be so damn ambitious. Next time, know what you're getting into before you volunteer."

"Jesus Christ!" Grant swore, slamming down his coffee cup. "Harrigan's a real fucking disaster. I've put up with him for a long time, but I think I'm finally going to have to write Uncle Ulysses. He's in personnel, you know?"

"So I've heard," Dobbs replied dryly.

Benoit lay with his arms behind his head, staring up at the whitewashed ceiling, watching it turn from pink to rose in the light from the setting sun. "Are you glad to be back?" Inge asked, snuggling into the crook of his arm.

"That's an understatement if I've ever heard one. I don't know how I got along without you for as long as I did."

"Me either." Inge smiled. Running her finger over the two wounds on Benoit's chest, she shivered slightly, realizing how close she had come to being a widow. "Did Jace say you were okay?"

"I'm fine. Just need to take it easy for a few days. Turns out it was a real blessing in disguise. Harrigan wanted me to go to Utah to try to find that deserter who kidnapped Cle. He seems to think he passed through here last summer and is with an emigrant train between here and California."

"Oh, no," Inge said, bolting upright. "You just got back. And Utah is not a very nice place to be right now if you're a soldier."

"I know that, darling. That's why I'm glad I don't have to go. Harry's going instead."

"Oh, God," she said, moving back to his side. "Harry's

always volunteering for everything. When is he going to learn?"

"Never, I hope." Benoit laughed. "Not if I want to be company commander."

"Jean! That's a terrible thing to say. You would feel very badly if Harry got killed."

"Maybe," he said, doubting that he would at all. "But from my perspective Harry's just a gigantic pain in the ass. That's something about your mother and Ashby," he added hurriedly, trying to change the subject. "How in hell did it come about?"

Inge giggled. "*Mutter* got another letter from Oregon, telling her again that she should come. When Jim heard . . ."

"From you, naturally."

"Of course from me. Who else?"

"So what happened?"

"So I told Jim that she had finally made up her mind to go to Oregon. He got this really strange look on his face. Said he didn't think that was such a good idea and he needed to talk to her about it. Next thing I know, *Mutter* is telling me that she and Jim are going to be married and she doesn't want to go to Oregon after all. Isn't that romantic?"

Benoit looked at her out of the corner of his eye. "Uh, yeah, I guess it is."

"Of course it is, you unfeeling lout," she said punching him playfully in the side.

"Oh," he gasped, feigning injury.

"Oh, Jean," she said anxiously. "I'm so sorry. I forgot about your wound. Did I pain you?"

"No, you didn't *hurt* me," he laughed. "Sometimes your English is as confused as your mother's."

"That isn't funny," she pouted, pulling away.

"Of course it isn't," he said soothingly, drawing her back. "It wasn't right for me to make a joke like that. I think your English is perfect," he said, stroking her back. "It's what really appeals to me about you."

"Oh, it is?" she said, turning to him with an impish grin. "And I thought it was this," she added, taking his hand and placing it on her breast.

Benoit felt his breath quicken. "Well, maybe it isn't just your English," he added, massaging her, feeling her nipple grow hard. "Why don't we talk about it later."

"Aren't you interested in reading your mail?" Inge asked a half hour later.

"What mail?" Benoit replied sleepily.

"The stage came through today. You got two letters."

"That's nice," he said, feeling himself drift off.

"No, Jean," she said, pushing his shoulder. "If you go to sleep now you'll be up all night."

"I feel like I could sleep for a week."

"You can sleep later. But not right now. You can either wake up and talk to me or you can read your letters."

"Why don't you read the journal I kept for you and wake me up in an hour?"

"No, no, no," she said, wagging her finger under his nose. "I've read it three times already. It makes me want to cry."

"Don't you have a book or something?"

"No. I do not have a book. You've been gone for weeks. I want to talk to you."

"What do you want to talk about?" he asked, putting the pillow over his head.

"I want to talk about your letters," she said, pulling the pillow off.

"Oh, Jesus, Inge, you just don't give me any rest."

"That's what wives are for. I'll get them for you," she added, slipping out of bed.

"Later, Inge. Please."

"No!" she said, stamping her foot on the floor of hard packed dirt. "Now!"

"God," he moaned, sitting up. "I had to marry a German."

"That's just because you're smarter than most people give you credit for." She laughed, tossing two envelopes in his lap. "One is from Cle . . ."

"Oh no, not him again? I wish he'd leave me alone."

". . . and the other is from your sister."

Benoit's eyes brightened. "Oh really? I wonder what she has to say."

"You won't know until you've opened it," Inge said excitedly, pushing him over so she could sit cross-legged on the edge of the bed.

Benoit's eyes skimmed the letter, stopping occasionally when he was unable to immediately decipher her writing.

"Well . . ." Inge prompted.

"Just the usual stuff. You can read it. Says Mother is doing very well . . . Armand is such a dear . . . Theophile was home for a few weeks during the summer break at the Naval Academy . . . how's he grown so tall and handsome . . . and," he paused. "Uh, oh."

"What is it, Jean? Is something the matter?"

"Listen to this. Let me read you what she says: "New Orleans has become a very strange place, t-Jean . . . ""

"That's what she calls me . . ." he explained.

"I know. Go on."

> . . . you wouldn't recognize the city any more.
> Everywhere there are preparations for war, not
> quite secret but not quite public either. All the
> young men, Theophile's friends and Armand's
> as well, talk about what an easy victory it is
> going to be over the North once the politicians

quit talking and let everyone get down to fighting. I think it is very frightening, t-Jean. The
thought of a war and possibly losing you and
Theophile and maybe even Armand although a
doctor would not be expected to be in the thick
of any fighting causes me absolute panic. But
everyone is saying that war is now inevitable,
that it is only a matter of time before the shooting actually begins. I don't think they are right,
my beloved brother, about an easy victory that
is. I think it will be a very terrible war. Armand
and Theophile both tease me about this. They
talk about what poor fighters the farm boys
from Ohio will make when it comes down to a
real battle, and about how all the generals who
are anybody are from the South, and how they
will flock to their homeland—they actually call
it that, as if we are not all Americans—when
the situation becomes critical. Theophile has
not said so definitively, but I'm sure he will
join the South. When I asked him why he
didn't just resign from the academy right now
if he felt so strongly about it and he just
laughed, saying something like how he needs
to stay as long as he can so he will have a better
understanding of what the enemy will be
thinking later. What really frightens me, t-Jean,
is the possibility that you and he will be fighting on opposite sides, that you may actually
end up trying to kill one another. I think this
bothers Mamman, too, although she doesn't
talk much about it . . .

Benoit stopped, letting the letter drop to the floor.
"I'm so sorry, Jean," Inge said, throwing her arms

around him. "I thought a letter from your sister would make you feel better."

"I know you did," Benoit said, returning her hug. "It isn't your fault. It's the damn politicians. They won't leave well enough alone. Jeb and I talked about this a lot when we were on the march. His theory is that some of those in Washington have decided there is a great deal of money to be made by promoting a war and that is why they are working so hard to see it happen. Jeb feels all this talk about slavery is just so much bullshit, that it's merely an attempt to hide the real reason: the North wants to take over the South's prosperous agricultural economy and they don't care how many people get killed in the bargain."

"Jean, don't you believe it's more than that? Don't you believe that slavery is really wrong?"

Benoit sighed. "Oh, God, Inge, let's not us fight about that. I don't think about slavery much one way or the other. My family is from the city; we don't own plantations *or* slaves. Very few Southerners do. I just know that slavery is a very emotional issue; it attracts fanatics from both sides."

Inge bit her lip. "You're right, Jean," she said slowly. "Slavery and those other things are dividing the country. We can't let them divide us, too. Are you going to open the letter from Cle?"

Benoit shook his head. "Not right now. I know what he says. He wants me to resign my commission and join the New Orleans militia."

Inge said nothing.

"I don't know what's right and wrong anymore, Inge. It seems like it was only a short time ago that I had very definite opinions on what was good and what was bad. Everything was black and white. Now, everything is gray. I'm beginning to believe there are no easy solutions, no easy answers at all."

Inge wiped a tear from her cheek. "One thing I do know is right," she said, trying to sound cheerful.

"And what is that?" Benoit replied, looking at her with eyes as sad as she had ever seen them.

"I think it is right," she said, bounding to her feet, "for me to go to the dining hall and sneak out a piece of *hefekranz* and bring it back for you. *Mutter* made a fresh batch just today."

❧ *12* ❧

Benoit had never seen Colonel Kemp in such a foul mood. "Goddamn politicians," he cursed, waving aside Frau Schmidt's offer of a fresh *Windbeutel*. "I can't eat any cream puff right now," he grumped. "Those people in Washington have ruined my appetite, maybe forever. They call me back there, take up two and a half months of my time, then don't want to listen to what I have to tell them."

"Exactly what point were you trying to get across?" Dobbs asked.

"Our so-called Indian policy," Kemp barked, fumbling in his pocket. "Where are my goddamn cigars? They must still be in my valise."

"I'll get you one, sir," Harrigan said quickly, starting to rise.

"No," Kemp said gruffly, waving him to his chair. "Strudelmeyer'll get one. George!" he barked giving the second lieutenant a fierce look.

"Yes, sir," Strudelmeyer said, leaping to his feet in such haste he turned over his chair. "I'm on my way, sir."

"Well, don't wreck the damn dining room while you're at it. Look in my valise. It's by my cot. Now, Dobbs," he continued as Strudelmeyer ran out of the room, "what was your question?"

"I asked what happened when you went before the committee, sir," Dobbs repeated softly.

Benoit smiled to himself. He had never seen his friend so subdued before.

"Damn idiots," Kemp said. "They think the solution is more troops. Kill the Indians. Burn their villages. Slaughter the buffalo so they'll starve to death. The whole damn town is consumed with war fever. War against the Indians. War against the South. And not a single, solitary son of a bitch on the committee has ever heard a shot fired in anger. Not one of 'em's ever seen his best friend blown apart by an artillery shell or held the head of someone who's had his guts ripped out by a large-caliber slug. I'll tell you all," he said, emphasizing every word, "my . . . cup . . . of contempt . . . runneth . . . goddamn . . . over."

Benoit looked up timidly. "Does that go for Senator Fontenot, too?" he asked, his voice a bare whisper.

"Dammit, Ben-oight, you're going to have to speak up. All that yapping in Washington has damaged my ear drums. What the hell did you say?"

"I said, sir," Benoit repeated a little louder, "if your comments are directed at Senator Fontenot as well."

Kemp's face softened. "Poor Emile," he said, shaking his head. "I felt sorry for him. He was the only one in that whole mealy-mouthed group who had any comprehension of what's going on out here. But there wasn't much he could do, with his sickness and all."

"Sickness?" Benoit asked in surprise. "I didn't know he was ill."

"Hate to be the one to have to break it to you, Ben-oight, but the senator has been stricken badly with consumption. It's come upon him quickly but very hard. The word is he's not expected to make it through the winter.

He looks like hell. Thin as a draftsman's line. White as the snow. Coughing up blood all the time. Its enough to make you want to cry. "

Benoit was stunned. Maybe that's what Cle was writing me about, he thought. I should have opened his letter. "No, sir, I didn't know about that. I guess that means that Congressman Couvillion . . ."

"That's right," Kemp interrupted, his face darkening. "He's being groomed as Emile's successor. But he may never make it. The town gossip is he's heavily involved in the Secessionist movement, in which case . . . oh, there you are Strudelmeyer. You found 'em, eh?"

"Yes, sir," Strudelmeyer panted. "Just where you said they'd be."

"Good, good," Kemp said, leaning back in his chair. "Goddamn," he said, biting off an end of the black cigar, "I'm going to have to learn to start curbing my temper. At my age, there's no sense getting all that upset over something I can't control. You have a light, captain?" he asked, turning to Harrigan.

"What happened in Washington is all history now," he said, puffing contentedly. "It's over with. I need to get caught up on what's been happening here. By the way, where's my honorary nephew, Alonzo. I mean, Roy," he said quickly, correcting himself.

"It's back to Alonzo," Dobbs said, relieved to see Kemp more himself. "There's a detailed report on your desk. He had a really rough time while you were gone. Captured and tortured by the renegades . . ."

Kemp's jaw dropped. "The hell you say. Where is he?" he added anxiously.

"He's, uh, at the Hog Ranch," Dobbs said tentatively. "He's formed an attachment . . ."

"Well," Kemp sighed, "if that's where he is, I'm assuming that he's a mite better."

"Yes, sir," Dobbs said hurriedly. "Physically, he's made a wonderful recovery. But the experience has left him a bit, uh, how shall I say this, emotionally unsettled."

Kemp gave the surgeon a keen look. "I want to know more about this, lieutenant. But not right now. Be in my office at zero seven-thirty. You can fill me in then."

"Yes, sir," Dobbs replied meekly.

"I was going through Fort Kearny and I got a preliminary report on the Cheyenne action, such that it was. I want to hear some more about that, too. In detail. All of you company commanders who were on the expedition, be in my office tomorrow at zero nine-hundred. Is that clear?"

"Yes, sirs," echoed around the room.

"While I was in Washington," he added, trying to sound nonchalant, "I had a chance to meet with Harry's much-mentioned Uncle Ulysses. In fact, we got rather tipsy together. I swear, that man can put it away. But all-in-all, we seemed to hit it off pretty well. Seems to me he's being wasted in personnel, but that's the army for you. Thought Harry might want to know that. Speaking of Harry," he said, looking around the room, "where is he? Is he out on patrol?"

Harrigan coughed. "Well, colonel, not exactly."

Kemp looked at him sharply. "What do you mean 'not exactly,' captain?"

"He's, ah, on a mission, sir," Harrigan stammered.

"A mission? You mean other than a routine patrol? What kind of mission?"

"It's sort of a long story, sir," Harrigan said, looking uncomfortable.

"You think we're going somewhere, captain?"

Dobbs leaned over and whispered to Benoit, "You're really going to see the shit fly now."

Briefly, Harrigan explained about Notch Henderson

and how he sneaked through Fort Laramie undetected and how he had sent Grant to bring him back.

"Let me make sure I understand this," Kemp said, his face reddening. "You sent Grant and thirty goddamn men off on a mission into *Utah*?"

"Yes, sss . . . sir," Harrigan stammered, the color draining from his face.

"Holy Jumping Jesus!" Kemp screamed, slamming his open palm on the table, turning over a coffeepot and setting the china to rattling. "Don't you remember what happened to Lieutenant Grattan? Who also incidentally happened to have thirty men under his command?"

"But this isn't Indians, sir," Harrigan said hurriedly. "These are white people . . ."

"White people who just happen to think they're at war with the army."

"Sir," Harrigan said, his hands starting to shake. "This isn't the same sort of situation. They're just going to arrest a deserter . . ."

"And Grattan was just going to arrest a Miniconjou."

"You think I did the wrong thing, sir?" Harrigan whined.

"Jesus, I almost feel sorry for the poor bastard," Dobbs said under his breath to Benoit.

"You know what I think, captain?" Kemp said his face so red Dobbs worried that he might suffer a stroke.

"N . . . n . . . no, sir."

"I think you ought to go back into civilian life, is what I think, captain. If you sent Grant off into goddamn Utah, when General Johnston has twenty-five hundred troops marching on Salt Lake City and the whole damn territory may go up in flames tomorrow, if you sent Grant and thirty-men . . ."

"Thirty-two, actually," interjected Harrigan. "He has Ashby and the German boy with him."

"Holy mother! You think that makes it better?"

"N . . . n . . . not n . . . n . . . necessarily, sir. I was just pointing out."

"Captain!" Kemp roared. "You asked me what I think. I think as I sit here tonight that I've made a grave mistake in judging your capabilities. I go away for two months and what happens? A young man who is as close to me as a son is captured and tortured by a group of bloodthirsty Indians, perhaps never," he said, shooting a glance at Dobbs, "to fully recover. At least that's the impression I have of what Lieutenant Dobbs has intimated. Although it was totally beyond your control, I'm not happy with my men being marched into the ground on an expedition with a highly questionable objective—which they apparently failed to achieve, by the way—and then not being used at all. I'm not happy that a deserter who kidnapped a congressman and made off with a small fortune in government money, was virtually under your thumb and you never even knew it . . ."

"Sir," Harrigan blustered. "I can't be everywhere at once."

"No one goddamn said you could, captain, but that's the tough part of command. As they say in the Navy, if it happened on your watch, you're responsible. I was telling you what I think and I don't want you to interrupt me again. Understand?" he roared.

"Yes, sir," Harrigan mumbled.

"*I* think," Kemp said, "your decision to send Grant into Utah was the dumbest thing I've heard since I left Washington. What I *think*, you puffed-up toady, is that you're depriving some village of its God-given right to a resident idiot. Now all of you get the hell back to your quarters. I'm going to have a cigar and brandy in solitude. And maybe even one of Frau Schmidt's cream puffs. Dismiss!"

"Damn," Benoit told Inge when they were alone in their quarters, "I used to think the upperclassmen at the Academy were good at reaming people out, but I've *never* witnessed a butt gnawing like that. And in front of all the officers—plus you and your mother—to boot."

"Poor Captain Harrigan," Inge said sadly, turning back the quilt, which was more than welcome since the nights already were appreciably cooler even though it still was officially summer. "I thought he was going to cry."

"Cry? I thought he was going to vomit. But don't feel sorry for him. He's brought it all on himself."

"That's a cruel thing to say, Jean."

"Cruel my foot. Don't forget that your brother and your stepfather-to-be are part of that detachment that Harrigan cavalierly sent off to Utah, even after Jace tried to tactfully suggest that he spend a little more time considering the options."

"Do you really think Erich and Jim are in danger?" Inge asked nervously.

Benoit looked at his wife and felt a wave of regret for his words, wishing he could bring them back into his throat. You numbskull, he said to himself, what do you want to go and get her worried for? "No," he said, trying to sound convincing. "No matter how mad the Mormons get at the soldiers they aren't going to take it out on a couple of innocent civilians, especially when one of them is little more than a boy. After all, they're God-fearing people. Their beliefs are just a little different from ours, that's all."

"I hope you're right," Inge said, looking somewhat relieved. "But if they get back all in . . ."

"*When* they get back."

"All right," Inge said, smiling. "*When*. As I was saying,

when they get back, I don't think it would be a good idea for you to let Erich hear you call him a boy."

Benoit laughed in spite of himself. "That's a good point, darling. I certainly don't want him taking after me."

"How'd it go?" Benoit asked Dobbs. He had been loitering outside the surgeon's office for twenty minutes waiting for him to return from his scheduled meeting with the colonel to brief him on Alonzo's condition.

"The only thing I can say is he's a lot calmer than he was last night. God, he was a wild man. I've never seen him like that before. He must be under a tremendous amount of pressure as well."

"He really chewed Harrigan's ass, that's for sure," Benoit commented.

"Yeah. And that bothers me, too."

"That's a strange thing for you to say. I didn't think there was any love lost between you and Harrigan."

"Oh there *isn't*. You can be sure of that. But I'm worried about what Harrigan might do. I don't want to see anyone else get hurt."

"Do? What could he possibly do?"

Dobbs shrugged. "Who knows? I'm just saying that I thought Harrigan was right at the breaking point before Kemp lit into him. No telling what might be running through his devious little mind now."

"Don't you think you might be overdramatizing it just a little?"

"Possibly." Dobbs nodded. "In any case, Harrigan was waiting outside Kemp's office when I left. Maybe they'll kiss and make up."

The thought of the burly Harrigan having any sort of physical contact with anyone, male or female, sent Benoit into a laughing fit.

"What's so funny?" Dobbs asked, staring at his friend.

"Oh, nothing," Benoit said, wiping his cheek. "I guess the strain of everything that's been happening is getting to me, too. What did you tell the colonel about Alonzo?"

"Told him the truth. What else could I say? I didn't want to trivialize it, but I didn't want to get him too upset either. I told him from a physician's point of view that Alonzo seemed to be recovering remarkably well."

"Is that all?"

"No," Dobbs said, shaking his head. "I told him about my concerns about the boy's mental state. I told him I thought some of it was perfectly natural, that it was going to take a long time for him to fully recover from an experience like that."

"And what did Kemp say?"

"He said he wanted me to go get him. That he wanted to see Alonzo face-to-face as soon as possible."

"And that's where you're going?"

"As soon as I get my kit. I need to do a routine check on the girls anyway."

"You want some company on the trip?"

"You don't have anything else to do?"

"Not when I'm on limited duty. The company's got the day off. Part of our reward for our so-called heroic duty in the battle with the Cheyenne. Most of the men are lounging around the barracks. Corporal Flannery can handle anything that comes up in the next few hours."

"You think you're up to the ride?"

Benoit laughed. "Jesus, Jace, it's only six miles."

"Okay. Let's go. We can be back by midafternoon."

They were halfway to the stables when Benoit pointed to the east. "Two Indians," he said, cupping his hand over his eyes. "Looks like they're headed straight for Old Bedlam."

"That's unusual," Dobbs mused. "Let's go see what it's all about."

"That's Red Horse and his friend," Benoit said in surprise when the two Indians got closer.

"Looks like they've been in a fight," said Dobbs, pointing to a long gash across Red Horse's ribs, beginning just below his left nipple and running downward for five or six inches.

Smiling at Red Horse to show his intentions were good, Dobbs leaned forward and ran his finger lightly along the edge of the wound, collecting some of the greasy substance that the Indian had rubbed on as a salve.

"What's that?" Benoit asked curiously.

Dobbs smelled it, then dabbed it on his tongue. Making a face, he slowly shook his head. "Damned if I know," he said. "I think it's buffalo tallow and some kind of herb, but it isn't something I've ever seen before. Wish I could see him in a week or so to determine if it works."

"His friend didn't totally escape injury either," Benoit pointed out, indicating Sad Bear's badly swollen nose and a deep cut across the back of his left hand, which also was covered with what looked to be the same salve.

"Judging from you two," Dobbs said pleasantly, "I'd hate to see the loser."

Although he did not understand the words, Red Horse sensed what Dobbs was saying. Smiling, he reached into the parfleche he had slung across his shoulder and produced two small deerskin bundles. Handing one to Sad Bear, he slowly unwrapped the other. There were two items inside, both dark brown, about three inches long and two inches wide. Both were wrinkled and covered with a thin white crust.

"That looks like salt," Dobbs said, staring.

Red Horse proffered the objects to Dobbs, inviting him to hold them.

Dobbs took them in his hand and stared at them closely. "Son of a bitch," he said softly, turning to Benoit.

"What are they?" Benoit asked.

"Ears!" Dobbs said with a smile.

While Dobbs was examining the contents of the first package, Red Horse was unwrapping the second. It contained only one object, larger and considerably more substantive. It also was dark brown and covered with salt.

Dobbs took it when Red Horse offered it to him. "Holy shit!" he said after studying it for several moments. "It's a heart."

Red Horse grinned broadly, pleased that Dobbs had apparently recognized the objects and understood their significance. Still grinning, he uttered one of the few English words he knew. "Blizzard!" he said, laughing heartily.

"Jace," Benoit said soberly once they had saddled their horses and ridden out of the post, headed southward toward the Hog Ranch, "something's been eating at me and I want to get your opinion."

"Sounds profound," Dobbs said, glancing at his friend.

"It is, Jace," he replied, spending the next twenty minutes telling Dobbs about the letters from Clement Couvillion and his sister, and about his long discussions with Jeb Stuart during the Cheyenne campaign.

"What do you think, Jace?" he asked earnestly when he had finished. "Should I resign my commission in the army and accept one in the New Orleans militia?"

Dobbs turned to stare at him, his eyes flashing.

"I can't believe you're seriously asking me that," he said angrily.

"What do you mean?" Benoit asked, taken aback.

"That you would treat your oath so lightly!" Dobbs

said furiously. "Does the army mean so little to you that you'd toss away your whole career to join—to even *consider* joining—a treasonable organization like a state militia. How could there be any doubt in your mind that the South is absolutely wrong, that the Southern insistence on continuing to practice the unconscionable custom of slavery is totally abhorrent. I can't believe that you would even think about lending your support to such an abominable cause."

"Hold on, Jace," Benoit replied, feeling his own temper rising. "I didn't say I *supported* slavery . . ."

"Then what the hell are you saying?"

"I'm saying that there's a hell of a lot more involved here than slavery."

"Tell that to Uncle Tom."

"Jesus, Jace, I can't believe you swallowed that crap from Harriet Beecher . . ."

"Swallowed it? Hell yes, I *swallowed* it. It's the goddamned . . ."

"It's about as true as that crap that John Brown is spreading . . ."

"And I guess you think it's all right to take a man and put him in chains . . ."

"Neither me nor anyone else in my family has ever . . ."

"So that makes it justifiable. It makes slavery . . ."

"Jace, let's get away from the slavery issue for just a minute. What about state's rights?"

"State's rights my ass!" Dobbs spat, his face reddening. "That's just an excuse by those power-hungry plantation owners . . ."

"They're not all plantation owners, Jace. Some Southerners actually *believe* that the federal government should not be the controlling power, that . . ."

"That goes against the Constitution . . ."

"*Your* interpretation of the Constitution . . ."

"And you've taken an oath to uphold the Constitution . . ."

"But I never took an oath to sell my soul to a group of greedy, money-hungry Northern politicians . . ."

"Yes, you did! You vowed to fight to uphold that Constitution. To give your life . . ."

"But if I don't believe what the politicians are saying, Jace. If I don't . . ."

"That isn't your decision to make. You're an army officer, for Christ's sake. You have a responsibility . . ."

"What about my responsibility to my family? To my brother? Do you think I want to take up arms against my brother? Against all my . . ."

"It isn't what you *want*, you thick-headed imbecile. It's what you've sworn . . ."

"Jace!" Benoit said, reining his horse to a stop. "Forget what I asked you. I think it's better if we drop the whole goddamned thing. Otherwise, in about two minutes we're going to be swinging at each other . . ."

"If that's what it takes to make you see reason . . ."

"Goddamnit, Jace, let's just drop it," Benoit said angrily. For several minutes they sat glaring at each other.

"Okay," Dobbs said at length. "I think you're right. It's not something we need to discuss right now."

"I'm glad you agree with *something* I've said," Benoit added, urging his horse forward. Good God, Benoit thought, staring at a dollar-sized white spot between his horse's ears, no wonder this country is so divided. If two old friends can't even talk calmly about the greatest threat to this country's existence that has ever been, it's no wonder strangers are at each other's throats.

For the rest of the way to the Hog Ranch, they rode in silence.

"How you feeling, Alonzo?" Dobbs asked cheerfully, banishing the argument with Benoit from his thoughts.

"Not bad," he replied, smiling in return. "Better than I did last week, anyway."

"Let me see your wound," Dobbs said, gently lifting the young man's arm. "Uuummm," he said, turning it this way and that. "It seems to be healing well. Is it giving you any problems?"

"It itches like hell," DeAlonzo replied. "And I keep thinking I feel pain in my hand but it isn't even there."

"That's normal," Dobbs replied. "You'll be feeling that for quite awhile. How you doing otherwise?" he asked, looking at him carefully.

"Let's take a walk," DeAlonzo said, looking quickly around the room. "Ellen's made a little hideaway out back, a place where the girls can go when they feel the need for a little privacy. It ain't fancy . . ."

"Lead the way," Dobbs replied. "By the way, where's Narcissa?"

"In the bar," DeAlonzo said. "I think she's chatting with Lieutenant Benoit."

"Okay," Dobbs replied. "Let's go for that walk."

"What is it you wanted to tell me?" he asked five minutes later, sinking into one of the rough wooden chairs Ellen had placed strategically around a smooth spot just on the far side of a small hillock. The space was just large enough for four chairs, which had been cobbled together by a carpenter from Fort Laramie in return for services rendered. The spot was designed as a sort of outdoor parlor to give the girls a place to relax and talk among themselves without being overheard by the steady stream of customers that poured into the establishment. The chairs were set facing west, looking out over a broad, flat plain dotted with juniper and stunted pines. In the evening, it was a wonderful place to come and watch the spectacular sunsets.

"I'm not quite sure how to express this," DeAlonzo said. "I was always better with a brush than I was with words."

Dobbs grunted noncommittally.

"You know," DeAlonzo said, nervously fingering a small stone he had scooped out of the dust, "that I was raised a strict Roman Catholic?"

"Doesn't surprise me." Dobbs smiled. "What with a name like Alonzo DeAlonzo."

"Yeah." DeAlonzo smiled. "Us paisans are big on Catholicism. At least my parents are. I kind of got away from the faith, though. Quit going to Mass. Quit taking the sacraments. Especially quit going to confession," he said, trying to sound lighthearted.

"Get to the point, Al," Dobbs prompted.

"There really isn't a point, I guess," DeAlonzo said softly. "It's just that the whole, uh, *experience*—is that the right word?"

"It'll do."

"Well, the whole time Blizzard was torturing me all I wanted to do was die."

"I can understand that."

"But not if you're a Catholic. Suicide is strictly forbidden. A suicide can't even be buried in consecrated ground."

He's rambling, Dobbs thought. But he seems to know which direction he's going in.

"But that never even crossed my mind when that son of a bitch was chopping off my fingers. The forbidden aspects of suicide, that is."

"I know what you mean," Dobbs added softly.

"It was only later. Once I was down here with Narcissa. She's a great girl, by the way," he said enthusiastically. "She's been wonderful to me."

Dobbs nodded without speaking.

"But once I was through the initial physical pain, I got to thinking about the spiritual side. Narcissa kept telling me to quit feeling sorry for myself, but she's not a Catholic so she didn't know the words a priest would use. If I had been home, Father Costello would have told me to concentrate on regaining my faith. Narcissa was saying the same thing. I had to quit looking at the bad side . . ."

"Very sensible," Dobbs said, feeling his spirits rise.

"So I started praying again. First time in years and years. And I started remembering all those stories I had heard in catechism. Those stories about the saints and martyrs. When I was a kid, I figured it was all bullshit, all that talk about how the Christians marched into the coliseum and faced the lions rather than give up their faith. I figured it was all just a big sales pitch to make us happy little Catholics. You understand?"

"I'm not a Catholic, but I understand," Dobbs empathized.

"No you don't!" DeAlonzo said forcefully. "You can't really until you've been through something like this."

"I lost my wife," Dobbs confided. "I know what loss is."

"Oh, I'm sorry," DeAlonzo said quickly. "I didn't realize."

"No way you could have known. But go ahead."

"Well, I started to think about all those saints and how much *they* suffered. When you put events in that perspective, losing a hand isn't too serious."

A-ha, Dobbs thought, the light dawns.

"I mean, it isn't the end of the world or anything. I still have one good hand. And I have my mind and my eye. Particularly my eye since an artist depends so heavily on his ability to visualize concepts. You understand?"

Dobbs nodded.

"And I have Narcissa, too. In other words, I've lost a

hand, but I've regained my faith. And as far as I'm concerned, that's more than a fair trade. Does that sound foolish?"

"Not to me." Dobbs grinned. "Not at all. And I'm sure it won't sound strange to Colonel Kemp. He's anxious about you, you know."

"I heard he was coming back soon."

"Got in yesterday. I met with him this morning and he wants to see you right away."

"Okay, let me go tell Narcissa I'm going to be riding up to the fort," he said, pushing himself out of the chair.

"Just a second," Dobbs said, laying his hand on his arm. "Just so I'm sure I understand you. You're going to keep on painting?"

"I'm gonna try." DeAlonzo nodded. "I'm going to see if I can learn to use my left hand."

"We might be able to devise a suitable prosthesis."

"Let's take that as it comes. The Lord will tell me what He wants."

"Does this painting include Indians?" Dobbs asked, watching DeAlonzo carefully.

"I d . . . d . . . don't know about that yet," he stuttered.

"Take your time in deciding," Dobbs said. "By the way, you may want to know that we got confirmation this morning that Blizzard's dead. The two Brulé who brought the soldiers to rescue you tracked him down and killed him."

DeAlonzo stared at Dobbs for several seconds.

"What I'm going to say may sound like a contradiction to everything I've told you," he said slowly.

"Try me."

DeAlonzo looked up. Dobbs saw that his eyes were burning. "I'm glad!" he said emphatically. "I hope that fucker suffered."

Dobbs laughed. "Don't say that to Father . . ."

"Lieutenant Dobbs!" a woman's voice called.

"It's Narcissa," DeAlonzo said in surprise.

"Lieutenant Dobbs," she said, hurrying to meet them. "You'd better come."

"Calm down, Narcissa," Dobbs said, grabbing her elbows. "Speak slowly and tell me what's happened."

Narcissa took two deep breaths. "It's Captain Harrigan . . ." she began.

"Captain Harrigan?" Dobbs asked, puzzled. "What about him?"

"He just rode up. He looked awful mad. Went storming into Miss Ellen's office, looking like he was going to bite her head off. Lieutenant Benoit went in right after him. They're all yelling . . ."

She was speaking to an empty spot; Dobbs was already running back to the building.

The first person he saw when he burst through the door was Ellen. She was standing behind her desk, leaning forward with all the weight on her arms. Her face was whiter than Dobbs had ever seen it.

"What the hell . . ." he began. Before he could finish the sentence, he saw Benoit, who was standing off to the side with his hands in the air.

"Come in, lieutenant," said a voice that Dobbs hardly recognized. "We've all been waiting for you."

Standing behind the door was Harrigan, his service revolver in his right hand. It was pointed straight at Ellen.

"What's this all about?" Dobbs said quickly, trying to sound authoritative.

"It's about you, you stupid, hardheaded son of a bitch," Harrigan barked, his voice three octaves higher than normal. To Dobbs, he sounded like a boy going through puberty. But there was nothing boyish about his eyes, which shone with the ferocity of a madman. Dobbs took in the scene, struggling to keep from panicking. His first thought, once he got his emotions under control, was that he had been correct; Harrigan had been unable to stand the pressure and had cracked like a pecan.

"You argument's with me then?" he asked, fighting to exude a calmness he did not feel.

"You're goddamned right it's with you."

"Then why don't you let them go," Dobbs said, nodding at Ellen and Benoit. "So we can discuss this in private."

Harrigan emitted what was supposed to be a laugh. To Dobbs it sounded like a mule braying.

"Close the door," he said, gesturing with the pistol. "Let's keep this cozy."

Dobbs kicked the door shut. "Don't you realize what you're doing, captain?" he asked, deciding to try reason.

"What are they going to do?" Harrigan asked, grinning horribly. "Take my rank away? Kemp already has ended my career. You heard him. The whole goddamned world heard him."

"He wasn't himself," Dobbs said, hoping to sound con- ciliatory. "He was tired after the long trip. Once he's had some sleep and has had a chance to think about it, he'll chance his mind."

"Oh, no," Harrigan said, waving the pistol like a schoolmarm's finger. "He repeated it all in his office this morning. Went through all my reports on what has hap- pened while he was gone. When he finished, he said the papers just confirmed what he had thought: that I'd fucked up royally and my career in the army was as good as over."

"Let me talk to him," Dobbs said soothingly.

"Why?" Harrigan said, making another attempt at a laugh. "You think you're God? You think you can get the mighty Colonel Kemp to reverse himself?"

"Well . . ."

"I don't know what it is about you, Dobbs. You have a vision of yourself as a goddamned paragon. You're not a bad doctor, at least as far as sawing off limbs goes, but you pretend to be a philosopher and a wise man. As far as I can tell, though, you're just a wise ass."

"Certainly some of what you say . . ."

"Don't try to patronize me, you son of a bitch," Harrigan said, shifting the pistol threateningly. "You try to make yourself out to be a very moral man, someone who has the power of life and death in his hands. But underneath you're just a filthy whoremonger."

Dobbs felt his face flush, his heart quicken. Control it! he told himself. Don't let him get to you! "I'm sorry you feel that way . . ." he mumbled, struggling to command his feelings.

"Oh, but I do," Harrigan said, nodding vigorously. "You see, I've been thinking about this for quite a long time."

"Thinking about what?"

"How I can humiliate you in front of your woman. Make her see what a coward and a two-faced prick you really are."

Dobbs looked at Benoit, who was shaking his head from side to side. Dobbs interpreted it to mean don't do anything.

"You see, Dobbs, I want you to grovel. I want you to get on your knees and beg me to be good to you, to apologize for all the bad things you said about me."

"I didn't say anything bad about you," Dobbs said, as placatingly as he could manage.

"Oh, yes, you have. I've heard what you say behind my back . . ."

A hard pounding on the door interrupted him.

"Everything all right in there?" DeAlonzo yelled through the thin panel.

"Tell him to go away," Harrigan hissed at Ellen.

"It's all right," she said weakly, so low that DeAlonzo could not hear.

Not getting any response, DeAlonzo turned the knob and swung open the door. Harrigan, who had been standing close behind it, was knocked temporarily off balance.

Seeing his predicament, Ellen tore open her desk drawer, frantically reaching for the pistol she always kept there as protection against rowdy customers.

"No!" Dobbs screamed at Ellen, lunging for Harrigan.

Turning more quickly than Dobbs had thought he could, Harrigan swung his revolver like a club, catching Dobbs a solid blow behind his right ear. The surgeon dropped to his knees, then fell forward on his face, unconscious.

Harrigan lifted his pistol and aimed it at Ellen, who had her pistol in her hands and was aiming it at his chest. Harrigan fired before she did. His bullet, fired at point-blank range, caught her squarely in the chest, driving her back into the wall. With little more than a gasp, she slid to the floor, dropping the pistol on the desk as she fell.

Shocked into action, DeAlonzo bent over and charged at the captain, ramming his head into Harrigan's groin.

Yelling in rage and pain, Harrigan kicked DeAlonzo to the floor, pointing the pistol at his head.

Benoit, who had scooped Ellen's pistol off her desk, aimed it at Harrigan and yelled.

"Stop! Don't make me kill you!"

Harrigan gaped in a kind of rictus of alarm. Ignoring DeAlonzo, he raised his pistol and aimed it at Benoit, his finger tightening on the trigger.

Both weapons went off at the same time. Harrigan's bullet zinged over Benoit's head, creasing the scalp as it went by. Benoit's, however, struck home. Hitting the tip of Harrigan's nose, it blew off the back of his head and sent his feet flying in front of him, looking, Benoit thought, like an acrobat trying to make a back flip.

"Jesus God!" DeAlonzo gasped, taking a quick look around the smoke-filled room which smelled heavily of gunpowder, blood, and feces, since Harrigan's bowels had emptied when he died.

When Benoit saw a second shot would not be necessary, he lowered the pistol and ran behind the desk to examine Ellen, realizing with a quick glance that there was nothing he could do.

Vaulting over the furniture, he turned Dobbs on his back. "Thank God," he sighed in relief when his friend moved, bringing his hands to his face and shaking his head.

"Are you all right?" Benoit asked anxiously, wiping the blood from his face.

"I think so," Dobbs replied. "What about Ellen?"

Benoit stared at him dumbly. "I can't understand you," he said. "What did you say?"

"Don't you speak English?" Dobbs said peevishly, his words mostly incomprehensible.

When he removed his hands from his face and looked up, Benoit found himself gawking at a cruel caricature of his friend. Dobbs's right eye was open wider than Benoit thought possible and tears were streaming down his cheek. From the nose over, the right half of his face sagged sharply downward and his mouth seemed to have shifted an inch or more to the left.

"Where's Ellen?" he tried to say. "Is Ellen all right?"

Benoit just gaped at him, unable to understand a word.

~*13*~

Benoit busied himself with the coffee, using the opportunity to study the two men who sat hunched over the table: Dobbs and DeAlonzo.

How they have changed, he thought, spooning water over the freshly ground beans. There's the man who wanted to be the world's next great painter of the noble Indian, a man who three months ago thought he knew exactly where his future lay, now a confused, one-handed wretch consumed by a newly-emerged religious fervor that borders on the obsessive. And next to him is one of the most gifted people I've ever known, a first-rate surgeon and dedicated scholar, reduced by the unpredictable actions of a maniac to a tragic shell of a man.

"Isn't that coffee ready yet?" Dobbs asked grumpily, prodding Benoit from his reverie.

It's been almost a month since the incident at the Hog Ranch, Benoit reminded himself, but I still can't get used to the new, constantly irascible Jason Dobbs. "Coming up, Jace," he said, trying to sound cheerful. "You want it real fast or real good?"

"And don't forget my implement," Dobbs added, turning his disfigured face toward his friend.

The blow that Harrigan had delivered with the pistol behind the surgeon's right ear had triggered a horrific change in Dobbs's physical condition. Two days later, in an attempt to explain what had happened, he had dragged Benoit into his office and made him sit. Striding to his shelf of reference books, he had returned with a thick text that he plopped in front of his friend. Flipping it open to a previously marked page, he had pointed with a shaky finger at a diagram depicting the human neural network. It was a facial nerve that was damaged, he said, tracing its location on the drawing, pointing out how it emerges from the brain through a small hole in the skull near the ear. When Harrigan hit him, it evidently pinched the nerve. The result was a paralysis—a palsy, he had called it—to half of his face. His right eye was frozen open, forcing him to wear a patch day and night. Also, since the right side of his face, including the corner of his mouth, was also frozen, there was a steady stream of saliva drooling down his chin. Wherever Dobbs went, he had to carry a kerchief to mop the dribble.

There was pain as well, he had explained to Benoit in the slurred, drunken man's voice caused by the lost ability to control his lips and tongue, an ever-present ache behind his ear which was worse than an abscessed tooth. But perhaps the cruelest blow of all was the partial loss of taste that turned the best of Frau Schmidt's meals into pap, that and the inability to drink directly from a cup or bottle. To consume Benoit's coffee, he had to slurp it through a reed, a device that Dobbs always referred to as his "implement."

"Here we are," Benoit said briskly, carrying two demitasse cups of coffee to the table.

"About time," grumbled Dobbs, reaching for a bottle of

dark liquid that sat on a shelf behind him. Eagerly, it seemed to DeAlonzo, Dobbs splashed a healthy measure of the liquid to his cup.

"What's that?" he asked inquisitively.

"A dollop of laudanum," Dobbs replied, speaking slowly so Benoit would not have to interpret. "It helps the pain here," he said, touching the area behind his ear, "and here," he added, slapping his chest over his heart. Sticking the reed in the cup, he sucked slowly, seemingly inhaling the dark liquid.

DeAlonzo shook his head sympathetically. "It must be very trying for you," he said, "but from what Jean has told me at least you have some hope of recovery. That's more encouraging than this," he said, waving the stump of his right arm. "I'll never grow another hand."

Awkwardly, he lifted his cup with his remaining hand, bringing it to his lips in a jittery movement that threatened to send the coffee splashing over the rim. Leaning forward, holding the cup well over the table, he took a small sip.

"You're becoming fairly proficient," Dobbs said, watching as DeAlonzo slowly and deliberately returned the cup to the saucer. "With practice, you're going to get better every day. In a year, you'll be using your left hand almost as well as you did your right. But there's nothing I can do about this," he said, pointing at his face, "except wait and see."

"It's going to heal itself, Jace," Benoit said encouragingly. "You told me so yourself."

"No," Dobbs said sharply. "What I said was *maybe* it will heal itself. The medical literature says about ninety percent of the victims of this facial nerve palsy eventually recover. But it may take as long as two years and recovery isn't always total. The difference between me and Alonzo is he can learn to paint with his left hand, but my recovery has to be complete. As long as this situation persists, I can't perform as a surgeon. This paralysis may not be life-threatening, but it could end my career. The colonel has put me on temporary leave, but sooner or later he's going to need someone who's fully capable."

"Don't even think about that, Jace," Benoit interjected confidently. "The snow's going to start flying pretty soon and we'll all be stuck here for the winter. You don't have to worry about being replaced before at least next spring."

"That's a lot of consolation," Dobbs grumbled.

Anxious to change the subject, Benoit turned to DeAlonzo. "How about you? I heard a rumor that you're going Back East."

"At least for awhile," DeAlonzo confirmed. "I feel this sudden need to see my fathers."

"*Fathers?*" Benoit asked, surprised. "Plural?"

"Yes," DeAlonzo replied with a smile. "Two of them. My natural father and Father Costello."

"Who's Father Costello?" Benoit asked, frowning.

"My parish priest," DeAlonzo said. "I told Jace about him the afternoon of the sho . . . ah, the afternoon when he was at the Hog Ranch."

"It's all right," Dobbs said. "You can say 'shooting.' The word doesn't add to my misery."

"Father Costello was my spiritual counselor when I was growing up," DeAlonzo explained. "I didn't pay much attention to him then, but now I think I'm ready for his advice. I want to talk to him about the reemergence of my faith."

In an unconscious movement, he reached into his shirt and removed his totem, the small prism he had carried since he was a boy. Idly swinging it back and forth, he watched as it caught the light and sent beams of color dancing around the small room. "I don't know why Blizzard never took this," he said distractedly. "Maybe he didn't know I had it or how much it meant to me. Anyway," he added, shaking his head like a wet dog, "as I was saying, I need to talk to Father Costello about something that has been nagging at me for the last few weeks. I've been thinking of maybe entering the seminary."

"The *seminary*?" Benoit said, his jaw dropping. "What about Narcissa?"

"A wonderful woman," DeAlonzo admitted. "She's going back with me. Now that the Hog Ranch has closed . . ."

"It won't be closed long," said Dobbs. "There's too much need for entertainment of that type out here. It just needs the right woman to come in and take it over."

Benoit watched as the surgeon wiped his cheeks, not sure if he was removing the tears that flowed unchecked as a result of the injury or tears that were caused by the memory of his loss.

Again DeAlonzo nodded. "As I was saying, Narcissa is going to go with me. I want my father, make that *both* of my fathers, to meet her."

Benoit could not resist a chuckle. "Don't you think it's rather strange to be taking Narcissa to meet your priest?"

"You mean because she's a whore?"

"Well." Benoit blushed. "I g . . . g . . . guess so. The whole idea seems a little odd to me."

"Mary Magdalene was a whore," DeAlonzo said. "Just because Narcissa had to sell her body to survive doesn't mean she's evil. She's saved my life. I was this close," he said, holding his thumb and forefinger a quarter of an inch apart, "from killing myself. But she took care of me and gave me new reasons to live. All Mary Magdalene ever did was wash Jesus' feet."

"I can see your point," Benoit said flushing.

"Narcissa loves the west," DeAlonzo continued. "I guess I do, too, but it certainly hasn't turned out to be what I expected."

"Amen to that," Dobbs mumbled.

"When I first came out here, I was full of idealism. My admiration of the Indians, based entirely on the portraits I had seen and the images I had created in my imagination, was without bounds. I had this conception of how they were a perfect people living in a veritable paradise. I had to learn the hard way that, while they have many, many fine traits, they are still just people. Like you and me and Jace and Uncle Al, we all have our strengths and our weaknesses. They have their bad people just like we do, but that doesn't mean they're all bad. Just as the fact that I met some wonderful Indians doesn't mean they're all good."

"That's a remarkably rational view," Dobbs said, "especially considering your experience."

"God helped me see that," said DeAlonzo. "I still feel my destiny is out here. But before I continue to pursue it, I need some advice."

"How does Narcissa feel about you going to see this priest and talking to him about possibly entering the seminary? Or haven't you told her?" asked Benoit.

"Of course, I've told her," DeAlonzo said, surprised at the question. "She's fully in favor of it. She thinks this religion thing—that's what she calls it, my religious thing—is something I need to deal with before I can fully recover from the experience. She wants me to face it now rather than later. She . . ." He paused. "What's that commotion?"

"I don't know," Benoit said, running to the window. "But it sure sounds like something's going on."

"Let me see," said DeAlonzo, who had to stand on his toes to peer out.

"It's Grant," Benoit said, turning excitedly to Dobbs. "The Utah detachment's coming in."

"Well, I guess we'd best go see what their fate has been," Dobbs said, rising unsteadily to his feet. "I just hope to hell they don't need my services."

"They sure don't look very *happy*," Benoit said as the three of them rushed onto the parade ground.

Colonel Kemp, who obviously had advance warning of the detachment's arrival, was waiting in front of the flag-pole to formally welcome them home. Already the crowd was starting to form behind him. In the front row, over Kemp's shoulder, Benoit could see Inge and her mother. When Inge saw him, she came running over, grabbing his hands and forcing him into a little jig. "I see Erich and Jim," she said happily. "They've come back all right."

Benoit quickly counted the troops. "They're *all* there," he said in relief. "I guess our worries were for naught."

"Do you see any extra?" Dobbs asked, straining to see clearly with his good left eye.

"What do you mean?"

"I mean did they bring back Henderson? The man they went to get."

"Oh, shit," said Benoit. "I've been concentrating so hard on the possibility that they might have to fight the Mormons that I'd completely forgotten about Henderson."

"I don't see him," said Dobbs. "Maybe they hanged him on the spot."

"Oh, they wouldn't do that," Benoit replied, sounding somewhat uncertain. "But they could have been in a shoot-out, I guess."

"I guess we'll find out soon enough," said Dobbs, smil-ing ruefully.

As the crowd cheered and waved, the detachment filed into the compound, crossing the parade ground and coming to a stop at the base of the flagpole. To Benoit's eye, they looked dusty, tired, and dispirited. Most of the men rode with their chins on their chest, as if they had been many hours in the saddle, and Grant, for the first time since Benoit had known him, was unshaven and long-faced, an unnatural condition for the normally ebullient soldier.

"Something's wrong," Benoit told Dobbs, a note of concern creeping into his voice. "Something just isn't right."

Although the crowd continued to cheer, the men stared at them vacantly, seemingly exhausted beyond the point of jubilation.

"I'd say they all need about forty-eight hours of sleep," Dobbs commented, watching with his one good eye as Grant dismounted and walked stiffly up to Kemp. Despite his fatigue, the lieutenant popped to attention and presented a snappy salute.

"At ease, lieutenant," Kemp said, returning the tribute. "I can see you're about dead on your feet but as long as everybody's here and curious as hell, why don't you tell us briefly what the hell happened over there."

"Nothing, sir," Grant said, disgust evident in his voice.

"Nothing?" Kemp asked, raising an eyebrow. "What do you mean 'nothing?'"

"I mean we, that is me and the troopers, never got into Utah at all. When we got to the border we discovered that Brigham Young had declared martial law just the day before and all army troops were prohibited from entering the Territory."

"And you didn't try to push that, did you?" he asked, looking closely at Grant.

"No, *sir*! I may be ambitious but I'm not crazy."

"Very wise of you, Grant." Kemp smiled. "But tell me quickly about Henderson. I notice you don't have a prisoner."

"No, sir. As I just said, the border was closed, but only to soldiers. That didn't include civilians. When we found we couldn't proceed, Mr. Ashby and young Erich asked if

they could go on and try to find him on their own. It was
clearly above and beyond, colonel."

"Sure as hell was. I hope you told 'em no."

Grant shook his head. "No, sir, I didn't. I figured we'd
come all that way and we weren't going to come back
empty-handed, so I let 'em go. I had tremendous confidence in 'em, sir," he added. "And my judgment proved
correct."

Kemp shook his head and sighed. "But they weren't
successful, I take it."

"Not exactly, sir."

Kemp looked at Grant curiously. Accustomed to dealing with political ambiguities, the colonel caught something in Grant's tone that indicated there was more to the
situation than what the lieutenant was saying.

"What precisely do you mean by 'not exactly,' lieutenant? I think you'd best explain that."

"Sir," Grant said, sagging just a bit, Benoit thought, "I
think it'd be better if Mr. Ashby explained. He was the
one that conducted the search, not me."

Kemp scanned the faces, looking for Ashby. "Ah, there
you are," he said, spotting him toward the rear of the
detachment. "Mr. Ashby, would you please come forward?"

Ashby nudged his pony to the front, stopping in front
of Kemp.

"I understand you and Mr. Schmidt went into Utah
after this deserter."

"Yessir," Ashby mumbled, making it one word.

"Well, did you find him?"

"Sorta," Ashby replied, shifting his wad of tobacco.

"Well, Jesus Christ man! Either you did or you didn't."

"Beggin' your pardon, colonel," Ashby drawled, "but
it's kinda a long story."

Kemp looked at him carefully. "In that case, Mr.

Ashby," he said crisply, "maybe you'd better come into
my office, have a seat and a glass of brandy while you
explain it all to me."

Ashby grinned. "I think that'd be right nice of you,
colonel."

Kemp waited until after dinner to share with the men
what Ashby had told him.

Once the dinner plates had been taken away and Frau
Schmidt, soon to be Frau Ashby, proudly marched in with
a still-warm *Schwarzwälder Kirschtorte*, a chocolate layer
cake filled with cream and cherries and flavored with
cherry brandy that she had obtained in trade from a
German emigrant passing through and had been saving
for a special occasion, Kemp rapped sharply on his water
glass.

"All of you know I don't much like making speeches,"
Kemp said, clearing his throat, "so I'll try to keep this as
objective as possible. But it won't be easy because I'm
mighty riled."

Benoit glanced at the slice of cake that sat untouched in
front of Dobbs.

"You going to eat that?" he whispered.

Dobbs shook his head almost imperceptibly and
pushed the plate in front of Benoit. "You don't know how
badly I wish I could," he said.

"All of you men know," Kemp said soberly, "how I've
always been a defender of the Mormon emigrants. While
other officers along the trail have shown a little, shall we
say contempt, for them, I've always felt they were as entitled to our protection just as much as anyone else."

Benoit and Dobbs exchanged glances, wondering what
Kemp was leading up to.

"But the report that Mr. Ashby gave me about his

excursion into Utah makes me wonder if all those others weren't right and I was wrong."

"Sir," said Adamson, preparing to mouth a question.

"Later, Zack!" Kemp said sternly. "Let me finish."

Adamson sagged back in his chair.

Kemp struggled to regroup his thoughts, staring vacantly over the men's heads for what seemed to Benoit to be an awfully long time.

"Okay," he said finally, his eyes coming back into focus. "Here's the story in a nutshell. I don't know how to dress it up, even if I wanted to."

Taking a deep breath, he plunged ahead. "That wagon train which we believed Henderson was with, the so-called Fancher train, was ambushed in a resting spot in southern Utah called Mountain Meadows . . ."

"By Indians?" Strudelmeyer said loudly.

Kemp nodded, angry at the intrusion. "Yes, god-damnit, the Paiutes were involved. But that's only half the story. Now let me finish without being interrupted. The next man who breaks in before I'm through is going to be conducting a prairie dog census for the next month.

"As I was *saying*," he continued, glaring around the room, "the emigrants were attacked, first by Indians and then by Mormons."

"Mormons? Attacking emigrants?" Dobbs gasped, the implication striking him like another blow to the head.

"I can see you're all shocked," Kemp said. "So was I. I couldn't figure out why the hell Mormons might want to attack a wagon train. As it turns out, they didn't really *attack* the train; it's more complicated than that."

If Kemp wanted the men's attention, he had it. A naked woman could have walked through the door and not an eye would have left Kemp's face.

"From what Mr. Ashby was able to put together—and it was a damn impressive bit of digging, I might add—

this is what happened: As the emigrants passed through Utah there was quite a bit of anger in their wake. Part of it, I'm sure, is a result of all the mess that has been stirred up by Washington. Maybe the emigrants themselves were not entirely blameless. But for whatever reason there was a lot of resentment floating around. Not that it excuses what happened.

"The train was almost out of the Territory when the wagon master, Alf Stuart, a generally detestable human being as some of you know, decided to call a halt at a popular camping spot called Mountain Meadows. Apparently, it had been a long, hard trip and Stuart wanted everyone to be fresh for the final push over the mountains and into California.

"As far as anybody knows, they weren't harming anybody, just camped peacefully to give the stock the chance to graze while they made final repairs to the wagons. They had been there a couple of days when they were attacked by a band of Paiutes."

"By God, that sounds familiar," Adamson whispered to Strudelmeyer.

Kemp shot the pair an angry glance, then picked up the narrative.

"The Paiutes weren't strong enough to overrun the camp, so they fought for a little bit before things settled into a standoff. The Indians couldn't win and the emigrants couldn't leave. That's when a Mormon muckety-muck, the resident Indian agent I'm told, came into the emigrant camp under a flag of truce. After meeting with Fancher and Stuart, this man, whose name is Lee, worked out a compromise. He told them the Indians would allow them safe passage as long as they were escorted out of the area by a group of Mormon militia.

"That must have sounded like a pretty good deal to Stuart and Fancher 'cause they said okay. After a bit, the militiamen showed up and Lee organized the march. Women and children were loaded into wagons and they went out first. The male emigrants were each assigned to a militiaman and the plan was for them to follow the wagons on foot.

"They started marching out, but they hadn't gone very far when Lee called a halt. At his command, the escorts opened fire on the male emigrants and other militiamen began slaughtering the women and any child old enough to understand what was happening. The gunfire was the signal for the Paiutes to come storming in, killing any emigrant who wasn't already dead. They must have had a good old time butchering, scalping, and raping. When they were finished, they left the bodies lying on the Plains to rot."

Kemp leaned back in his chair, looking suddenly exhausted. "That's about all we know right now. But I want to say if it's the truth—and I have no reason to doubt that it isn't—it'll go down in history as one of the most dastardly deeds ever perpetrated in the west. I don't want to get started talking about how these so-called God-loving Mormons could ever do something so horrible because I might be doing them a big injustice. But it'll eventually come out. You can bet on it. And that's all I want to say about it unless some of you have some questions."

For several minutes, the officers sat in stunned silence, each trying to come to his own terms with the information.

"Sir," Adamson said after what seemed like a long time. "Are we sure they're really dead? That they didn't just go ahead and cross the mountains and disappear into California?"

Kemp shook his head. "Mr. Ashby saw the bodies."

"What's the casualty count?" asked Strudelmeyer.

Kemp shrugged. "Nobody knows for sure. By the time Mr. Ashby got there, it was a week or so after the massacre. The scavengers had been at the corpses. It was damn near impossible to get an exact count, but he figures there were a hundred and eighteen or a hundred and twenty men, women and children. Some of the real little ones are rumored to have been spared but no one knows where they are. They've just sort of disappeared. Any more questions?"

Dobbs whispered to Benoit, who turned to Kemp. "Sir," he said, "should we assume that Henderson was among those killed?"

Kemp bobbed his head. "Good question, lieutenant. I think the answer is yes. If the information about Henderson being with the group is correct we have to assume he was still with 'em when they were massacred. There's no basis for assuming that he would have stayed behind in Utah, since the Mormons don't want anyone there other than fellow Mormons. We haven't recovered the payroll money, and I doubt we ever will, but we have to reckon he's dead."

Kemp looked around the room, watching the men as they talked excitedly among themselves. Picking up his knife, he rapped on his water glass a second time. "I'm not through for the night, gentlemen."

When they had settled into a respectful silence, he reached into a case that was sitting on the floor beside his chair and extracted a sheaf of papers.

"These are copies of General Sumner's reports on the Cheyenne Expedition which were forwarded to me from Fort Leavenworth. I just got 'em this afternoon. Since so many of you were part of the fiasco I thought you might want to hear what happened after you turned around."

"Hip, hip, hooray!" Adamson said loudly, pounding on the table.

"Control your enthusiasm, lieutenant," Kemp said somberly. "It isn't a very pretty picture either. I'll give you the highlights," he said, flipping through the papers.

"A day or so after you left, Sumner took the cavalry after the Cheyenne. He didn't find them, but he found their village, or what was left of it. There were about three hundred lodges still there and he burned 'em all, along with all the buffalo meat the Indians had been saving for the winter. Eventually, they wound up at Bent's New Fort, where Sumner commandeered the wagon train that was carrying the annuities for, among others, the Cheyenne. He distributed the goods to the other tribes, but he seized the Cheyenne's share, destroying the arms and ammunition on the spot. Then they went on back to Fort Leavenworth. They never did find any sizable group of Cheyenne they could fight with."

"What does all this mean, colonel?" Adamson asked. "Was all our effort wasted?"

Kemp nodded grimly. "Pretty much, lieutenant. The way I see it, nobody's happy now. Sumner is furious because he couldn't kill any more Cheyenne and the Cheyenne are bitter because the army came looking for 'em in the first place, not to mention the fact that some of their best warriors were killed and their winter supplies destroyed. So they're not only wounded, they're in danger of mass starvation. If you want my prediction, it's this: The trouble has only begun."

"Why do you say that, colonel?" Strudelmeyer asked.

"It's simple, son," Kemp said with a sigh. "The other tribes are going to look at what Sumner's done to the Cheyenne . . . they're going to remember what Harney did to the Lakota . . . and they aren't going to be feeling very friendly toward the army. I still say much of this could have been avoided if it hadn't been for those numbskulls in Washington. But that's the way it is. The politicians start the wars and we have to fight 'em. It isn't going to change in my time and it isn't going to change in yours. My prediction is, it's only going to get worse. Add the Indian troubles to what's going on Back East over slavery and state's rights and talk of secession and a war between the states, and I'm afraid I end up a mighty pessimistic man."

Benoit turned to Dobbs, intending to ask his opinion. "Jace," he began, then stopped, watching as Dobbs lowered his coffee cup below the table and surreptitiously filled it with a brown liquid poured from a small silver flask.

"What's that?" he whispered, his brow furrowing.

"What?" Dobbs said, surprised.

"What's that in the flask?"

"Just some medicine," Dobbs said. "For the ache in my head."

"Laudanum again?"

"What if it is?" Dobbs whispered back.

"I think you ought to go easy on that stuff," Benoit said, looking worried.

"Well," Dobbs said slowly, staring at Benoit with his good eye, "what I think is you ought to mind your own damn business."

Benoit shook his head sadly. Before he could reply, Inge came over and whispered in his ear. "Okay," Benoit said, nodding.

"Colonel Kemp," he asked loudly.

"Yes, Ben-oight, what is it?"

"Begging your indulgence, sir," he said with uncharacteristic reticence, "do the reports from Colonel Sumner say anything about Werner and Wilhelm?"

Kemp sighed heavily. "Jesus Christ, Ben-oight, I've been hearing about those two kids ever since I've been here and I reckon it's about time we put the issue to rest.

Those boys are *gone*, you understand. G-O-N-E! They've disappeared somewhere up in the Black Hills with a bunch of people that now hate the sight of us. The army and the Cheyenne are at war. That shouldn't be too difficult for you to comprehend. If we ever see those kids again, it'll be purely by accident. And if you ask me about them one more time, you'll be cleaning horse stalls all winter. Do I make myself clear, Ben-oight?"

"Yes, sir," Benoit said, his face turning scarlet. "Perfectly, sir."

After dinner none of the officers hung around the dining room as they usually did, clustering around like old women exchanging gossip and opinions. Sobered by the evening's developments, they all hurried back to their quarters, seemingly half in shock.

"It's getting colder," Inge said, pulling her shawl more tightly about her as she and Benoit hurried across the parade ground, headed for their own tiny room.

"I smell winter," Benoit said, sticking his nose in the air. "You think it's too late to light the stove?"

"I don't know about you, but I'm going to bed," Inge replied. "I want morning to hurry up and be here. Maybe tomorrow will be a better day."

"It's been a depressing night, that's for sure," Benoit said, opening the door and waving Inge inside. "Can you believe that massacre? A group of *Mormons*, for God's sake. Killing unarmed men, women, and children. I mean just slaughtering them in cold blood. That makes my skin crawl. It just doesn't make sense."

"I believe Jim," Inge replied. "If that's what he says happened, it must be the truth."

"And then Kemp's pessimism," Benoit said, tossing off his jacket and unbuttoning his shirt. "I think he's changed since he's been out here. The job must be wearing him down."

"He *does* look older these days," said Inge. "Will you unbutton me?"

"Why do they make these damn buttons so small?" he asked rhetorically. "You know . . ." he said reflectively.

"Ooooh, come on, Jean. Finish the buttons. I'm freezing."

"Okay. Okay. I'm hurrying. There."

"Thank God," she said, pulling the dress over her head. "This bed is really going to feel great," she said, pulling back the quilt.

Benoit sat on the edge of the bed. "Inge," he said somberly, staring at his feet. "Does it seem to you like the whole world's going straight to hell?"

Inge peeked out, staring at him with one bright blue eye. "What do you mean?"

"Everything that's happened tonight. It just gets me down."

"Come to bed," she said quietly. "I want to hold you."

"The situation in Utah," Benoit said, pulling off his right boot and tossing it across the room. "The troubles with the Indians. The fact that there's virtually no hope for us ever seeing Wilhelm and Werner again," he added, pulling off his left boot and throwing it after the other one.

Standing, he unbuckled his belt. "And then there's Jace," he said, fumbling with the buttons on his trousers. "Damn, it's cold. My fingers feel like they're frozen. I'm scared half to death for him. He looks like shit and he's taking too much of that laudanum. I'm afraid he's going to kill himself."

"Do you think you should talk to the colonel about it?" Inge asked.

Benoit gave her a strange look. "Are you kidding?

Kemp is not going to listen to listen to anything I have to say. You saw how he jumped all over me about the boys."

"That was my fault. I shouldn't have asked you to do that."

"It doesn't matter. If it hadn't been that, it would have been something else. Seems like no matter what I say to him, it's wrong."

"Wait, Jean," Inge said as he prepared to slip under the covers.

"Huh?"

"Would you get a blanket? I don't think this quilt is going to be enough."

"Okay," he said, crossing the room and digging into a wooden chest where they kept the bedcovers.

"You know, Inge," he said, climbing in beside her. "I'm really confused. I don't know what to do."

"About what," she said, snuggling up against him.

"Anything. Should I resign my commission and take Cle up on that offer with the New Orleans militia? Everybody says there's going to be a war. That it's inevitable. And I don't want to have to fight against Theophile and cut off relations with my family."

Inge stroked his cheek. "Don't worry too much about that, Jean. When the time comes you'll make the right decision. I know you will."

"And what about Jace? I sure as hell can't go running off to New Orleans and abandon him in his condition. He's like a brother. Maybe even closer."

"You aren't going to abandon him. I don't think you could. But let's don't talk about it anymore tonight."

"You're right. Tomorrow's bound to be a better day." Benoit shivered. "By God, it *is* getting colder. I'm going to get another blanket. I *hate* these goddamned winters."

Jumping up, he padded across the room and dug into

the chest a second time. "Oh, great!" he said, glancing out the high window above the chest.

"Jean," she mumbled sleepily. "Will you *please* settle down and come to bed?"

"It's snowing like a son of a bitch," he said, sliding under the covers.

"Shhh," she said, placing her finger on his lips. "Go to sleep."

Benoit lay staring at the ceiling, a jumble of thoughts racing through his mind.

"Inge," he whispered a few minutes later.

"Oh, for God's sake, Jean," she said peevishly. "What is it *now*?"

"I was just thinking . . ."

"Is this something I really need to know tonight?"

"Uh-huh."

"Okay," she sighed. "Tell me. And then be quiet and go to sleep."

Benoit pulled her closer. "There would actually be two good reasons to take Cle up on his offer."

She lifted her head off his chest and looked at him. "And what would they be?"

"It almost never snows in New Orleans," Benoit grinned. "And everybody there can pronounce my name."

KEN ENGLADE is a bestselling author of fiction and nonfiction whose books include *Hoffa*, *Hotblood*, and *Beyond Reason*, which was nominated for an Edgar Award in 1991. He lives in Corrales, New Mexico.

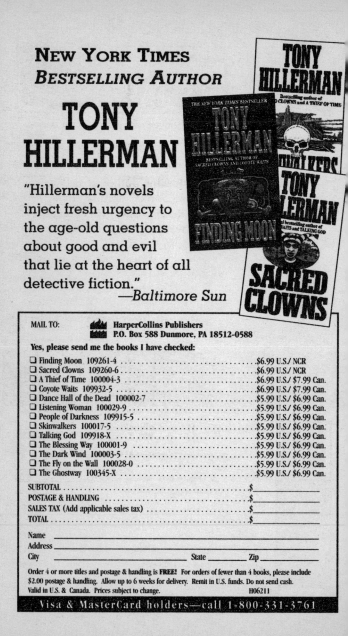